Out of
Thin Air _____

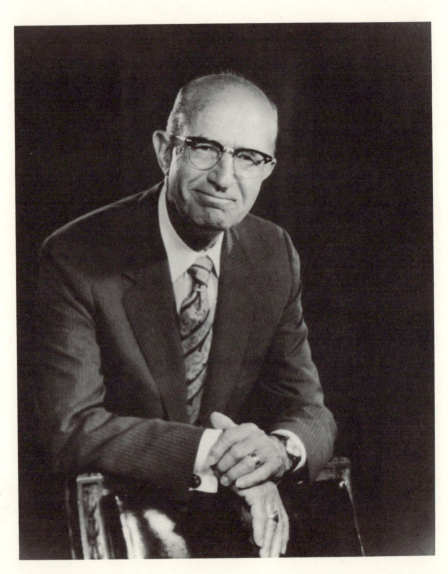

Leonard Pool.

Out of
Thin Air _____

A HISTORY OF
AIR PRODUCTS AND CHEMICALS, INC.,
1940–1990

Andrew J. Butrica _____

with the assistance of Deborah G. Douglas

PRAEGER

New York
Westport, Connecticut
London

Library of Congress Cataloging-in-Publication Data

Butrica, Andrew J.
  Out of thin air : a history of Air Products and Chemicals, Inc.,
1940–1990 / Andrew J. Butrica with the assistance of Deborah G.
Douglas.
      p. cm.
  Includes bibliographical references and index.
  ISBN 0–275–93765–8 (lib. bdg. : alk. paper)
  1. Air Products and Chemicals, Inc.—History. 2. Chemical
industry—United States—History. 3. Gas industry—United States—
History. 4. Pool, Leonard Parker, 1906–1975. 5. Industrialists—
United States—Biography. I. Douglas, Deborah G. II. Title.
HD9651.9.A37B88 1990
338.7′66′00973—dc20   90–39618

Library of Congress Catalog Card Number: 90–39618
ISBN: 0-275-93765-8

First published in 1990

Praeger Publishers, One Madison Avenue, New York, NY 10010
An imprint of Greenwood Publishing Group, Inc.

Printed in the United States of America

The paper used in this book complies with the
Permanent Paper Standard issued by the National
Information Standards Organization (Z39.48-1984).

10 9 8 7 6 5 4 3 2 1

Contents

3.   Survival and Strategies   51

     The Move to Emmaus   52
     An Appeal to Wall Street   55
     A Surprising Source of Cash   57
     Trail Blazing   59
     The Dawning of the Oxygen Age   65
     Weirton   67
     New Strategic Directions   70
     Looking Abroad   74
     Hustling for Business   76
     Revolt by the Board?   78

4.   Air Products Comes of Age   83

     The Cold War Heats Up   84
     Liquid Oxygen for Rockets   84
     Santa Susana   89
     The Three Bears   94
     A New Lease on Leasing   98
     Process Engineering for the Chemical Industry   101
     The Technological Supermarket   105
     Accomplishments   106

5.   The Technological Enterprise and Its Culture   109

     Leonard Pool's Values   109
     The Hard Realities of Labor Policy   112
     Pool's Philosophy   113
     Safety and Quality   118
     The Complexities of the Culture   119
     The Beginnings of R&D   126
     Patents   128
     Institutionalizing R&D   130
     Into the Future   133

PART III.   THE MODERN FIRM EMERGES   137

6.   Charting a New Course   139

     Organizing for an Enlarged Scale of Operation   141
     Remaking the On-site Concept   144
     Into the Merchant Gas Business   147
     The Defense and Space Markets   155

Figures and Tables

Figures

Tables

Acknowledgments

October 1, 1990, marked the fiftieth anniversary of the founding of Air Products and Chemicals, Inc. This book is the centerpiece of the company's celebration of that anniversary. It grew out of an interest on the part of many former and present employees. Concerned with the complexity of the project and with creating a quality product, William Kendrick, Vice President of Public Affairs, turned for advice to Arnold Thackray, the Director of the Beckman Center for History of Chemistry at the University of Pennsylvania. Together, Kendrick and Thackray co-chaired a History Advisory Committee whose other members included Professor Louis Galambos, editor of the papers of Dwight D. Eisenhower at the Johns Hopkins University, Professor John Smith of Lehigh University, and key present and former employees of Air Products.

I am indebted to the members of the History Advisory Committee for their comments, suggestions, enthusiasm, and support. Many other Air Products employees, past and present, facilitated the researching and writing of this book. It is a pleasure to acknowledge the help of those individuals who participated in the initial round of oral history interviews undertaken by Professors Smith and Thackray or who later gave their time to talk with me. My special thanks go to Carl Anderson, Chuck Anderson, Dex Baker, Jim Boyce, Robert Craig, Ed Donley, Lee Gaumer, Mark Halsted, George Hartnett, Dorothy Hoffner, Joe Kaminski, Andy Mellen, Lanny Patten, Frank

Pavlis, Walter Pool, Harry Quigley, Alain Régent, Brian Rushton, Don Shire, Bill Thomas, and Andy Woytek.

Eleanor Maass used her professional skills to help create an historical archive at Air Products. Dozens of employees have contributed documents, artifacts, and other memorabilia to that archive. Special thanks go to two people who assisted "above and beyond the call of duty." Dorothy Hoffner, who served as History Office coordinator, arranged for the acquisition of the valuable papers of Lee Twomey; and Minnie Pillivant, of the Detroit office, tracked down precious records on Charles Rider, father of Dorothy Rider Pool.

Thanks go to those outside Air Products who provided valuable assistance in a variety of ways: Jay Brill (U.S. Air Force, retired); Richard Leyes (National Air and Space Museum); Anne Millbrooke (archivist, United Technologies); Larry Owens (University of Massachusetts); Laurel Putman (Superior Air Products); John Sloop (NASA); and Darwin Stapleton (Rockefeller Archive Center).

I must especially acknowledge the help of the three academic members of the History Advisory Committee. John Smith generously shared his knowledge of the chemical industry in the twentieth century. Louis Galambos offered innumerable suggestions on how to develop the structure of the book, and extensively critiqued its early drafts. Arnold Thackray worked closely with me at every stage of the project, and the final shape of the narrative owes much to his experience as an historian and his skills as an editor. Finally, I am pleased to thank Deborah Douglas, who, in addition to carrying out preliminary research, assisted greatly in the late stages of text preparation and took on many other tasks.

Andrew J. Butrica

Introduction

This book tells the story of the first fifty years of one major corporation, Air Products and Chemicals, Inc. The story is exciting—full of struggle, determination, crisis, and heroic endeavor. Words like entrepreneurship, sales, finance, engineering, technology, and human resources describe the history of Air Products. So, too, do concepts like being a late entrant to an established industry, struggling to find market niches, seeking for comparative advantage, establishing a discrete set of skills, moving into wholly new but related fields of endeavor, and breaking through to the level where economies of scale and scope would allow the firm to enjoy a secure future as a major player on a global basis. The story is one of success, plain luck at some points. But it also contains its share of hard knocks, disappointments, and mistaken strategies.

Air Products started as a consequence of the entrepreneurial vision and drive of one individual, Leonard Pool. Over the course of fifty years, Pool's precarious venture has grown into a diversified, multinational corporation. Initially, that growth took place wholly within the industrial gas business. Struggling to find its way, Air Products pioneered such concepts as leased "on-site" plants and "piggybacking," as well as being the first U.S. firm to enter European and other overseas gas markets. The early part of the Air Products story forms an important chapter in the wider history of the industrial gas industry.

Since the industry's beginnings at the turn of the century and until well after World War II, it operated under a peculiar set of constraints. The fundamental raw material—air—was free and available everywhere, yet transportation of the packaged products, principally oxygen, was inordinately expensive. Markets were local. It was this fact that allowed upstart Air Products, which entered the business late, a chance for success.

On the eve of World War II, Leonard Pool founded his firm to meet the needs of mid-level consumers. He believed that those consumers were inadequately served by the big suppliers, themselves pre-occupied with larger-scale developments. Pool was a shrewd opportunist who thought to combine existing technology with a novel marketing concept. Instead of delivering oxygen in cylinders, he proposed to build and then to lease oxygen generators. Those generators would be placed on-site at the facilities of customers with moderate demand. In this way, Pool sought to overcome the limitations imposed by transportation costs, and to exploit a market of wider geographic scope from one fixed manufacturing plant. The idea was ingenious. Industrialists who reviewed Pool's plans encouraged him. However, no immediate orders were forthcoming. Pool's fledgling firm faced its first crisis.

The hallmark of an entrepreneur is flexibility. As the storm clouds of World War II thickened, Pool changed course and seized the chance to sell his generators to the military. While his leasing concept had to lie dormant, his start-up organization blossomed into a significant corporation. The only trouble was that, at war's end, Air Products once more faced a dearth of customers.

The next fifteen years were tremendously exciting. During this time, it was completely uncertain as to whether or not the company would succeed. The determination and drive of Pool and his colleagues were tested to the limit. Major developments in the market for industrial gases, in the number and combinations of gases consumed, and in the technology by which they were produced, all spelled opportunity to those alert enough to read the signs, and bold enough to act. For Air Products, the three areas critical to success proved to be engineering, sales, and finance.

First, there was the struggle to engineer and to build an enormous, changing array of process equipment. As a small organization playing "catch-up," Air Products offered not so much the lure of radically new technology as the willingness to combine familiar elements in more efficient ways. Every job was a fresh challenge for the company's engineers, requiring great creativity and stamina. Second, there was the necessity of selling. Here the key was listening to the customer. Management came to be based on the belief that if a customer could articulate a need, Air Products could certainly engineer a solution. Finally, the whole operation was premised on the availability of cash. Leasing meant that remuneration came only after equipment was built. The company drew upon traditional resources such as public stock offerings, but it also formed innovative relationships with insurance and banking firms to secure the capital needed for survival and growth.

In the years following World War II, the industrial gas business was itself transformed. An abundant supply of cheap oxygen became available with the introduction of tonnage plants. Leonard Pool's on-site concept became the norm, even as Pool himself ingeniously found a way for his own small company to acquire an early mastery of tonnage technology. Air Products was thus able to obtain a growing share of a growing market, and begin to move away from the strategies of the late-entrant toward those of the industry trend-setters.

In the 1950s, both the U.S. military and the largest commercial producers began to emphasize the advantages of liquid oxygen. Then, in order to provide fuel for the space effort following *Sputnik*, the military sought to develop large-scale hydrogen generation, purification, and liquefaction processes. One key to Air Products' success was the way in which it took advantage of those opportunities. Tonnage liquid processes, which the firm developed for the military, were rapidly transfered to the commercial sector. By 1960, Air Products was not only able to compete directly with the largest industrial-gas companies for major orders for oxygen plants, it was also clearly established as a leader in liquid hydrogen technology.

Two other, linked innovations were critical to Air Products' ability to break loose from the pack and to take on the major players. One was the set of financial arrangements—the indenture—that gave the company access to the capital required to finance tonnage plants. The second was the idea of piggybacking, a concept as ingenious as the original on-site notion. Piggybacking, in which Air Products was a pioneer, involved building excess gaseous or liquid capacity at an on-site plant. The cost of this excess capacity was far smaller than that of a separate plant, which meant Air Products had a competitive advantage as it once again played the late-entrant game of catch-up, this time in the expanding merchant market for gases delivered by tube trailers, tankers, and other vehicular means.

In the 1960s, the chemical, petrochemical, electronics, and food industries provided strong growth prospects to Air Products. By now the company was set on exploiting those opportunities of scope and scale offered by the emergence of truly national and international markets for industrial gases, and by its own larger size. A move into Europe, as early as 1957, was one important element in the firm's new strategy, a strategy which depended on the extension of its marketing and distribution networks, and on the strengthening of its managerial structure. It was in the 1960s that Edward Donley and Dexter Baker began to put their imprint on the company, as they wrestled with these issues of scope and scale.

Oxygen, hydrogen, and the other industrial gases are, of course, "building block" chemicals. The earliest U.S. industrial gas firms had quickly recognized this, and had long since developed their own activities in chemicals. Air Products itself diversified into chemicals in the 1960s, with ventures into a range of process intermediates. Using the profits of the industrial gas business and the company's by then considerable ability to secure financing, it soon acquired top positions in a number of specialized chemical markets. Air Products entered its second stage of diversification in the 1980s, when it had a painful learning experience in the construction-engineering business before consolidating its attention on the emerging high-temperature technologies of cogeneration, trash-to-steam, and flue-gas desulfurization.

As Air Products grew, it switched its attention to fresh markets and continuously pursued new strategies. What remained constant were the roles of engineering, sales, and entrepreneurship, and the steadily growing skills base of its people.

As the story of Air Products unfolds over the following pages, certain themes will emerge. Government contracts played a critical part in the company's first years. World War II orders to build mobile oxygen generators literally kept the company alive. In the 1950s, Korean War and other military orders for generators swelled sales, while development contracts for tonnage liquid-oxygen and liquid-hydrogen plants provided Air Products access to an important, emerging technology. In the 1960s the company deliberately moved into both owning and operating plants for the military, while also concentrating on selling rocket fuel to the civilian NASA space agency. By 1970, federal contracts accounted for a small percentage of company business, although government-funded development and supply contracts would remain important for a number of markets, among them NASA, the helium conservation program, wastewater treatment systems, and the synfuels industry.

In the 1970s and 1980s, management issues would come steadily to the fore, as Air Products wrestled with how to develop and deploy the skills of its growing ranks of employees, and how to strengthen its management structures. Financial and legal issues; career development and public relations; research and development; all needed to be conceptualized in fresh ways as the company became a major, multinational corporation operating in a more technologically demanding and faster-changing world.

Right from the start, process engineering has been one engine of growth at Air Products. The recruiting and husbanding of the firm's process, design, and project-engineering talent has been a key issue. The ability to initiate and carry out engineering projects of ever-increasing magnitude, from the tonnage plants of the fifties to the trash-to-steam plants of the eighties, contributed substantially to the company's growth. Engineering helped shape the company's culture. The enduring style of Air Products—its customer focus and hungry emphasis on sales and growth—emerged from the interaction of the values and personality of Leonard Pool with the engineering skills of his colleagues, and the opportunities offered by the industrial gas business. Pool's initial decision to build an oxygen generator foreshadowed the company's diversification into other chemical processes and, later, into other forms of process engineering in the areas of the environment and energy.

The success of Air Products also owes much to its developing management style, to its willingness to pay attention to fostering human resources, and to its seizing of opportunities for growth that were afforded to all American industrial gas companies in the second half of the twentieth century. As global demand grew steadily, Air Products became the second largest industrial gas supplier in the United States, and fourth in the world, because it successfully institutionalized the determination to grow. The very entrepreneurial drive which characterized the company took it into some painful learning experiences. In the 1970s, it moved too far from its core areas of expertise, and then retrenched. In the early 1980s, it entered into synfuels-linked activities, which shrank precipitously as oil prices collapsed. However, by 1990, Air Products was firmly established as a large, still-growing multinational corporation, operating in the three areas of industrial gases, chemicals, and environmental and energy systems. The history of how this came about is told in the following pages.

PART I ——————————————

THE ROOTS OF ENTERPRISE

For almost four centuries Americans have been launching new enterprises to provide products and services needed in this country and in foreign markets. Far more of these ventures have failed than have succeeded. Those that have survived and flourished have without exception been led in their early years by men or women of unusual energy and determination, entrepreneurs with a vision and the ability to convert ideas into successful businesses. So it was with Air Products, a multinational, high-tech corporation today, but initially only one man's dream.

To understand this transformation, it is necessary to understand the man, Leonard Pool—his origins, family, and ideas. Out of those roots in the early decades of this century came the complex enterprise we know today. Our story also grows out of the realities of the industrial gas business in the years prior to World War II. By 1940, the American oxygen industry was well established, with several large and prosperous firms. Air Products was a latecomer to the ranks of that industry. However, its precarious situation changed with the onset of war. If the beginnings were humble and the risks were great, Pool and his colleagues knew how to make opportunity their ally.

1

The Entrepreneur and the Engineer

> Leonard spoke about building cathedrals, and other grand things—completely out of context. It was so unreal that I didn't take him seriously.[1]

Our story begins with Leonard Parker Pool (1906–1975). Pool was a driven, decisive individual. His restless dreams and his determination were to give birth to a multinational, high-tech corporation with 1990 sales approaching $3 billion. But to understand Pool, we must go back in time to the era when railroads were king.

Railroads in the United States underwent massive expansion in the decades following the Civil War, as the West was settled and the country industrialized. The railroads became extraordinary business empires, consuming vast quantities of iron, steel, labor, and capital. They provided jobs and opportunity to tens of thousands, including the Pool family. In Leonard's first twenty years of life, railroads defined his world. It was a world of skilled mechanics, of engineering innovation, and of expanding opportunity.

Working on the Railroad

Leonard's paternal grandfather, Ira G. Pool, was of English descent, part of the aristocracy of labor in late nineteenth-century America. Superintendent of the Soo Railroad shops in Minneapolis, he and his wife raised a large family under comfortable circumstances. Leonard J. Pool (1868–1926; henceforth L.J. Pool) and his several brothers and half brothers grew up to join their father in the shops of the Soo Railroad. One son, Ira G. Pool, Jr., eventually rose to be a vice president of the Great Northern Railroad. Another, Edward Pool, became a manager on the Erie line. L.J. Pool became a boilermaker and an inventor of sorts. Family legend has it that he devised several tools for working on steam boilers and developed an arrester to prevent sparks on Western locomotives.

Life was secure for L.J. Pool when, around 1890, he met Emma E. Ludford (1869–1952). Born in London, England, Emma had emigrated to Almonte, Ontario, a small town near Ottawa. In 1887, at the age of eighteen, she moved to Sault Ste. Marie, Ontario, abutting Michigan's upper peninsula. Emma was courted by and married L.J. Pool. The couple settled in Minneapolis, where they had four children. The first three, Ira J. (1892–1943), Fred (1896–1897), and Hazel I. (1898–1918), were born within six years. The "baby" of the family, born eight years later on November 5, 1906, was Leonard Parker.

Emma Pool was an emotional, tenacious, and intelligent woman. Her life was her family. With neither the gift for friendship nor an inclination to be social, she depended heavily on her husband, who dominated the family. L.J. Pool was a kindly father but a strong disciplinarian. When he had cash in his pockets, he spent freely on his family, giving them everything he could. But cash was not always on hand. Because of his spending habits, the family suffered occasional privation. In addition, his moves from job to job, typical of railroad craftsmen, bred in young Leonard a sense of insecurity.[2]

In 1909, when Leonard Pool was three, his father left Minneapolis for a position with the Chicago, Milwaukee, and St. Paul Railroad in Deer Lodge, Montana. It was there that Leonard's mother, already in her forties, gave birth to two more sons in rapid succession, George F. (1910–1973) and Walter D. (1911–   ). About this time, L.J. Pool's health began to fail. In 1913 he took a job as a boilermaker-foreman in the bustling railroad center of Meadville, Pennsylvania. In 1915, less than two years after the move to Meadville, Emma Pool, now forty-six, gave birth to yet another child, Betty Jane (1915–1931). Leonard's role had changed from that of being the baby to that of being the middle child in a large family.

Leonard Pool was ambitious from an early age. There was also no doubt that he was talented. He was an excellent student, enjoying grade school. In 1918 his oldest sister Hazel died. Leonard briefly

Leonard Pool, wearing spectacles, at the center of a group of Pool family members and friends. The two boys to Leonard Pool's right and left are his brothers, Walter and George, respectively.

entertained his first "impossible dream": a career in medicine. Later, he told his brother Walter that the family had lacked adequate medical attention: "If someone was sick we didn't always have the wherewithal to get the care needed."[3] Seeking to assure that others would have access to good medical care later became a driving force in his life.

In the years immediately after World War I the Pool family was in precarious circumstances as L.J. Pool's health deteriorated. When Leonard entered high school in 1920, he had to divide his time between his studies and efforts to bolster the family finances. Eventually, he dropped out of school and started the fatiguing work of locomotive repair in the Erie Railroad shops. Here Leonard learned the new metalworking skills of oxyacetylene cutting and welding, a technology brought into prominence by World War I and the expansion of the oxygen industry.

The Oxyacetylene Industry

No place on the surface of the earth is devoid of oxygen, for oxygen is one of the two main ingredients of the air (the other is nitrogen). Nonetheless it was only in 1774 that oxygen was first isolated and its properties described by Joseph Priestley, in England. The great French chemist Antoine Lavoisier quickly elucidated the crucial role of oxygen in combustion, respiration, and a host of chemical reactions. But in 1900 oxygen was still a laboratory curiosity—produced when needed by chemical reaction, by the electrolysis of water, or by a newly invented machine, the oxygen "generator" of Carl von Linde.

Linde, a professor of mechanics at the Technical Institute in Munich, Germany, not only devised but also made commercially viable a way of generating oxygen "out of thin air." In Linde's machine, air was liquefied by a process of compression, followed by cooling and rapid expansion. When the liquid air was fed into a distillation column, the oxygen, which boils at a higher temperature than nitrogen, could be separated out, brought to room temperature, compressed into cylinders, and transported to customers. Linde's machine performed the feat of turning air, free and available all over the earth, into a saleable commodity—oxygen gas.

In 1906, the year of Leonard Pool's birth, Carl von Linde visited Cleveland and dined with a personal friend, Myron T. Herrick, and other local capitalists. Herrick and his associates were so interested in Linde's machine that in 1907 they formed a syndicate, the Linde Air Products Company, to acquire his American rights. Linde Air

Products installed its first oxygen generator, capable of producing 1,000 cubic feet of oxygen per hour (conventionally designated today as one ton per day) in Buffalo, New York.[4]

One major use of oxygen derived from the invention of an oxyacetylene torch in France in 1901. The flame produced by burning a mixture of acetylene and oxygen is remarkably hot. That flame can be used for cutting and welding iron and steel. To increase oxygen sales, Linde began to make and sell acetylene gas as well as oxyacetylene welding equipment. During the First World War, the Navy and large-scale metalworking firms made extensive use of oxyacetylene equipment. The result was an explosive growth in demand for what came to be referred to as "industrial gases."[5]

Oxyacetylene cutting and welding was the largest use for oxygen and for acetylene in the United States. Acetylene was made from calcium carbide and water. Linde Air Products moved aggressively to develop its central position in the nascent industry. In 1917, Linde and four other companies and their subsidiaries formed the Union Carbide and Carbon Corporation. By this move, Linde not only assured its future as the largest American industrial gas producer, but also signaled the affinities between the industrial gas business and the wider chemical industry.

The same booming wartime demand gave rise to Linde's major competitor, the Air Reduction Company, Inc. That company was organized in 1915 around air separation technology developed by Georges Claude, founder of the French firm, Air Liquide. Air Reduction's sponsors included Percy Avery Rockefeller, nephew of oil magnate John D. Rockefeller. In 1916, Air Reduction broke ground in Philadelphia for its first oxygen generator. The following year, it built or bought several acetylene plants and moved into the manufacture of cutting and welding torches.[6]

The technology of oxygen manufacture, and of its industrial use, was thus successfully transplanted from Europe to the United States. By the 1920s, oxyacetylene welding and cutting had a variety of applications: to manufacture and repair railroad, industrial, marine, automotive, aeronautical, and electrical equipment; to build up worn rail ends; to cut up scrap metal; and to weld pipe joints on oil, gas, water, and steam lines. The two principal markets were the steel industry and the railroads.

Linde (Union Carbide) and Air Reduction, the main American companies, became large and profitable enterprises with several geographically dispersed plants from which to serve customers. A typical plant might generate 1,000 cubic feet per hour of oxygen (enough to fill all the space in an average house, each day). The oxygen was pumped into heavy steel cylinders, which were returned for filling when empty. The cylinders weighed around 130 pounds and were designed to contain 18 to 20 pounds (216 to 240 cubic feet) of oxygen at pressures of 2,000 pounds per square inch and higher. Thus only about one-eighth of the weight of each cylinder shipped was usable product. The economics of cylinder transportation limited the geographic reach of each plant. The great size of the country, and the growing demand for oxygen in the "roaring twenties," would mean that there was plenty of room in America for other players, and for other ideas about how to play the game of making gases and profits "out of thin air."[7]

Pool's Pancake Days

By 1924, Leonard Pool had acquired a working knowledge of the railroad repair and oxyacetylene welding businesses. A family crisis led him into the new experience of salesmanship. L.J. Pool, who had suffered from high blood pressure for a number of years, experienced a partial stroke and was unable to work for almost a year. In October 1925, he was in a bad automobile accident. Four months later, after massive strokes, he died at the age of fifty-seven, leaving a negligible estate.

Leonard's role changed yet again. He now became the *de facto* father of the family still at home. Ira J. Pool, the oldest son, was away in Baltimore working for the railroad. Fred and Hazel were dead. The younger children—Betty Jane, ten; Walter, fourteen; and George, fifteen—were not old enough to work full-time. Emma Pool, who became heavily dependent on Leonard, decided to return to Minneapolis, where her three brothers and several of her husband's relatives lived. In the summer of 1926, Emma, Betty Jane, Walter, and Leonard moved to Minneapolis, while George was sent to live with Ira.

Leonard Pool found work at a service station in Minneapolis, where he picked up some knowledge of car repair. While looking for a better job, he began to imagine ways of improving automobile engines. He thought one might feed oxygen-enriched air into the carburetor. But he soon abandoned automobiles and any thought of their improvement, when he snared a position as a traveling salesman for the Pillsbury Flour Company.

Pillsbury was a well-managed, innovative concern. Leonard Pool sensed opportunity in its growing ranks. Along with several other young men, he won a place in its training program and was taught how to sell pancake flour to restaurants and retail outlets. At the end of the training period, the top student was allowed to pick his territory. Pool, competitive and hard-driving, was that top student. He immediately went to the library to learn about population trends. On the basis of his research, he chose Detroit. He reasoned that the growing automobile industry would require an increasing number of blue-collar workers, who would eat a lot of pancakes. Leonard moved in May 1927. The following year, Emma brought Walter and Betty Jane to Detroit, where they shared his apartment.

Leonard became a successful salesman for Pillsbury, but he did not like peddling pancake flour or Saturday night pancake socials. The welding industry was buoyant in Detroit. Soon Leonard was working for the C.H. Dockson Company, which assembled and sold welding equipment made from components manufactured elsewhere. Typical of many such small companies, Dockson was a family business run by Charles Dockson and his wife Ida. Their son Sterling was a salesman, and he and Leonard sold equipment to shops and scrap yards. Leonard saw first-hand how a small family business worked. And he was able to combine his knack for salesmanship with the technical knowledge of welding he had gained when working for the railroad.

Pool was ambitious to be his own boss. In 1929, while still working for Dockson, he started his first business venture, a part ownership in a Detroit automobile junkyard. His brother, Walter, was employed there. As Leonard soon discovered, junkyards were highly competitive. The venture failed from a lack of capital. By then, Pool had already started another job. This latter opportunity arose from his encounter with Harrison Bird, Detroit branch manager of the Burdett Oxygen Company, which resold welding and cutting equipment, and sold cylinder oxygen and acetylene. The two men took a liking to each other. Bird offered Pool a position selling equipment and gases on a route.

The year 1929 was momentous for Leonard Pool in another way. It was then that he met and began to date Dorothy Rider (1900–1967), a young woman six years his senior. She would become Leonard's rock and anchor, playing a crucial role in the founding of Air Products. Dorothy had graduated from the Detroit Teacher College and the University of Michigan (1921) and taught French in Detroit's

Dorothy Rider Pool, circa 1933, shortly after she and Leonard Pool were married.

public schools. She was the only child of Charles Rider (1872–1938), the founder of the Paris Laundry chain and an investor with holdings in Detroit real estate, in the Fisher Body Company (later taken over by General Motors), and in a dozen other local concerns.[8] Despite her father's substantial assets, Dorothy Rider was an unassuming person. She worked hard and was frugal. Both qualities would be important in the difficult years ahead.

Dorothy and Leonard married on December 19, 1931. The match was intriguing: the older, wealthier woman and the aggressive but impecunious young suitor. While Dorothy became a stabilizing force in Leonard's life, she never tried to dampen his desire to run his own business. For a few years, he stayed with the Burdett Company, but he was determined not to be just a hired hand.

Testing the Waters

In 1934 Leonard Pool began to plan his second business venture. The oxygen industry was showing signs of recovering from the depressed sales of the early thirties (Table 1). Pool was convinced that he could make a success, selling cylinders of oxygen and acetylene to welding shops and other small users. That meant acquiring gas cylinders, which were expensive. Thousands of dollars would have to be raised just to get started.

Pool turned to his boss, Harrison Bird, for financial support. Together they set out to raise $25,000, a difficult task in the Depression year of 1934 when capital was hard to find. The partners had little success. Eventually Pool met Walter Yenzer of Toledo, Ohio, who was also in the oxygen business, and anxious to become involved. In the course of 1935–1936, with oxygen sales looking up, the trio raised $28,000 by selling stock to their friends. In addition, Charles Rider, Leonard's father-in-law, invested $50,000 in the venture. Rider became Vice President, when Pool incorporated the Acetylene Gas and Supply Company on May 4, 1936.

A few months later, Pool's employer, the Burdett Oxygen Company, was caught up in the wave of mergers sweeping through the industrial gas business. In order to meet increasing demand in the mid- and late-thirties, the more progressive oxygen manufacturing firms acquired new plants from which to deliver cylinders, and acquired smaller concerns.[9] Better roads, more powerful trucks, and larger and more reliable generators all helped this consolidation. Linde, the industry leader, was active in acquiring oxygen and acet-

Table 1
U.S. Production of Oxygen, 1919–1939

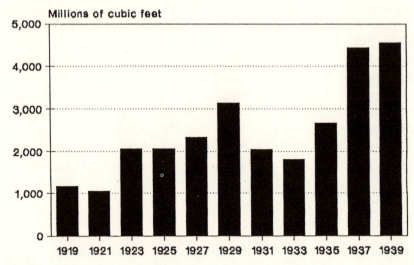

SOURCE: U.S. Census of Manufactures.

ylene plants, as was the industry's second largest firm, Air Reduction. In 1933, the National Cylinder Gas Company was organized, and by the end of the decade it in turn had acquired enough plants to become the third largest producer. Burdett was bought out by yet another player, Compressed Industrial Gases, Inc. (CIG). CIG, though organized only in the late twenties, was an important instigator of mergers and buy outs.[10]

Leonard Pool worked for CIG briefly after the Burdett Oxygen buy out, before resigning and devoting himself full-time to the fledgling Acetylene Gas and Supply Company. He and his partners rented a warehouse off Grand River Avenue in Detroit and purchased second-hand cylinders and a truck. They bought gases from National Cylinder Gas and resold to small welding and machine shops. The company grew and prospered, gradually acquiring some important accounts.

Leonard Pool's venture became successful enough in its turn to attract a buy out offer from Compressed Industrial Gases in late 1938. Perhaps because their only alternative was to be undersold and crushed in the marketplace, Pool and the other investors in Acetylene Gas and Supply accepted $140,000 worth of CIG stock for their company. Pool cashed in some of his shares and paid back the money he had borrowed. As part of the deal, he became manager of railroad sales for CIG in Chicago. Soon he was promoted to manager of the

Detroit branch, a position he held until 1940. Pool ran local gas operations, and also oversaw the start-up of new generators in Shreveport, Louisiana, and Evansville, Indiana.

By this time, the Pools were getting along well financially. Dorothy, besides being a teacher, was prosperous in her own right. Her father had died on February 14, 1938. His will appointed Dorothy executrix and bequeathed to her an estate worth nearly $100,000.[11] Leonard, for his part, had his job and his remaining CIG stock. He was able to support his mother and to help his brother Walter through medical school at the University of Michigan.

Leonard's Entrepreneurial Vision

While the Pools were prosperous, Leonard was still unhappy. It seemed that in his work he could do nothing which pleased the head office. His aggressive, restless drive could not be contained by a subordinate position in a large organization. Under the terms of the agreement with CIG, the company could not fire him for five years, and Pool was barred from starting a similar business in Detroit for that same period. Groping around for an "out," in the spring of 1939 he came up with a new idea.

Industry practice was to generate oxygen in gaseous form at centrally located plants, and to distribute it in cylinders. Pool's simple and ingenious idea was to avoid the cost of shipping heavy cylinders by building inexpensive generators that could be installed on the site where the oxygen would be utilized. Pool did not stop there. He reasoned that customers could be persuaded to lease these on-site plants, paying for the oxygen they consumed at a metered rate like electric power or natural gas. In a final, elegant touch he anticipated providing an incentive to stimulate demand: the more oxygen a customer used, the cheaper the rate would be. Everyone would be happy.

By eliminating the cost of shipping cylinders, the charges to the user could be a great deal less. Meanwhile, Pool himself would enjoy a steady revenue from the leases. In short, Leonard reasoned, he would keep the "cow"—the oxygen plant—on the customer's premises, and sell the "milk"—the oxygen—on the spot. This was quite different from the practice of the leading companies like Linde and Air Reduction, which kept their "cows" on their own centrally located sites. It was also quite different from the strategy of several small companies which offered to sell generators to customers and were thus relieved of the problems of delivering "milk." Pool believed his new concept would give him the best of both worlds.

The major consumers of oxygen in 1939 were in the steel industry, where per ton use of oxygen had increased 75 percent during the decade.[12] That growth was driven by technological innovations developed by Linde, the industry leader. In 1931, Linde had begun promoting a special blowpipe capable of making oxyacetylene welds of exceptional strength at greatly increased speed. A far greater factor in expanding the use of oxygen in steelmaking was the Lin-De-Surfacer, a massive scarfing machine, which replaced hand-held torches and saved time. The new machine automatically removed, or "scarfed," surface defects from hot slabs of steel, while they were being rolled to the desired thickness. Depending on the size of the machine, oxygen consumption ranged from 28,000 to 250,000 cubic feet per hour (that is, 28 to 250 times as much as Linde's original Buffalo plant produced).[13]

In order to supply those unprecedented quantities of oxygen, European technology was once again transplanted. Linde licensed from Germany and adapted to its own needs the Heylandt process of making and distributing oxygen in liquid form. Liquid oxygen at −297°F was pumped into large, insulated cylinders and shipped by rail or truck to the point of consumption, where it was converted into gas for customer use. The Heylandt process saved on cylinders and delivery costs and was congruent with Linde's emphasis on supplying customers from its own centrally located plants. Linde's liquid production and distribution technology put it in a unique position to serve the largest oxygen consumers.[14]

Pool did not envision direct competition with Linde in this new, liquid market. Instead he focused on the world with which he was familiar, the market among smaller consumers. They still purchased their oxygen in gaseous form, in cylinders. Perhaps Pool could interest some of these customers, with big enough consumption, in the virtues of an on-site plant. Cracking even this limited market was an audacious goal. Pool, the high school drop-out turned salesman, would have not only to acquire the technology necessary to make oxygen generators, but also to raise considerable capital to finance their construction and ownership. And he would have to create a niche protected from the cylinder salesmen of giants like Linde and Air Reduction, and from all the other smaller suppliers of generators or cylinder gases. Even if his concept was correct, he would need great supplies of entrepreneurship, opportunism, and luck. In short, he faced all the problems of a late entrant to an established market.

While he had some experience in raising capital and possessed his own limited financial resources, Pool's concept was a completely untested one. Worse still, he lacked any of the engineering skills needed to design and construct oxygen generators. Pool knew that the cost of the machine was critical to his success. If the price was too high, the great savings his lease plan offered would vanish.

It was possible to purchase generators from one of the few American companies that manufactured them, such as the Independent Engineering Company of O'Fallon, Illinois; Superior Air Products of Newark, New Jersey; or the Gas Industries Company of Pittsburgh, Pennsylvania. Alternatively, generators could be imported from France or Germany. However, the clouds of war that were gathering in Europe suggested that importing machines was highly risky. And both options lacked the independence which Pool desired in every aspect of his work.

Leonard Pool was above all an entrepreneur, willing to take risks. He believed that the market for oxygen was about to open up dramatically. Demand had risen from its Depression low of the early thirties. The looming possibility of a second world war signalled the likelihood of a further sharp increase. On January 12, 1939, President Franklin D. Roosevelt had delivered a special message on national defense, and in April Congress had responded with a measure calling for the U.S. to build 6,000 aircraft. The demand for aircraft was symbolic of an expanding market for every sort of war materiel, and especially for iron and steel. The design, manufacture, and leasing of oxygen plants in the United States looked plausible to Pool.

Persuaded of the virtue of his ideas, Pool decided to push ahead in the late spring of 1939. To sell his concept he resolved to build a demonstration generator. With this in mind, he wrote to the Dean of Engineering at the University of Michigan, outlining his ideas and asking for some candidates to interview. The school sent several students, including Frank Pavlis.

The Engineer Meets the Entrepreneur

Frank Pavlis was the first in his family to graduate from college. He was gifted, and won a four-year scholarship. He also worked as a laboratory technician and later as a chemistry lab instructor, while attending the Michigan College of Mining and Technology.[15] His lab duties and course work ate up most of his time, but Pavlis still found it possible to be a member of the college debate team. In this as throughout his career, he was a man interested in ideas and in the plausibility of arguments. When he received his B. S. in 1938, he was first in his class. His high marks won him a graduate fellowship at the University of Michigan in Ann Arbor, a leading school in chemical engineering.

Pavlis received a Master's degree with honors in 1939. His main interest was petroleum engineering. Petroleum companies were big, and the prospects they offered seemed secure. When a representative of Shell Oil came to the campus to conduct interviews, Frank Pavlis won a job offer. Nonetheless, he replied to the inquiry from Leonard Pool and asked for an interview. Pavlis described himself as "twenty-two years of age, physically sound, single, and still sufficiently plastic to adapt myself whole-heartedly to a type of work that promises to lead to a worthy end."[16] The interview turned into a lecture. As Pavlis later noted: "it was more a case of listening to Leonard's business plans than it was an in-depth interview. He was very optimistic about the future, completely in contrast to the other interviewers at the university, who still were Depression-minded and kept reminding us we'd be fortunate to get any job at all. Leonard spoke about building cathedrals, and other grand things—completely out of context. It was so unreal that I didn't take him seriously."[17]

Pavlis and the others interviewed agreed that Leonard Pool was too enthusiastic. They underestimated the man:

> Several weeks later he appeared on campus and conspired to get me alone by offering me a Coca-Cola. He started the conversation by asking me the direct question: "When are you coming to work for me?" I told him that I had not decided to work for him. I also mentioned my Shell Oil opportunity and described its attractiveness. Then he stuck out his chin, as he did many times in later years, and said, "Well, you may not have decided to work for me, but I have decided that you will." I pondered the two offers for several days, and decided to join this man who was a dreamer. . . . [18]

After graduation Pavlis presented himself at the office Pool had established in space rented from the General Cartage Company of

Detroit. Leonard explained that he wanted to build a small generator capable of producing 350 cubic feet per hour of oxygen. Pool asked Pavlis to give him the specifications for the air compressor, a crucial part of the plant, so that he could order it immediately. But Pavlis, who had never seen an air separation plant, had to return to Ann Arbor to collect the thermodynamic data he needed. After he had been there a few days, he received a telegram from Pool: "YOU SHOULD HAVE ENOUGH DATA. REPORT FOR WORK ON MONDAY AND ORDER COMPRESSOR."

The two men pushed ahead with the project. Neither of them had the practical skills in soldering and brazing necessary to build the demonstration unit. It was customary for Pool to have Pavlis visit his and Dorothy's home in Canada on Saturday nights to drink beer and talk with the locals, who were mostly French Canadians. One such local was Paul LaChappelle, who knew soldering and brazing and was unemployed. Leonard invited him to join the team.

Whenever he could get away from Compressed Industrial Gases, Pool looked in on Pavlis and LaChappelle and offered friendly suggestions. At night, Pavlis did the designing and mechanical drawing work. During the day, he and LaChappelle pounded the plant together with a few dilapidated tools, including a drill press and a grinder purchased by Pool. By the middle of February 1940, Pavlis calculated that he had spent 1,950 hours on the project, including 800 hours working on the heat exchanger and connections, 350 on the caustic scrubbers and air compressor, and 250 on the distillation column.[19] Pool poured his capital and salary into the second-hand machinery and hundreds of component parts needed for the plant. He cashed in his personal insurance policies and overdrew his bank account. For Pavlis, too, "It was a sort of nightmare. I still wonder how we did it. . . ."[20]

By the summer of 1940, after a year's labor, the plant was working reasonably well. The distillation column had a tendency to pulse, sounding like a heaving horse, but it could produce 359 cubic feet of 99.5 percent pure oxygen per hour, slightly exceeding the original goal. Leonard Pool the salesman now wheeled into action. He arranged demonstrations of the oxygen unit, just as the war in Europe was sending shock waves through the United States. In May 1940, Holland and Belgium had fallen to the Germans, Dunkirk was evacuated, and Roosevelt asked Congress for 50,000 aircraft. Pool's belief in a sharply increased need for oxygen was being fulfilled. And his

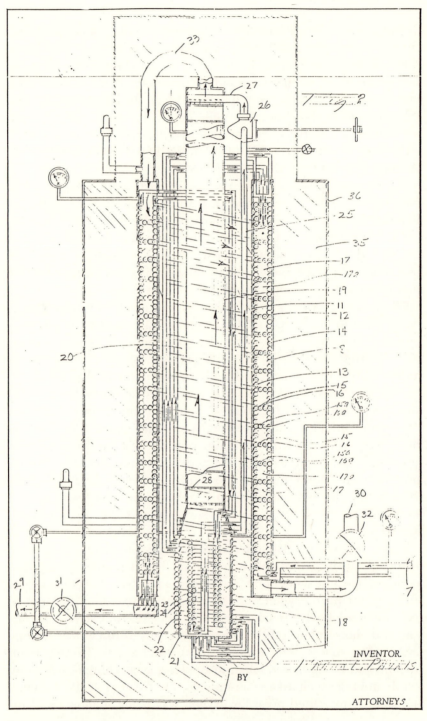

Patent application drawing of the Pavlis prototype generator.

ideas about possible customers were changing. He was able to persuade even Charles Kettering, a General Motors' vice president and one of America's most famous engineers, to attend a demonstration.

"Kettering was a very plain fellow that you could meet in the laboratories. You wouldn't know he was General Motors' chief research officer,"[21] Pavlis later recalled. At the demonstration, it proved necessary to improvise. The presence of liquid oxygen, as indicated by a gauge on the instrument panel, was the principal way of telling that the plant was working. But, horrible to relate, Pavlis had not had time to get the plant fully running, because Kettering arrived two hours early. In desperation, he quickly established a false reading on the gauge, making it appear that the plant was functioning. Kettering, examining the generator, remarked that it had the steadiest gauge he had ever seen (and well it would have been, since the valves were closed). Leonard replied, "yes, the plant runs very well." After Kettering left, Leonard congratulated Pavlis on the demonstration. "But Leonard," Pavlis explained, "the plant wasn't really running." Pool's reaction was a reprimand that included several expletives.[22]

Others who came to look included James Lincoln, the president of the Lincoln Electric Company, and officials of the Ford Motor Company, including the chief engineer. It was not necessary to sell the Ford representatives the on-site supply concept—Ford already owned several German-built generators. However, Ford was not immediately interested. Neither was Nash-Kelvinator, whose chief engineer also visited the prototype. An increased demand for oxygen was one thing. Obtaining plants from an untested source, and buying the new concept of leasing, were something else again. While these results were discouraging, Pool and Pavlis had little left to lose. Leonard resigned from Compressed Industrial Gases to devote himself full time to the generator project.

Carl Anderson and Engineering Excellence

As both men knew, their first tasks were to improve the demonstration unit, which had unstable operating characteristics, and to establish production facilities. They needed help from someone with a solid understanding of generator design and manufacture, someone with years of experience in the field. At this crucial juncture, Pool learned about Carl Anderson, an engineer with just the sort of experience the project needed. Pool quickly invited him to come aboard.

Anderson, who was forty-two at the time, had graduated from Cleveland's East Technical High School in 1916 and had then enrolled in the mechanical engineering program at Case School of Applied Science.[23] He had worked during the summers for General Electric's Cleveland Wire Division. In the autumn of 1918, he left Case to work as a civilian for the Army Air Corps. He also applied to the Tank Corps but could not serve because of a heart murmur. He then worked briefly in Washington, D.C. before returning to the Cleveland Wire Division. He spent the academic year 1919–1920 at Purdue University, studying electrical engineering. Graduating with a B.S. in 1921, Anderson went back to the Cleveland Wire Division as a project engineer.

For a time he worked on the design and construction of distillation column caps and trays for the production of argon gas, used in General Electric's new Mazda C lightbulb.[24] Anderson's next task involved an oxygen generator. In 1924 he joined several of his colleagues from the Cleveland Wire Division in designing and building air separation plants for I. H. Levin, a company organized two years earlier by Levin, Lee Twomey, and D. Tonkonogy. The firm reorganized more than once, and in 1925 became the Gas Industries Company, headquartered in Pittsburgh.

Carl Anderson became superintendent, engineer, and project manager, directing a work force of about ten people. He remained with the firm until 1939, designing, constructing, and operating air separation plants and electrolytic cells for the production of hydrogen and oxygen. The company prospered and became a technological leader in the American branch of the industry. This became apparent in 1927, when Charles Berger, an executive of the Gulf Refining Company, became interested in using oxygen in the manufacture of aluminum chloride, a catalyst in cracking oil.[25] Looking for a study of the best available processes for making oxygen, he turned to Gas Industries. As part of the study, Levin contacted Matthias Fränkl in Augsburg, Germany. Fränkl had certain patents covering the use of a new type of heat exchanger, or regenerator, which he had developed in the twenties. His process proposed using a novel form of heat exchange (which would take place in the regenerator) that was soon recognized as a critical breakthrough for the design of oxygen plants. An air separation system incorporating the Fränkl regenerator promised to supply oxygen in much larger quantities than any previous generators. This was the origin of "tonnage oxygen" plants that found extensive use in the steel industry many years later. Gas Industries purchased a third interest in Fränkl's company, which was known as MAPAG.

Anderson traveled to Augsburg to look at Fränkl's regenerator. He became convinced that the equipment was not appropriate for Gulf's needs. As he toured the German shops, it appeared unlikely to Anderson that the regenerator would meet its inventor's performance claims. Further, after viewing the operation first hand, it seemed that the problems of designing a process cycle based on the Fränkl concept could not be readily solved. He cabled the home office not to continue in the venture. Gulf had already ordered one of the Fränkl-type regenerators from Gas Industries but, as a result of the unexpected recommendation, the order was cancelled. Gas Industries, in a quandary, turned to Hazard Flammand, a Frenchman who had also developed new technology for air separation. Early in 1928 Anderson moved to Douai, France, to begin work on the design of a new oxygen generator based on Flammand's technique.

Satisfied that the design was sound, Anderson sailed for the United States and an appointment with Charles Berger of Gulf, who approved it. Gas Industries built the unit in Pittsburgh and successfully installed it at Port Arthur, Texas, in 1929. The plant produced 6,000 and later 8,000 cubic feet per hour of 99.8 percent pure oxygen, as well as over 99 percent pure nitrogen. It was one of the largest oxygen generators built up to that time in the United States and represented an impressive new level of oxygen purity. Moreover, it established the technical abilities of Gas Industries and underscored the engineering expertise of Carl Anderson. It also once again illustrated the dependence of American companies on European technology.

Despite the financial and technological successes of Gas Industries in the 1920s, the company fell upon hard times. As the Depression set in, customers for oxygen generators virtually vanished. One opportunity that kept the firm solvent came from overseas. In August 1936, an agreement was reached between Gas Industries, Sydney Allen (a London banker), and other parties. The agreement included purchase of British rights to Gas Industries' patents and working drawings. The company formed as a result of the agreement was the Saturn Oxygen Company, Ltd. The creation of Saturn took Carl Anderson to Great Britain to help supervise the manufacture, installation, and operation of oxygen generators. Anderson also took clients from England to Wright Field in Dayton, Ohio, to examine a mobile oxygen generator built by Gas Industries for the Army Air Corps, in 1933.

In 1939 Anderson turned down the position of Managing Director of Saturn, and returned to the United States. Ill with double pneumonia, he did not resume work at Gas Industries until the early spring of 1940. When he did return, Anderson found only a skeleton staff of one man who ran the office and sold spare parts for plants. Anderson left to join the Kerotest Company, a firm designing high-pressure petroleum valves. While that work was interesting, it was a waste of his two decades of experience with oxygen generators.

Longing for a change, Anderson was open to challenge when, in September 1940, he met Leonard and Dorothy Pool. He did not have high expectations. He was hesitant about joining Pool's venture because he wanted a job with stability. But Leonard, ever the salesman, explained his plans to build and install on-site plants and derive a steady stream of revenue from leasing. As Anderson later recalled:

> Leonard was a wonderful salesman, a very positive salesman. When he told you something, he made you believe that what he was telling you was the truth. He was very positive about what he wanted done and how to do it. He didn't always know how to do it, but he knew someone like myself could do it if I got down to the work. . . .

Anderson came to share Pool's excitement. "I thought he was very smart, because his concept was different from our concept [at Gas Industries] and I could see that if you owned the producing equipment and you sold the gas, it would be like keeping the cow and selling the milk."[26]

Notes

1. Frank Pavlis interview, 2 February 1988, Air Products History Office, Trexlertown, PA (hereafter APHO).

2. Walter Licht, *Working for the Railroad* (Princeton, N. J.: Princeton University Press), pp. 76, 220–230, 232.

3. Walter Pool interview, 25 January 1976, APHO.

4. William Haynes, ed., *American Chemical Industry*, 6 vols. (New York: D. Van Nostrand, 1949), VI:433–434; "The Linde Story," *Focus* 2 (Summer/Autumn 1982): 5.

5. Haynes, VI:434; "The Linde Story," pp. 5–7, 13; Charles F. Brush to Fred W. Woof, 7 March 1907, Charles F. Brush Papers, Special Collections, Freihergen Library, Case Western Reserve University, Cleveland, Ohio.

6. Haynes, VI:6; *Poor's Financial Records: 1940 Industrial Manual* (Poor's Publishing Co., 1940), p. 1880; *Moody's Manual of Investments, American and Foreign: Industrial Securities* (New York: Moody's Investor Services, 1940), p. 1961.

7. Haynes, VI:6; *Poor's Financial Records: 1940 Industrial Manual*, p. 1880; Union Carbide and Carbon Corporation, *Annual Report for the Year 1931*, p. 36.

8. Last Will and Testament of Charles Rider, December 2, 1930, Probate Court of Wayne County, Liber 5103, C320104; *The Story of Fisher Body: A Tradition of Craftsmanship* (Detroit: General Motors Corp., 1949), pp. 6–7.

9. Acetylene Gas and Supply Company incorporation papers, APHO; *Poor's Financial Records: 1940 Industrial Manual*, p. 1597.

10. Haynes, V:189 and IV:46; *Poor's Financial Records: 1940 Industrial Manual*, p. 2050; Union Carbide and Carbon Corporation, *Annual Report for the Year 1935*, pp. 10–11.

11. Charles Rider obituaries in the *Detroit Free Press*, 15 February 1938, p. 20 and the *Detroit News*, 15 February 1938, p. 27; Last Will and Testament of Charles Rider, 2 December 1930, APHO.

12. Union Carbide and Carbon Corp., *Annual Report for the Year 1939*, p. 19.

13. "Union Carbide II: Alloys, Gases, and Carbons," *Fortune* (July 1941): 94.

14. "Oxygen: Past, Present, and Prospects," *Chemical Engineering* (January 1947): 126. Another advantage was that containers for liquid oxygen, which was transported at atmospheric pressure, were much lighter than cylinders holding gaseous oxygen, which was compressed to very high pressure. The reduction of container weight meant that more oxygen could be transported.

15. Now Michigan Technological University, Houghton.

16. Frank Pavlis to Leonard Pool, 31 March 1939, APHO.

17. Frank Pavlis, "Why Write a Story about Air Products," manuscript, 30 January 1988, p. 6, APHO.

18. Frank Pavlis interview, 2 February 1988, APHO.

19. Frank Pavlis' handwritten ledger, 1939, APHO.

20. Frank Pavlis interview, 2 February 1988, APHO.

21. Frank Pavlis interview, 2 February 1988, APHO; Stuart W. Leslie, *Boss Kettering* (New York: Columbia University Press, 1983), pp. 296–313.

22. Frank Pavlis interview, 2 February 1988, APHO.

23. Now Case Western Reserve University.

24. Leonard S. Reich, *The Making of American Industrial Research: Science and Business at GE and Bell, 1876–1926* (Cambridge: Cambridge University Press, 1985), pp. 84, 86; James A. Cox, *A Century of Light* (New York: Benjamin Company, 1979), pp. 64, 147, 149–150.

25. Peter Spitz, *Petrochemicals: The Rise of an Industry* (New York: John Wiley & Sons, 1988), p. 126.

26. Carl Anderson interview, 2 February 1988, APHO.

2

Air Products at War

While Leonard Pool's first focus was on assembling the engineering team he needed, he was beset by other problems. To move ahead he would have to build an effective organization, gather capital, and perfect his product. Above all, he had to find customers and create a secure niche in the market. In the helter-skelter of responding to available opportunities, the young firm would move far beyond the initial vision of leasing on-site oxygen generators. Pool's ambition drove him to pursue every opportunity—and many opportunities were presented by the unusual demands of a wartime economy.

Chancing It

Of the numerous problems Pool faced, the easiest to solve was that of incorporation. He simply walked down the street to a local firm of lawyers and announced that he wanted to organize a company. The lawyer who handled the business was James Spencer, who would play an important role in the Air Products story. The papers of incorporation were signed on September 30, 1940 and filed on October 1: the Industrial Gas Equipment Company was born. The stated purpose of the concern was "to manufacture, produce, rent, lease, sell, and service equipment for the production of gases and to manufacture, produce, and sell gases of all kinds; and to own, lease, hold, and acquire real estate and property and equipment useful thereto."[1] Pool's venture, of which he became President and Treasurer and his

UNITED STATES OF AMERICA

The State of Michigan

TUEBOR

CIRCUMSPICE

MICHIGAN CORPORATION AND SECURITIES COMMISSION

TO ALL TO WHOM THESE PRESENTS SHALL COME:

I, *Howard M. Warner*, Commissioner of the Michigan Corporation and Securities Commission, Do Hereby Certify That Articles of Incorporation of

INDUSTRIAL GAS EQUIPMENT COMPANY

were duly filed in this office on the ___1st___ day of ___October___ A. D., Nineteen Hundred and Forty_____and the said Company is authorized to commence its business in conformity with Act 327, Public Acts of 1931.

FORM NO. 22

In testimony whereof, I have hereunto set my hand and affixed the Seal of the Commission, in the City of Lansing, this ___First___ day of ___October___ A. D. 194_0

Howard M. Warner
Commissioner.

Papers of incorporation of Air Products, *né* the Industrial Gas Equipment Company.

wife Dorothy Secretary, would need all of the license provided by this broad statement of purpose.

The authorized capital of $50,000 consisted of 500 common shares of $100 par value each. Leonard Pool was the only stockholder. Two hundred shares were issued to him in exchange for the transfer of title to the demonstration oxygen plant, to all materials, tools, dies, patterns, and drawings owned by him, and to "all patents, patent applications or patent rights owned or controlled by him and relating to the manufacture of oxygen gas, or the design, construction and manufacture of plants for the production of oxygen gas."[2] Pool envisioned patenting the prototype generator. In June 1940 Frank Pavlis had contacted a lawyer, who drafted an application and specifications, and had drawings prepared. But neither Pavlis nor Pool took the patent idea beyond that preliminary step.

As if he did not have enough problems to cope with, in mid-October Pool learned that the name "Industrial Gas Equipment Company" had already been used in Michigan. Carl Anderson's proposal of Pool Air Products was rejected, but Pool liked the name Air Products. The company was renamed. At the same time, Leonard turned to another family member for help in opening the company's first office and shop. His brother, Walter Pool, also had an entrepreneurial bent. While teaching pathology at Wayne State University's College of Medicine, he had created a "school" of mortuary science. Walter had an understanding with the university that it would turn the "school" into an academic department after a period of time (which it did in 1943). But for the moment, Walter was able to help Leonard's new company with space for offices, drafting, and light manufacturing, as well as with modest clerical support.

Air Products had meager prospects. Staff turnover was rapid. Leonard Pool was a hard taskmaster, but he was careful to husband the engineering talent he had recruited. The value Pool placed on that talent would strongly shape the company culture. Frank Pavlis and Carl Anderson officially joined the payroll in October 1940, and Pool added a draftsman, Don MacLeod, a native of Windsor, Ontario. MacLeod would later play a role in the company's manufacturing department. Anderson was vital to the venture, and Pool gave him a salary equal to his own and the title Vice President of Engineering. Anderson also became a member of the Board of Directors. He had the status, but not the power, of a partner in the firm.

Unbeknown to Anderson, his old employer, Gas Industries, filed for bankruptcy that December, providing Pool with his first lucky break. The company's assets, which remained in legal limbo because of a claim by a Gas Industries customer, represented a treasure trove of engineering and manufacturing information. Anderson and Pool learned about this development from John Swindell, an unemployed Gas Industries draftsman, who had been retained by the trustee of the bankruptcy court in January 1941 to compile an inventory of the company's assets. As this was being done, Pool followed Anderson's recommendation and hired Swindell. A month later, Swindell, acting on his own behalf, offered the trustee $250 for all the production equipment, including molds, fixtures, and patterns; all drawings, blueprints, and other engineering records; and all domestic and foreign patents owned by Gas Industries. Conveniently, these assets had been appraised at only $247.80! The trustee attempted to determine if there were other parties interested, and was unable to find any. When he offered these technical assets for sale at a private auction on March 19, 1941, Leonard Pool and John Butler (a friend in the gas business) bought them for $1,625. Butler put up the actual money, and Pool acquired some of the assets from him by paying in monthly installments.[3]

The property Pool acquired consisted of ten American patents, and production drawings for electrolytic cells and air separation plants. The value of the patents was questionable, since many dated from the 1920s and were no longer valid. The most recent patent was already four years old and had only minor utility. The real value of the acquisition lay in the production drawings. With them, Air Products could leapfrog months if not years of design work and launch directly into the manufacturing of equipment. It could, that is, if and when it managed to land its first order.

Keeping the Wolf from the Door

It was now eighteen months since Pavlis had signed on. Desperate for work, Leonard Pool secured a small order from the Rotary Electric Steel Company of Detroit, for the redesign of an oxygen cutting torch. It was not the sort of thing for which Air Products had been organized, but it was at least a beginning. Meanwhile, working capital—a normal problem for entrepreneurial ventures—was tight. Pool's funds had been depleted in financing the design and construction of the demonstration plant. He borrowed from his wife and from his brother Walter. He also paid himself, Pavlis, and Anderson partly in stock.

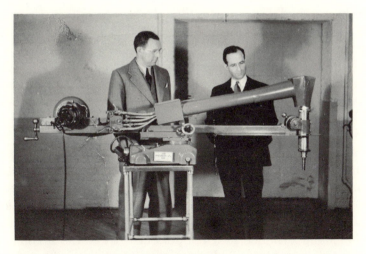

Carl Anderson and Leonard Pool with the company's first order, an
oxygen cutting torch, in early 1941.

As Pool knew, it was vital to keep Anderson at work redesigning
the prototype generator that Frank Pavlis had put together:

> I saw the chief problem was that the distilling column had
> problems with entrainment and flooding of the column by the
> liquid as it came down . . . I knew exactly what was happening
> . . . the downcoming pipes going from tray to tray were not of
> proper size. This they couldn't get out of a textbook. I took the
> designs that we had from Gas Industries and we adapted those
> to build new heat exchangers, and a new column which had all
> the advantages that we had determined through the testing at
> the General Electric Company. Then the plant worked per-
> fectly.[4]

Pool also used Anderson for other experimental engineering work.
Several times in 1941, he asked if there was a better way of com-
pressing oxygen into storage cylinders or pipelines. Standard compressors used a water-based lubricant, which had the disadvantage
of introducing water vapor into the oxygen gas. The vapor had to be
removed by chemical drying or adsorption to obtain dry gas for transport in cylinders. Anderson knew that neither the Germans nor the
Americans had succeeded in solving the water vapor problem.

One possible solution was to pump the oxygen in a liquid state.
Because of its focus on making and transporting liquid oxygen, Linde

regularly pumped oxygen as a liquid. The technique devised by
Linde's impressive staff of research scientists and engineers was to use
graphite and asbestos packing in the liquid oxygen pumps, which
leaked after fifty hours of operation. Equally unsatisfactory was the
method patented in 1932 by Anderson's former boss, I.H. Levin.[5]

Leonard was not in the least discouraged by such technological
roadblocks. He said: "Andy, go home and give it some more
thought and see if you can come up with something."[6] After a period of much frustration and after going over the different patents
on pumping volatile liquids, Anderson suddenly saw a partial solution: subcool the oxygen fed to the pump. Nitrogen has a lower
boiling point than oxygen. Hence gaseous nitrogen from the top
of the distillation column could be used to subcool the oxygen
and the pump cylinder to a temperature below the boiling point
of oxygen. Subcooling would eliminate one major problem by pre-
venting the oxygen from reaching its boiling point, vaporizing,
and causing the pump to vapor lock.

Air Products' liquid oxygen pump seemed likely to give it a technological edge, but the pump's practical development was many
months away. Besides, Pool still had to drum up the customers.
Here, as later, Carl Anderson's links to General Electric proved
helpful. Anderson's brother Nils was employed by General Electric's Carboloy subsidiary, where 2,000-ampere electrolytic cells
were used to generate hydrogen for sintering tungsten and other
carbides. Carboloy had purchased its electrolytic cells from Gas Industries. These were the same cells which Anderson had built as a
Gas Industries employee and for which Air Products now owned
the production drawings. Through the intervention of Nils Anderson, Carboloy contacted Air Products and awarded them a contract
for replacement cells. A temporary reprieve had been granted to
the hard-pressed organization.[7]

By July 1941, Air Products was employing nineteen workers, in
addition to Pool, Anderson, and Pavlis. Anderson, like Pool, was
spending all his time on administration. Pavlis, with MacLeod and
one other draftsman, made up the engineering operation. The bulk
of the new employees were constructing cells for Carboloy. Soon the
firm landed an additional contract to build electrolytic cells, this time
for the Tennessee Copper Company, another old Gas Industries Company customer. And Pool's persistence finally began to pay off in
military contracts.

The United States was stepping up its production of war materiel.

Don MacLeod with a liquid oxygen pump.

The Lend-Lease Act, made law in March 1941, authorized the manufacture, sale, loan, lease, and transfer of war materiel to Britain and all other countries deemed vital to the defense of the United States. (In July 1941, the Soviet Union alone requested nearly $2 billion worth of military aid.) Since war materiel normally involved steel, that meant a concomitant demand for oxygen. Pool knew his best hope lay in the military market. He intensified his efforts to win military orders, not only in Washington, D.C., but also at the Army Air Forces' national procurement center at Wright Field, Dayton, Ohio. Oxygen had a role not only in the repair of aircraft by welding, but also as a gas breathed in high-altitude flight. After all, Anderson had built a mobile generating unit for the Army Air Forces as long ago as 1933.

In June 1941, Leonard Pool, Carl Anderson, and their wives drove to Dayton. On an earlier trip, Pool had been unable to find anyone at Wright Field who was interested in mobile oxygen units. "Don't call us; we'll call you," he was told. But Leonard Pool was determined not to give in. He picked up the base telephone book and methodically went through it, calling people. He finally reached a Captain Robert Turner, an engineering officer with Aero-Medical Laboratories. Turner said, "We have been looking all over for Anderson," whom he knew from Gas Industries and the mobile oxygen generator designed by Anderson and I.H. Levin.[8] Anderson and Pavlis worked day and night and produced drawings for an appropriate mobile unit within two weeks.

In 1933, the Gas Industries mobile generator had been seen as an interesting but esoteric piece of equipment. Those were extremely lean years for military procurement. By the spring of 1941, however, Robert Turner had decided that the Army Air Forces would soon need oxygen on many, widely dispersed airfields, perhaps in remote foreign climes. Turner liked the Air Products design and funds were available for experimentation. He gave the company a $51,000 development contract.[9] At last Air Products had an order for an oxygen generator. The company had also broken into the military market, even though it was selling generators, not leasing them.

Electrolytic cell construction and the Army Air Forces development contract enabled Pool to keep running, but the firm was acutely short of working capital. Leonard turned to his wife Dorothy seeking aid. She loaned Air Products $14,000. While her motive was "to help a struggling husband," Dorothy received 6 percent interest and a promise of repayment by September 10, 1941. The loan was secured by assignment of the company's accounts receivable with Carboloy and Tennessee Copper, as well as by a mortgage on all of the company's tangible property and equipment.[10]

In November 1941, just as the orders for electrolytic cells were running out, Pool found someone to try out the leasing concept with which he had started. That person was Anthony Taylor, purchasing agent for the Rotary Electric Steel Company, which was in need of additional oxygen capacity. The company did not believe it had any place to put an on-site generator, but Pool, desperate to push his concept of "keeping the cow and selling the milk," suggested installing the original Air Products' demonstration plant in the boiler house. It was not a choice an engineer would have made. When Frank Pavlis started to install the unit, he found the heat so intense that he had to buy a pair of shoes with extra thick soles. Nevertheless, with this installation, Air Products was in the leased on-site generator business. At last, things were looking up.

Leonard Pool's persistence in seeking military orders also began to pay off in other ways. He learned in Washington that the Navy intended to convert fourteen World War I generators, originally designed to produce nitrogen for the synthesis of anhydrous ammonia, to produce oxygen for use in naval shipyards around the country.[11] Once again, the Anderson–Gas Industries connection was to prove crucial in getting new business.

Pool approached the Navy and suggested Air Products for the work of converting one of the generators that was to be located at the Norfolk Navy Yard at Portsmouth, Virginia. Pool noted that Carl Anderson had already installed a 1,000 cubic-feet-per-hour oxygen plant at the Navy Yard, when he was with Gas Industries in 1928. Anderson was invited to Virginia to discuss the proposal, but after visiting the site he made an odd recommendation. He advised the Navy to contact Air Reduction, the plant's original manufacturer, if it wanted to pursue the idea of conversion. He did state, however, that Air Products could build a new 6,000 cubic-feet-per-hour generator based on old Gas Industries drawings. Impressed by Anderson's candor, the Navy abandoned its conversion plan for the Norfolk plant and awarded Air Products a contract in November 1941. With this $156,000 project, it began to appear that if Pool could keep Air Products afloat long enough, the company would find its salvation in the military market.

Pearl Harbor and the Lessons of War

On December 7, 1941, the Japanese bombed United States military installations at Pearl Harbor. American entry into the war dramatically increased the demand for oxygen. The war also cut off America from the major foreign suppliers of oxygen-generating equipment. This had little effect on Linde or Air Reduction, which had been building their own plants for many years. However, the very few American sellers of generators were barely able to supply the dozens of independent producers and distributors of oxygen, let alone the armed services. The Navy, the Army Air Forces, and the Corps of Engineers badly needed mobile and stationary units to place on aircraft carriers and at airfields. As events would soon make clear, the manufacture of reliable and safe mobile plants small enough for on-site use at airfields demanded novel rearrangements of available technology. And it was here that Leonard Pool's pioneering efforts with his demonstration generator began to pay unforeseen dividends.[12]

The military had been accustomed to relying not on its own generators, but on gas shipments from Linde and Air Reduction, who supplied oxygen gas in cylinders and, in the case of Linde, liquid oxygen in insulated tank cars and trucks. That left the Navy, Army Air Forces, and Corps of Engineers uncertain where to find mobile generators. Linde and Air Reduction were not themselves interested in manufacturing unfamiliar small plants for this specialized market. Thus, Air Products found itself no longer a late entrant to an established domestic business, but one of several contenders offering to supply a new product in a wartime market. The challenge to Air Products and other small suppliers was to come up with appropriate designs and to accelerate production without lowering the quality of their products. The success of Air Products in meeting this challenge stands in sharp contrast to the experience of its competition.

In a great rush, the Army Air Forces placed sizable orders with known contractors. Chief among those contractors was the Independent Engineering Company. Before Pearl Harbor, it had already won over $3 million in military contracts and, in February 1942, it obtained a $1.7 million contract for mobile oxygen generators.[13] Air Products also managed to pick up some sizable crumbs, thanks to the connection it had made with Robert Turner and the Army Air Forces. In February 1942, Air Products received an $836,000 production contract for fifteen 600 cubic-feet-per-hour mobile trailer-mounted oxygen units. The generator was model 281–4, which stood for the fourth revision of design number 281 that the company's engineers had made.

Independent Engineering expanded its production capacity in 1942 and turned out 20 mobile units per month based on total orders for about 400 plants. But the military grew discontented with the quality of these mobile generators. As a memorandum of April 20, 1943 stated, "the Engineers report is very definite that the design is imperfect. Originally designed as a 1000 cubic foot plant it has been rerated as 600 cubic foot and that reduced capacity is less than 70 percent efficient."[14] According to the War Production Board, Independent's generators exploded frequently, needed repairs too often, and required too many operators. Nonetheless, the Independent contracts were not cancelled in the first years of the war because the military acutely needed oxygen plants. Superior Air Products, the other major supplier of mobile generators, had not completed a single unit by April 1943.

Needing to accelerate production of, and research and development on, mobile oxygen generators, the military turned to Vannevar Bush and the National Defense Research Committee (NDRC). The NDRC spent over $4 million on generator research between 1943 and 1945. To turn research knowledge into a production model, the NDRC asked the M.W. Kellogg Company to carry out engineering studies and development work. The Clark Brothers Company, Inc., of Olean, New York, was asked to develop a lightweight oxygen compressor, a reciprocating expansion engine (based on designs from S.C. Collins and F.G. Keyes of the Massachusetts Institute of Technology), and the tools and techniques to manufacture an appropriate heat exchanger. Relying on that development work, the Army Air Forces eventually placed orders with Kellogg and Clark for twenty mobile plants.[15]

Air Products, which did not receive a slice of this particular pie, nevertheless quickly proved itself capable of supplying mobile generators which produced substantially more than their rated capacity and which used fewer war-critical materials (e.g., steel, copper, and aluminum) in their construction than those built by their competitors. In addition, Air Products plants weighed less, saved shipping space, operated on less power, and were simpler to run. Low-cost production and operation would become the hallmarks of Air Products engineering. In the autumn of 1944, after using Superior Air Products and Independent Engineering plants, the Soviet Union specified Air Products equipment when requisitioning plants through the Lend-Lease Program. Air Products contracts with the government grew from $156,000 in 1941 to more than $7 million in 1944.[16] Implicit in these numbers is the fact that Pool and his colleagues were not only meeting the challenges of engineering and of sales, but also the challenges of how to run a growing operation.

Technological Innovation

The success of the Air Products units was due to their technological reliability. Virtually every generator included the special liquid oxygen pump which Carl Anderson had invented. The pump and the overall design of the 281-4 and subsequent generators gave Air Products an edge over its competitors. Knowledge of that edge provided Leonard Pool with additional motivation (not that he needed any) to take on projects that were even more challenging.

One principal use of the mobile generators was on military airfields, to supply oxygen for the crews of high-flying aircraft. High pressure gas cylinders inside aircraft would explode when hit by gunfire. The Army Air Forces decided to store the oxygen aboard the aircraft in a liquid state. Air Products turned to Clarence Schilling as consultant on this problem.[17] Schilling was a skilled craftsman and "natural" engineer who had eleven years of air separation experience at the Cleveland Wire Works. The A-1, which Schilling helped to develop, was a trailer-mounted unit which generated either 1,000 cubic-feet-per-hour of oxygen gas or seventy pounds-per-hour of liquid oxygen. The A-1 was much lighter than the 281-4 and was powered by an air-cooled Continental aircraft engine used on AAF trainers such as the Stearman PT-17 and the Fairchild PT-23. The use of this engine had a special appeal, because the Army Air Forces already had a cadre of mechanics trained to repair it. Air Products only had to train enlisted personnel to run and repair the compressor and liquefaction components.

Another, even tougher challenge came with the Army Air Forces' request for six generators capable of producing 60 pounds of liquid oxygen per hour. The catch was that these generators had to be operational on aircraft repair ships serving in the Pacific.[18] Since the pitch and yaw of a ship disturbed the flow of gas and liquid in the distillation column, a difficult engineering problem had to be solved. Schilling set to work to redesign the column. In traditional columns, the liquefied air was separated into its constituent parts as it passed through a sequence of trays placed one above another. The nature of gas flow was controlled by the size and arrangement

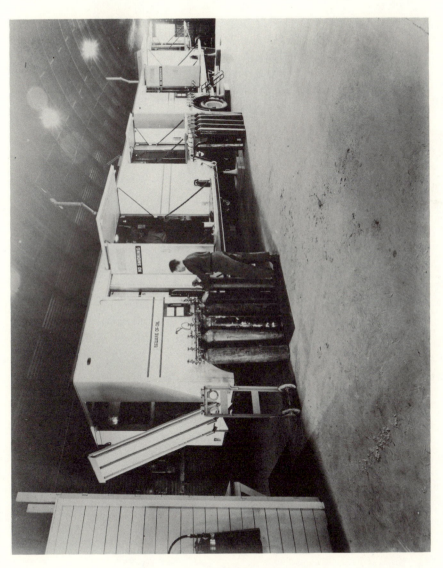

Model 281-4 mobile oxygen generators being used in Alaska by the U.S. Navy to fill cylinders, May 1944.

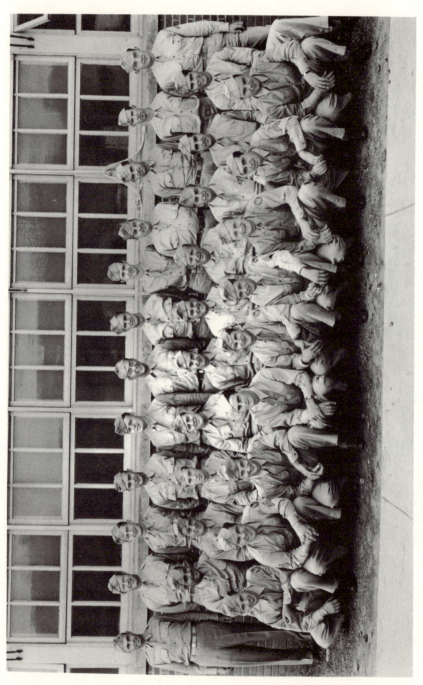

The First and Second Aircraft Repair Units, two of many crews trained by Air Products in the operation and maintenance of its mobile oxygen generators, in June 1944.

of the bubble caps on these trays. However, the bubble caps became dysfunctional when the column tilted, as would happen on a ship. Schilling developed a system that minimized this problem; the trays had built-in pockets and a network of tubes which connected each pocket to the ones directly below it. These tubes were positioned so that no matter how the column was tilted, liquid would quickly redistribute itself with only a momentary interruption in service.

In addition to those technical challenges, Air Products was faced with the need to train non-technical people in the operation and maintenance of its generators. Hundreds of Army Air Forces, Navy, and Corps of Engineers enlisted men and officers, most of whom lacked any technical experience or instruction, were taught at company facilities in Detroit and Chattanooga. Also, detailed handbooks of operating, maintenance, and safety instructions were written and published for use by those trainees. A fortunate outcome of this training program was the hiring in due course of several participants, including Ray Patterson, Bill Say, Bill Schmoyer, and Ed Perlman, as peacetime employees in Air Products' Operations Department.

As the company's business grew, Anderson's informal network of contacts was of great help. Lee Twomey, the former chief engineer of the Cleveland Wire Works, served as a consultant, and Clarence Schilling, who was initially employed as a consultant, later became a permanent employee. Leonard Volland (a former employee of both the Cleveland Wire Works and Gas Industries), who had extensive experience designing distillation columns and trays, and Mark Halsted, a high school graduate with some drafting experience, were hired in 1942. The following year, Air Products added two engineering graduates of Detroit's Lawrence Institute of Technology: Jack Graeffe, a refugee from Nazi Germany, and Edward Donley, who was hired as a designer. Both would later prove vital to the company.

To help strengthen the sales effort, Leonard enlisted his brother George in 1943. George Pool had been a district manager for Compressed Industrial Gases, then for the National Cylinder Gas Company, before he took charge of government contracts as Air Products' Vice President in charge of sales. George dealt with key officials of the War Production Board, freeing Leonard to spend more time on entrepreneurial and managerial matters.

(*front, l–r*) Leonard Pool, Frank Pavlis, (*back, l–r*) Don MacLeod, visiting Soviet engineer, Carl Anderson, Len Volland. Many of the company's mobile and stationary generators went to the Soviet Union as part of the Treasury Department's Lend-Lease Program.

Finances

Leonard Pool knew that, on the eve of Pearl Harbor, Air Products had stood on the edge of bankruptcy. The 1941 fiscal year had ended with a deficit of $33,000 on sales of only $8,300. Pool had even considered taking a full-time job in order to keep the business going. The firm had to hold a special shareholders' meeting on December 15, 1941, to issue common stock to officers and employees in lieu of salary. While most of this stock went to Leonard Pool, a significant block went to Carl Anderson and Frank Pavlis, and a few shares were paid to Olaf Dybvig, a mechanic, and Don MacLeod.

Air Products was a cash-starved corporation well into 1943, even though it was gathering important military contracts. Some of the pressure was relieved when the company began to receive progress payments and advances on contracts. Leonard Pool quickly learned how to take advantage of these special conditions. For instance, a September 1944 contract for $2,790,000 to supply the Army Air Forces with forty A-1 generators permitted the company to receive 10 percent of the sale price up front, in addition to the usual advance payments.

At the end of fiscal year 1942, the company turned its first profit: a scant $235 before taxes, on net sales of $44,491. During the same period, the company signed contracts to supply some $3.8 million worth of oxygen generators. In fiscal 1943, net sales of $1 million yielded an income before taxes of $150,000. By fiscal 1945, net sales would reach $5 million, with pretax income of nearly $500,000. As these figures indicate, Air Products had cleared the gate by 1943. Even so the Board had to increase the authorized capital of the company yet another time in 1944 and to use shares to pay its officers and employees.

Detroit to Chattanooga

As wartime business picked up, Air Products abandoned Walter Pool's mortuary school and moved into an old ice house at 14000 Brush Street, which had both a crane and a high ceiling. Even these facilities were inadequate for the production of oxygen generators in any significant number. By November 1942 the company had contracted to build 68 units, including 1 for the Navy, 12 for the Corps of Engineers, 16 for the Army Air Forces, and 39 for the Treasury Department Lend-Lease Program, for shipment to the Soviet Union.

When the war was over, Air Products had built a total of 241 generators, 151 of which were sent to the Soviet Union under the Lend-Lease Program.[19] A complicating factor was the diversity of models produced. The Navy called for a stationary, 6,000-cubic-feet-per-hour oxygen unit, while the Army Air Forces wanted a trailer-mounted, 600-cubic-feet-per-hour oxygen unit, and the Corps of Engineers a trailer-mounted 500-cubic-feet-per-hour oxygen and 100-cubic-feet-per-hour nitrogen plant. Later contracts would add even more complexities, and the company produced no less than thirteen varieties of generators for the war effort.

There were well-defined limits to growth in Detroit. Manpower and construction space were tight. Manufacturers such as Ford were swamped with orders for tanks, military trucks, and aircraft. Thus the search for larger quarters became linked to a search for a more extensive labor supply. The Army Air Forces, the company's major military customer, offered to erect a building provided the company found the land. George Pool went to the War Production Board in Washington and explained the situation. The Board offered three sites: a building at a former New England stone quarry; a Pittsburgh foundry; and a vacant railroad-repair shop in Chattanooga, Tennessee. Air Products chose the Chattanooga site at a special meeting of the Board of Directors on September 20, 1943. The new plant had two ten-ton cranes, a high ceiling, and abundant floor space (approximately 96,000 square feet on 17 acres of land). Chattanooga also offered an adequate, if unskilled, labor supply.[20]

Air Products was able to afford the renovation and equipping of the Chattanooga site because of Defense Plant Corporation (DPC) funding. Organized in August 1940, the DPC was a special agency of the federal government that financed, constructed, and owned industrial plants needed for the war effort. These plants were run by private businesses through a lease or a management agreement. The DPC was particularly active in the aviation industry, and in the production of aluminum, magnesium, aviation gasoline, synthetic rubber, steel, ordnance, and chemicals (including oxygen).[21]

There was a substantial amount of public financing available to enlarge oxygen and acetylene production. The three largest producers, Linde, Air Reduction, and National Cylinder, as well as the industry's other firms (including the Burdett Oxygen Company, the Southern Oxygen Company of Bladensburg, Maryland, and the Chicago and Cincinnati facilities of Liquid Carbonic, Inc.) all benefited. The underwriting of facilities to *manufacture* oxygen *generators* was

Mobile and stationary oxygen generators under construction at Chattanooga.

another matter, however. Only one company other than Air Products, Independent Engineering, expanded oxygen generator production facilities to accommodate war needs. Unlike Air Products, Independent underwrote its expansion entirely with private capital.[22]

The government financed the move of Air Products from Detroit to Chattanooga at a cost of $600,000, including over $125,000 for machine tools and other equipment.[23] The relationship with the DPC and the War Production Board was clearly beneficial to Air Products, because it allowed the company to get into large-scale production with an adequate labor force. Air Products had entered the war with only 13 employees. Its work force expanded to 70 before leaving Detroit. Pool brought to Chattanooga the cadre of experienced engineers and draftsmen recruited in Detroit—Anderson and Pavlis, as well as Volland, Donley, Graeffe, MacLeod, Halsted, and Swindell—but he hired a fresh crew of shop employees from the local work force. Within three months the company was again producing oxygen generators. By May 1944, Air Products had 280 employees and was looking for more. Soon, the plant was operating three shifts and turning out four to six units a week.

Wartime demand had created a new market, that for mobile generators, in which Air Products became the leading player. And wartime financing by the government had enabled the company to take advantage of its opportunity.

Problems and Frustrations

The company celebrated the success of fiscal 1943 by declaring its first dividend: $15 per share. A year later, in celebration of continuing progress, the Board of Directors voted to share the corporation's prosperity with employees by creating a profit-sharing plan that set aside 10 percent of profits (before federal taxes) each year. The creation of the plan, however, required the approval of the Treasury Department, and as late as March 1945, approval was still not forthcoming.

This difficulty was but a foreshadowing of other problems with the government, stemming from the Renegotiation Act of 1942. The purpose of the Act was to control war profits by private industry doing work under contract. It stipulated that each contract in excess of $100,000, later $500,000, would contain a renegotiation clause for the recovery of any part of the contract price found to represent excessive

Table 2
Air Products Sales and Profits, 1941–1945

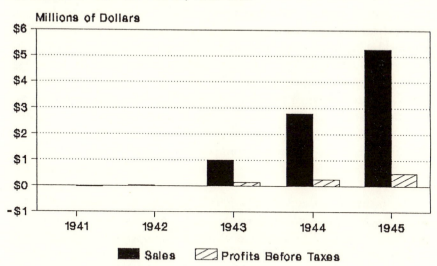

profits. The Act remained in force for the duration of the war and for the following three years.[24]

The company's success in bringing down the military's cost of mobile oxygen generators suggested that it had received excess profits. Leonard Pool went to Washington in December 1944, to negotiate with the Army Air Forces and the War Contract Price Adjustment Board. The Board made a substantial reduction in the refund requested by the Army Air Forces for fiscal 1943. Pool agreed to a compromise refund of $235,000, less tax credit. This painful experience was repeated in the renegotiation bargaining for fiscal 1944. The firm's profits suffered. Air Products posted net profits of $73,700 in 1943 but only $66,000 and $97,000 for fiscal 1944 and 1945, even though pretax income in these three years increased steadily from $150,000 to $500,000 (Table 2).

Nevertheless, the Pools, Pavlis, and Anderson could be pleased with what they had achieved in technology, in business, and in the war effort. They had built the company's reputation and its resources, both human and financial. They had produced excellent plants for the military. And they had made enough money to put some aside for what was expected to be a difficult transition to a peacetime economy.

The Chattanooga plant was entirely too large for any orders the company was likely to have in the immediate postwar years. Pool and his colleagues considered the question of a long-term location in the fall of 1944. They agreed to establish a reserve fund for the expense of a return to Detroit after the termination of war contracts. Free of the restraints of his earlier agreement with CIG, Leonard Pool—abetted by his brother George—was also considering entering his old business of selling cylinder oxygen and acetylene gas. He intended to open up at least one but probably more sales territories. Pittsburgh and Cleveland, two of the great industrial centers, appeared to be the most promising. The estimated capital needed for each territory was about $500,000. The company would also have to make a large capital investment in constructing plants to lease. Seeing these awesome sums on paper led to the decision not to declare dividends for both 1944 and 1945.

The future once again looked uncertain in the autumn of 1945, when Great Lakes Carbon Company of Chicago made an offer to buy out Air Products. The offer was a ninety-day option to purchase the company for $400,000. All war orders had been cancelled after victory over Japan on August 14. Leonard Pool, his colleagues and family had to give the offer serious consideration in light of the firm's uncertain future.

Notes

1. Articles of Incorporation, Industrial Gas Equipment Company, Air Products, Inc., Board of Directors Minute Book, no. 1, APHO.

2. "The Minutes of First Meeting of Incorporation of Industrial Gas Equipment Company, 30 September 1940," Air Products, Inc., Board of Directors Minute Book, No. 1, APHO.

3. Bankruptcy papers, Gas Industries Company, Case No. 20,988; "Payroll—Salary, 1940–41," APHO.

4. Carl Anderson interview, 2 February 1988, APHO.

5. "The Linde Story," *Focus* 2 (Summer/Autumn 1982): 18–19; U.S. Patent 1,921,531, 3 February 1932.

6. Carl Anderson interview, 2 February 1988, APHO.

7. *Moody's Manual of Investments, American and Foreign: Industrial Securities* (New York: Moody's Investor Services, 1940), pp. 1869–1870; Carboloy Corporation, "Carboloy Cemented Carbide for Reducing Wear on Tools and Machine Parts," (np: 1936), pp. 2–3.

8. Carl Anderson interview, 2 February 1988, APHO.

9. The date of this verbal contract is noted in "Field Generation of Oxygen," minutes of a meeting held at the Pentagon, 16 April 1943, p. 20, National Archives, Washington, D.C. The official date of the contract was

26 January 1942. Civilian Production Administration, *Alphabetical Listing of Major War Supply Contracts* (Washington, D.C.: Government Printing Office, 1946), p. 36.

10. Dorothy Rider Pool, "The Biography of a Business: Air Products Then and Now," APHO.

11. The generators were being operated by the Tennessee Valley Authority (TVA) at Muscle Shoals, Alabama. "Memorandum on Use of Muscle Shoals Equipment for Oxygen Production," 7 April 1942, National Archives, Washington, D.C.

12. William Haynes, ed., *American Chemical Industry*, 6 vols. (New York: D. Van Nostrand, 1949), VI:6–7; "The Linde Story," p. 10.

13. Civilian Production Administration, *Alphabetical Listing of Major War Supply Contracts*, p. 1624.

14. R.H. Snider to J.W. Flatley, Memorandum, 20 April 1943, National Archives, Washington, D.C.

15. W.A. Noyes, Jr., ed., *Chemistry: A History of the Chemistry Components of the National Defense Research Committee, 1940–1946* (Boston: Little, Brown, 1948), pp. 352–353. Amounts spent on research by the NDRC were supplied by Professor Larry Owens, who is preparing a history of the NDRC.

16. D.P. Morgan to F.O. Carroll, letter, 4 March 1944; D.P. Morgan to Guy N. Giroux, letter, 25 April 1945; James A. Lawson to J.W. Wizeman, memorandum, 3 February 1945; Andrew Ross, "Portable and Semi-portable Oxygen Generating Plants for the Military," 1 August 1945, APHO; "Russian Hydrogen and Oxygen Program," 12 June 1942, National Archives, Washington, D.C.

17. Clarence Schilling was educated at Cleveland College.

18. Noyes, pp. 354, 357–358.

19. In addition, sixty-four were sold to the Army Air Forces (including forty-one A-1s) and thirteen each to the Corps of Engineers and the Navy.

20. Reconstruction Finance Corporation, Defense Plant Corporation, Plancor No. 1837.

21. See Gerald Taylor White, *Billions for Defense: Government Financing by the Defense Plant Corporation during World War II* (University: University of Alabama Press, 1980) and Clifford Judkins Durr, *The Early History of the Defense Plant Corporation* (Washington, D.C.: Committee on Public Administration Cases, 1950).

22. War Production Board, *War Manufacturing Facilities Authorized through August 1944* (Washington, D.C.: Government Printing Office, 1945).

23. Ibid.; Reconstruction Finance Corporation, Defense Plant Corporation, Plancor No. 1837, National Archives, Washington, D.C.

24. Richards C. Osborn, *The Renegotiation of War Profits*, Bureau of Economic and Business Research Bulletin Series, No. 167 (Urbana: University of Illinois Press, 1948), pp. 17, 21.

PART II

COMING OF AGE

As the war ended, Leonard Pool, his family, and his colleagues at Air Products had every reason to think hard and long about the future. The war had provided an unexpected opportunity, with its demand for small, mobile generators. However, with the return of peace, government contracts—the company's central business—were being cancelled. In the private sector, the company was a minor, little-known organization which faced the prospect of intense competition from Linde, Air Reduction, and National Cylinder Gas, the major producers and distributors of industrial gases at that time. Air Products had been unable to establish a solid footing in the leasing business, the niche Pool hoped to fill. Capital, as always, was in short supply. The challenges were daunting and the risks great.

During the years from 1945 to 1957, Air Products would struggle to survive and to develop a business strategy. By 1957, these efforts were successful and the firm was on solid footing (Table 3). Air Products, by that time, would be established in the leasing and the tonnage gas businesses. It would have a large and growing trade with the federal government. In addition, the company entered the traditional cylinder gas business and began to produce and distribute new gases such as argon, helium, and hydrogen. Finally, Air Products strengthened its reputation in process engineering. The search for a strategy proved successful. Pool's venture had come of age. If still far from being the equal of industry leaders, like Linde, on their own ground, Air Products was a going concern. For some years following the war, however, the outcome was in serious doubt.

Table 3
Air Products Sales and Profits, 1945–1957

Millions of Dollars

3

Survival and Strategies

In 1945, Leonard Pool declined to sell Air Products to the Great Lakes Carbon Company. A year later, he received another offer, this time for $2 million in cash. Still he refused to sell. Pool was determined to make his company a success, even though the cancellation of military orders meant virtually starting over. Once again he faced the entrepreneurial challenges of finding capital and a market for the company's products. The basic difficulty was that Pool sought to compete in an established industry, replete with its market leaders and many minor players. Lacking either a radical technological innovation (like the Xerox machine or the Polaroid camera) or a plentiful supply of capital, Pool and his colleagues put their faith in their drive, determination, and ingenuity.

As reconversion to a peacetime economy began, Pool could call on resources he had not had in 1940: a reputation for the ability to deliver what was promised, a tradition of joining creative ingenuity to excellent engineering, a knowledge of generator design, and experience in managing a manufacturing operation. These assets would be important during the troubled years of the late 1940s, as Pool tried first one strategy and then another to make Air Products a profitable company. The year after V-J Day was one of particularly acute uncertainties, and of major decisions. Would the company survive? Where would it relocate? Could it lease or sell generators in the civilian market?

Air Products tried a variety of approaches in the immediate postwar years. The firm looked for more military contracts, sold oxygen generators and electrolytic cells overseas, leased generators in the United States, and launched a cylinder gas and welding equipment business. Amidst the chaos of this array of strategies, Air Products faced the problems of moving from Chattanooga and of financing its operations. By the end of 1946, the company had found toe-holds in a variety of markets. Unexpectedly, its major source of revenues was from overseas sales of generators. Financial matters remained a cause of serious concern. During the first quarter of fiscal 1947, Air Products had a loss of nearly $68,000. By the end of the year, that figure had grown to $240,000, although the sting of the loss was softened because an Internal Revenue Code provision permitted the company to use an income tax "carry-back" to reduce the figure to $83,000.

The Move to Emmaus

While questions of corporate strategy occupied Leonard Pool's mind in 1945, the most immediate question was the timing of the return to Detroit. Air Products' lease in Chattanooga was coming to an end. The market for the company's generators seemed likely to be quite small and unpredictable in the immediate postwar years. The major markets lay in the Northeast and Midwest, and being in the South added to transportation costs. There were also problems with union labor in Chattanooga.

The company's first home had been Detroit. The Board had voted in 1944 to establish a reserve fund for the return to that city. As the time to move came close, Detroit's own labor problems made it seem a less desirable location. Pool and his colleagues agreed to survey the field. They decided to focus on the country's "steel belt," extending from the East Coast westward to Indiana and Illinois. They knew that Air Products was hard pressed for cash and would not be able to afford an expensive plant.

In January 1946, Dick Turner, Personnel Director in Chattanooga, began the search. His quest took him to the Blainsville, Indiana, and the Youngstown, Ohio, areas. For a time, Ashtabula, Ohio, appeared as if it might be the next home of Air Products, but Turner continued his odyssey into Pennsylvania and the great steel region centered around Pittsburgh, then eastward through Greensburg and Latrobe, Johnstown, Altoona, York and Hanover, Columbia and Lancaster, then northward through Pottsville, Reading, the Lehigh Valley, and Wilkes-Barre. He went south to Hagerstown, Maryland, and then looked at buildings in Camden, Haddon Heights, and Berlin, New Jersey, across the Delaware River from Philadelphia.

A special shareholders' meeting on March 13, 1946, again discussed the move. The Defense Plant Corporation had received and accepted an offer of $360,000 for the Chattanooga facility. Now Air Products would have to leave. In best Hollywood style, the telephone rang. Dick Turner, making a long-distance call, informed the meeting that his first choice was a plant with about 25,000 square feet of floor space in Emmaus, Pennsylvania. For $75,000 Air Products could purchase the machine shop of the Donaldson Iron Works. The Board of Directors approved the move on the spot and instructed Carl Anderson to complete the transaction.

The site selected was in the Lehigh Valley, in the hinterland of Philadelphia. The Valley—originally settled by the Pennsylvania Dutch—had an industrious work force attracted there by the iron mines and foundries which had flourished in the nineteenth century. While most mining had ceased before World War I, steel had become ever more important. The nation's second largest producer, Bethlehem Steel Company, was the dominant firm; other substantial companies included the Pennsylvania Power and Light Company, Mack Trucks, Inc., Lehigh Portland Cement Company, and Lehigh Structural Steel. World War II had made all of these firms prosperous. The Donaldson Iron Works was situated in Emmaus, a town of less than 10,000 bordering Allentown and Bethlehem, the major cities of the Valley. For decades, Donaldson had been the largest company in Emmaus, employing 500 men at its peak, but it had shut down because of labor difficulties.[1]

The move was an enormous logistical challenge. Since the Chattanooga site had been sold, Air Products had to pack up and ship its equipment forthwith. The new site had to be readied. Repairs, boilers, power supplies, and offices all had to be completed. There was a shortage of housing for employees making the move to Pennsylvania. Ready or not, Air Products moved into its new facilities on Friday, May 7, 1946. It would be a considerable while before the renovations were actually completed. The price was much higher than expected. The final cost of setting up at Emmaus was between $125,000 and $150,000.

There were other immediate problems. Skilled labor was in short supply. Workers did not wish to change jobs. Few were interested in the night shift. There was a lack of young machinists because of a lack of apprenticeships. With moving and remodeling taking place at

The original Emmaus plant.

the same time, stores and production materials were lost or destroyed. A railroad strike prevented the delivery of machine tools from Chattanooga. Workers had to be shifted from one department to another to get jobs done. By April 1947 the situation had reached a critical level. Mark Halsted, now Production Manager, wrote to Leonard Pool, "Something drastic must be done . . . [about] our inability to produce oxygen plants with the situation as it now exists. Unless [a plan is agreed to and] acted upon . . . you can expect that our production schedule will fall even farther behind and become more or less hopeless."[2]

The resettlement in Emmaus exacted a heavy toll. Productivity and morale were low—a new manufacturing staff was being trained—and the expense of developing the facility cut deeply into profits.

An Appeal to Wall Street

The move to Emmaus was not the only drain on resources in 1946. Pool's original idea of leasing on-site generators implied a capital-intensive strategy. Air Products would also need capital if it was to sell oxygen on the retail level by entering the cylinder gas business. At the end of 1945, however, Air Products had cash and deposits of only $63,000. It held $85,000 in earned surplus and could expect $338,000 when the government paid its final invoices. Air Products desperately needed an infusion of capital.

The Board of Directors found a temporary respite by borrowing approximately $300,000 from the Hamilton National Bank of Chattanooga, using an assignment of the cancellation claim on the Army Air Forces contract as security. However, what was needed was not more debt, but more equity. Leonard Pool's first idea was the sale of stock to friends and relatives. George Pool, Leonard Volland, and two other employees between them purchased eighty-five shares at $100 each. Such purchases were well meaning and welcome, but severely inadequate for Leonard Pool's ambitions. To underwrite those ambitions, he would have to turn to the nation's capital markets. Jim Spencer put Pool in touch with the New York firm of Reynolds & Co., who were stockbrokers and investment specialists. Reynolds liked Pool, and especially his idea of on-site leased generators.

In May 1946, Air Products went public. The recapitalization plan called for the authorization of 1,180,000 shares. Two kinds of shares, Class A (180,000) and common stock (1,000,000) were issued, both at a par value of one dollar a share. Each class A share was entitled

to an annual dividend of fifty cents and was convertible into two shares
of common. Preexisting shares of Air Products stock were converted
into "units" of new stock (a unit consisted of one share of Class A and
one share of common stock). A block of common stock was offered at
par to Reynolds & Co. partners, families, and employees, as well as
to members of the Air Products Board of Directors. Another block
of common stock was reserved for sale at par to Air Products officers
and key employees. The rest was offered to the public.

The results of the offering were surprising and pleasing. Reynolds
and Air Products people alike snapped up their allotments. Members
of the public were enthusiastic. The price of the stock rose, even
though the official prospectus circulated by Reynolds & Co. clearly
stated that dividends would not be forthcoming in the immediate
future. The common shares reached a high of more than nine dollars.
In December 1946, a second offering of shares at 7½ reflected the
market's continued expectations, and netted a very satisfactory return
for Air Products. Gradually, the price declined and by October 1947,
a further offering of common shares went for only 5¼. With this sale,
the company ended its ventures into the national capital markets for
several years.

What made Air Products so interesting to Wall Street was Leonard
Pool's novel concept of leasing on-site generators. Carl Anderson
knew only too well that building and then selling generators was a
"feast or famine" business. "To keep the cow" was a powerful idea,
in that it offered the prospect of a steady flow of cash through the
sale of "milk." But a herd of "cows"—oxygen generators—would be
expensive to acquire and maintain. Part, but only part, of that expense
could be offset by lease income. Large supplies of equity would be
necessary if Pool was to build and then lease generators to the companies that needed oxygen. The idea of leased equipment was in
vogue thanks to the success of IBM, which leased all its equipment.[3]
But, as Frank Willard of Reynolds & Co. wrote in 1948: "The principle
of leasing equipment instead of selling it, like the International Business Machines Co. and others, is a great business, but takes time to
establish."[4]

For investors, it was sufficient that Air Products had a novel idea,
an entrepreneurial leader, and a wartime track record. For the company itself, the issue of how to make leasing both saleable to customers
and profitable to Air Products was still murky. The 1946 and 1947
infusion of equity capital bought time. The sale was also symbolic of

an important change. Leonard and Dorothy Pool no longer enjoyed total control.

Leonard was still the largest stockholder but he and his wife now owned only 43.6 percent of the Class A and 5.5 percent of the common shares outstanding. As part of the underwriting agreement, Pool also guaranteed the election of at least two directors from Reynolds & Co. The Board had previously been comprised entirely of Pool's colleagues and nominees.[5] Now it was enlarged to accommodate three "outsiders," Herbert Grindal, Frank Willard, and Lawrence Marks.[6] The first steps had been taken along the traditional path by which a family firm dominated by one outstanding entrepreneur becomes a large, public corporation run by professional managers. It was years before the journey would be complete, and in 1946 it was far from clear that it would ever take place.

A Surprising Source of Cash

In the lean years immediately following World War II when capital and cash flow were major, anxious questions, bank loans or "going public" provided two means of raising necessary cash. But to keep the company afloat, the overriding reality was that orders had to be won. In the U.S. domestic market at least, this was difficult because history was repeating itself. The World War I boom in industrial gases had been followed by a slump in the immediate postwar years. So now, sales of oxygen fell sharply in 1945 and again in 1946 (Table 4). The moment was inauspicious.

Surprisingly and inadvertently, Air Products found its salvation overseas. In the words of Frank Pavlis, "At the end of the war, Air Products was much better known around the world than it was in the United States. The company literally subsisted on the revenues it obtained by the sale of air separation plants to customers throughout the world."[7] The overseas civilian demand for oxygen generators, and to a lesser extent for electrolytic cells, was tied to the reputation the firm had built up during the war. The generators shipped overseas had become advertisements for the company's products. Foreign governments and companies sought out Air Products. The first major market in the postwar period was thus one which was quite unforeseen. Ironically, it was also a market for sales of plants, not for leasing.

During the war, Air Products had sold a stationary generator to the Assam Oxygen Company of India. Even the original generator

Table 4
U.S. Production of Oxygen, 1941–1960

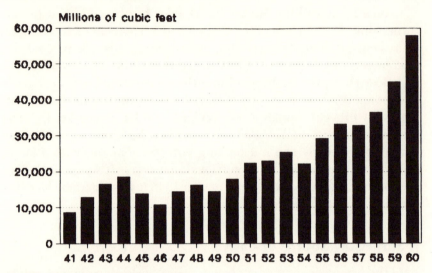

SOURCE: U.S. Census of Manufactures.

built by Pavlis and leased to Rotary Electric Steel, but later returned to Air Products, was exported in 1944 to Guatemala City for the Industrial Supply & Equipment Company, Inc. In addition, the company built a small skid-mounted generator for the Stone & Webster Engineering Corporation, which installed it in Iran, and a stationary plant for the Netherlands Purchasing Commission, which installed it in Batavia (now Djakarta). These modest achievements gave little inkling of what lay ahead.

Beginning with the sale of an oxygen generator to Laboratorios Alpha in Mexico in December 1945, overseas sales rapidly outstripped domestic sales of generators, and all other company business. Three-quarters of the units made by the firm between August 1945, and August 1948, were installed abroad. A little over half were in South America, the remainder going to Europe, the Middle East, South Africa, and China. The dollar value of overseas sales climbed. In fiscal 1947, export sales were $334,000 and in 1948, $561,000. After that, business dropped off. In fiscal 1950, foreign generator sales were only $198,000 (52 percent of total generator sales), because foreign customers lacked exchange dollars. Fortunately, domestic demand for oxygen had passed through its postwar trough by then, and the number and dollar value of generators sold or leased in the United States began to pick up.

Trail Blazing

The lease of generators in the United States, the trail-blazing idea with which Leonard Pool had initially thought he would develop and market his firm, was not lost sight of even in the war period. As early as December 1944, while the company was busily engaged in building mobile units for the war effort, Pool landed his second lease customer, Ross-Meehan Foundries of Chattanooga. The next lease customer, the Weirton Steel Company of Weirton, West Virginia, a subsidiary of the National Steel Corporation, would prove to be of far greater importance for the success of the firm.

Weirton, like many other steel companies, was interested in experimenting with enriching its blast furnaces with oxygen. But Weirton was an Air Reduction customer. (At this period Air Reduction and, of course, Linde continued in their traditional practice of neither selling nor leasing plants, but simply delivering oxygen to their customers in whatever amount was desired.) Leonard and George Pool, the salesman-entrepreneur and his salesman-brother, proved equal to the challenge. On October 31, 1945, the National Steel Corporation agreed to lease three 2,000-cubic-feet-per-hour generators for a period of five years to supply oxygen for its experiments at Weirton, West Virginia, and Steubenville, Ohio. The decision was not quite as miraculous as it first appeared. In characteristic risk-taking fashion, Air Products won the order by accepting National Steel's insistence that two generators be installed at Weirton by January 1, 1946, only two months later! As Leonard Pool recalled: "There was no way these plants could have been built and put in operation in that short period of time, but I agreed anyway."

Pool had a card up his sleeve—actually two cards. He knew that Air Products had generating plants of the correct capacity under construction for the Lend-Lease Program, which the government was going to ship to Russia: "I went to Washington and persuaded them to cancel the contract. Then Len Volland took over and got the plants ready for Weirton. On Christmas Eve, they went into operation. . . . "[8] Air Reduction, Weirton's traditional supplier, had felt confident—overly confident—that Air Products could not deliver in time. They had severely underestimated George and Leonard Pool's versatility.

A still bigger break came in June 1947, when Air Products signed a lease agreement with the Ford Motor Company for its River Rouge steel plant. Ford was one of the largest users of oxygen in the United

States. At the time, it was supplied with liquid oxygen by Linde, but it also owned on-site plants. Thus, to Ford, it was the economics of leasing that was at issue. Ford losses after the war were fearsome and cost reduction a matter of survival.

The Ford people had seen the original Pavlis generator in Detroit during the summer of 1940. Now they were impressed that the company was following up its wartime successes by supplying Weirton, and that Weirton was happy. How George and Leonard Pool made the sale is not recorded, but Ford gave Air Products a lease that required delivery on four times the scale of the Weirton contract. Air Products undertook to install four on-site generators capable, in combination, of supplying over half a million cubic feet of oxygen a day to be used in welding and in scarfing hot blooms, billets, and slabs. Liquid oxygen was also to be produced for use at the Ford Hospital in Detroit. Finally, Ford was to receive at no cost over one and a half million cubic feet a month of by-product nitrogen to be used in a number of ways, among them creating controlled atmospheres for heat-treating operations, blanketing inflammable liquid storage tanks, and spray painting.[9]

Leonard Pool's "impossible dream" of 1939 had faced three obstacles. First, he had to be able to build generators—a challenge met through his learning experiences with Pavlis and Anderson. Second, he had to find customers for leased plants. The sequence from Rotary Electric Steel to Ross-Meehan to Weirton and to Ford suggested that it would prove possible to find customers, given the wartime track record of Air Products, and the salesmanship of Leonard and his brother George. But the third great challenge still had to be faced— not how to finance one or two leased plants, but how to underwrite the construction and ownership of a large number simultaneously.

It was not possible to float a stock issue for every fresh lease agreement. Searching for a way forward, Leonard Pool approached insurance companies and banks in Philadelphia, in Hartford, Connecticut, in New York City, and elsewhere, looking for loans. He had no luck. One potential lender offered $180,000 over three years at the then daunting rate of 9.25 percent a year (about three times the going rate). Another wanted Air Products to pledge the entire assets of the company. Finally, Leonard Pool struck a deal at home. The Allentown National Bank, where the company had an account, loaned Pool the money he needed, requiring only the leased generators as collateral.

The loan's short payback period (three years) placed a huge financial burden on the leasing concept. Frank Pavlis had earlier developed cost estimates, profitability projections, and the basic elements of the lease contracts using altogether more optimistic assumptions. Now he had to reset minimum lease revenues much higher in order to pay back the loan in three years. The results were twofold: the price of oxygen to the customer would increase and the leased plants would operate at a loss. The only benign solution would have been to obtain longer term financing. But that was not possible given the paucity of the firm's postwar profits and its lack of either an established credit history or sophistication in financial matters.

Nonetheless, Air Products pressed its attempt to persuade potential customers of the virtues of leasing. The range of generators was standardized. The smaller plants made up the "R" series, such as the R-200, R-750, R-1000, and R-1250, which were equipped with a freon refrigeration quick start-up feature. Larger generators constituted the "E" series, like the E-2000, E-2500, E-5000, E-6500, and E-12,000. The "E" units were equipped with expansion engines to cool part of the intake air and thereby to operate at lower pressures. The number following the "R" or "E" signalled the generator's rated hourly capacity in cubic feet. In theory, an advantage of standardized units was the ability to group them to furnish a volume of oxygen corresponding to the customer's needs, without designing a special plant for each customer. In practice, each of the very small number of customers in the domestic marketplace was unique.

Leasing was a new idea. No one, including Leonard Pool, knew who the customers would be. In the 1930s oxygen had been purchased by a large number of small consumers who bought cylinder quantities (e.g., welding shops), and by a smaller number of larger consumers who might be served not only by cylinders but also by liquid conveyed by truck. Some large consumers even had on-site plants, which they had bought outright. The main industrial gas companies, Linde and Air Reduction, had concentrated entirely on supplying oxygen, and had not troubled themselves building plants for sale. (This was one reason Air Products had been able to win military orders for plants in World War II.) The few customers interested in owning on-site plants, like Ford, had bought those plants from one of a variety of smaller suppliers like Gas Industries or Superior, or from European manufacturers.

In 1939, Pool had thought in part that his new idea would avoid the expense of hauling cylinders. The snag was that even the smallest on-site plant would produce more gas than most cylinder users

An R–750 generator leased to Grede Foundries, Inc., of Milwaukee, Wisconsin. It was typical of the generators sold and leased by Air Products in the 1940s and 1950s.

wanted. In the changed conditions that prevailed after 1945, it turned out that on-site leased plants were most attractive to large customers with growing needs for oxygen. The real selling point behind Pool's idea of leased on-site oxygen generators was its combination of what a gas supplier like Linde did with what a generator manufacturer like Superior could offer.

Air Products had to receive a certain flow of income in order to cover the debt incurred on construction of a plant, so it insisted on a contract which required the customer to pay a minimum sum each month regardless of whether it consumed any oxygen or not. Beyond that, there was a variable rate. Thus the unit price decreased as consumption increased. Leasing appeared to promise a large customer a saving of 15 to 35 percent on the price paid for oxygen delivered by Air Products' competitors. That was the case, for instance, for a generator leased by the Fisher Body plant of General Motors in Flint, Michigan, in 1949. The total cost of oxygen to Fisher for the month of June averaged 36.9 cents per 100 cubic feet. If Fisher had taken its oxygen not from a leased on-site plant but from the supply network of Air Reduction, the same volume of oxygen would have cost 45 cents per 100 cubic feet.

In addition to direct economies, leased plants presented the indirect advantage of assuring an oxygen supply in the event of a labor strike or other problem at the industrial gas supplier. Thus, while leasing proved a hard sell in situations where the customer already had an on-site generator or liquid service, the obstacles could be overcome with the kind of sales ingenuity for which George Pool became known. Weirton provides one example. In that case, the ability to meet a ridiculously tight schedule gave Air Products the edge. Another example was provided by the Granite City Steel Company of Granite City, Illinois. Linde was supplying the company by pipeline, from a liquid-storage facility. Yet George Pool leased a generator to Granite City. To make the sale, he cut capital and operating costs by installing second-hand generators and an oxygen storage bank utilizing cheaper National Cylinder tubes. He also gave Granite City highly favorable oxygen rates. A unit of oxygen (100 cubic feet) cost only 9 cents when consumption exceeded 3.5 million cubic feet per month. At other Air Products leased facilities, the charge for the same rate of consumption was as much as 50 percent higher.

Ingenuity of the kind displayed at Weirton or Granite City could go only so far in securing orders. The Air Products sales force became instilled with the kind of savvy that allowed an individual salesman, upon discovering that his potential customer had no interest in leasing, to switch his tactics quickly and offer to sell a generator instead. As a consequence Air Products made a number of important generator sales. While the first customers were small industrial gas companies in the South, Air Products soon was supplying oxygen plants to larger producers and by 1949 to Air Reduction itself.

The firm continued to sign lease contracts from time to time. The main thrust of efforts to win customers was in the steel industry, where oxygen reigned as king. Air Products also sought to lease equipment to railroads, hospitals, and the chemical and petroleum industries. The Chairman of the Board, Will Dodge, who had at one time been the General Sales Manager of Texaco, tried to hold open the door to the petroleum industry.[10] In 1948, he contacted oil companies in the United States and Venezuela. However, none of his extensive canvassing led to a lease contract.

The hospital market also seemed promising. It was pursued by Bill Thomas, a chemistry graduate of Indianapolis' Butler University, who had worked under George Pool at the National Cylinder Gas Company in Philadelphia. At Air Products, Bill Thomas began a systematic exploration of the hospital market for leased plants. He rapidly discovered that Linde dominated this market too, through its ability to offer not only oxygen but also medical equipment and support for research into new medical uses of oxygen. Nonetheless, in 1947, Thomas succeeded in landing his first lease agreement, a small, 200-cubic-feet-per-hour generator at Hartford Hospital in Hartford, Connecticut. Subsequently, two other leases were obtained. The market, however, never really panned out—Linde's hold was too strong. The venture did provide the company with an important selling point: salesmen could assure potential customers that the generators were safe, since they were installed in hospitals.

Over the five-year period following World War II, lease revenues gradually increased and, by 1950, accounted for 38 percent of net sales (Table 5). In addition to the Weirton and Ford accounts, the most important leases were with the Jones & Laughlin Steel Corporation and Bethlehem Steel. Despite the generally depressed domestic market (U.S. oxygen production did not equal the 1944 wartime peak until after 1950), Air Products was making *some* progress.

Table 5
Air Products Lease Revenues, 1946–1960

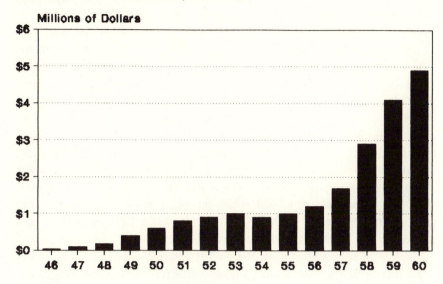

Millions of Dollars

The Dawning of the Oxygen Age

In the 1920s, researchers, industrialists, and dreamers had thought of many possible uses of large quantities of oxygen in the metallurgical, chemical, and other industries. However, the high cost of oxygen, whether produced electrolytically or by air liquefaction, made all such plans impractical.[11]

The picture had begun to change in the 1930s, thanks to the work of Matthias Fränkl in Germany. Fränkl developed a process, based on his innovative regenerator, that was capable of producing large quantities of low-purity (90–95 percent), low-cost oxygen. Up to that time, a normal (high-purity) oxygen generator was considered large if it generated 10,000 cubic feet per hour, that is, ten "tons" of oxygen a day. Fränkl's generator was of a completely different order.

Fränkl's prototype generator had not impressed Carl Anderson when he first saw it in 1927. But Fränkl persevered with improvements to his design. Eventually, Fränkl and engineers and scientists from other countries succeeded in creating improved designs which incorporated Fränkl's regenerator and fulfilled the dream of providing cheap, abundant oxygen for industrial processes. The Fränkl regenerator was used to manufacture acetic acid and other chemicals by I.G. Farben at Höchst, Germany. The outcome of World War II opened up opportunities for American companies to exploit this technology; the I.G. Farben unit was actually dismantled and shipped to the United States. This was one of the most important fruits of the military "technical teams" that scoured Germany after the war.[12]

Tonnage oxygen plants were soon being designed to serve both the chemical and the steel industries in the United States. In the chemical industry, Hydrocarbon Research, Inc., of Trenton, New Jersey, planned to build a pair of one-thousand-ton-per-day plants for the partial oxidation of natural gas for Carthage Hydrocol at Brownsville, Texas, and another pair for Standard Oil of Indiana at Hugoton, Kansas. Linde, after starting up a 200-ton-per-day experimental generator in August 1946 at its East Chicago, Indiana, research lab, set out to design tonnage plants for both the chemical and the steel industries. By 1949, it was building a 360-ton-per-day plant for an ammonia synthesis process for Du Pont at Belle, West Virginia, and a 135-ton-per-day generator for the Wheeling Steel Company of Steubenville, Ohio.

Despite Linde's headstart, Air Reduction managed to beat its larger competitor to the punch and supply the first tonnage oxygen to the U.S. steel industry.[13] In 1946, Air Reduction arranged to site a 150-ton-per-day generator at the Bethlehem Steel Company's plant in Johnstown, Pennsylvania. Bethlehem wished to carry out large-scale experiments with the use of oxygen in open-hearth and blast furnaces. Open-hearth furnaces attain a temperature of 3,300°F when heated by gas or petroleum flames. By adding a stream of oxygen, the temperature can be raised to 5,000°F, thereby hastening melting time and quickening the chemical reactions which take place in the melt, chiefly the conversion of carbon into carbon dioxide. Allegheny Ludlum, Wheeling, Bethlehem, and other steel companies estimated that the capacity of open-hearth furnaces could be increased at least 25 percent. Similar savings were expected in blast furnaces converting iron ore into pig iron. In theory, a tonnage oxygen plant could greatly augment a company's steelmaking capacity. Air Reduction's pioneering plant provided hard data.[14]

Tonnage oxygen was an opportunity for Air Products to enter on the ground floor of what in America was a new segment of the industrial gas business. In other words, it was an opportunity to escape the handicaps the company routinely faced as a late entrant to an established industry. By now, the firm had substantial experience in designing and building conventional oxygen generators. Moreover, Air Products had Carl Anderson, who had inspected a Fränkl plant at Augsburg, Germany, as long ago as 1927.

Believing that tonnage plants would be a key technology of the future, Leonard Pool did not hesitate to license two German patents from the Office of The Alien Property Custodian. Patents, however, were only part of what was necessary. Mastery of the new technology could only be acquired by the discipline of actually designing and building a tonnage plant. How, then, to acquire the funds, the experience, and the orders necessary to compete? And how to do this while moving to Emmaus, going public, and struggling to sell the leasing concept? The answer reveals much about the combination of drive, opportunism, and foresight that was to carry Air Products forward.

Weirton

As we have seen, Air Products had installed two conventional oxygen generators at the Weirton Steel works in West Virginia in late 1945. Those generators were used in Weirton's first, small-scale experiments in improving furnace operations. More to the point, the plants gave Weirton substantial savings compared to the cost of the oxygen it was obtaining from Air Reduction.

Julius Strassburger, Manager of Maintenance and Service at Weirton, had handled the original lease arrangements. Like many of his peers in the steel industry, Strassburger wanted a tonnage plant in order to realize further economies in steel production. He had been following German tonnage oxygen developments since before World War II. After the war, Weirton engineers quickly made their own extensive investigation of tonnage oxygen. Early in 1947, they invited proposals for a 400-ton-per-day plant from different firms, including Linde and Air Reduction. The competition was formidable. Air Products was a David among Goliaths.[15]

Unlike its competitors, Air Products had not even built a pilot or experimental tonnage plant, and it lacked the financial resources to do so. But the company had established a reputation with Julius Strassburger, through its conventional leased plants. Air Products had shown that it could deliver oxygen cheaply and that it could deliver quickly. Strassburger began discussing the design and construction of a tonnage plant with Clarence Schilling and other Air Products engineers. The Air Products Engineering Department undertook preliminary work "on spec." The company was still recovering from its costly move to Emmaus. It scarcely seemed a propitious time to embark on an expensive, risky project. Nor could Air Products afford to tie up large sums of capital. But Leonard Pool conceived a way whereby the firm could design and build the Weirton tonnage plant, gain the experience it needed, and avoid a drain on capital. In turn, Weirton obtained what no other competitor thought to offer: a tonnage oxygen generator almost at cost.

With the help of his brother George, Leonard Pool proposed that Air Products build a tonnage plant for Weirton on a cost-plus-fixed-fee basis and charge Weirton a continuing fee for assistance after the facility was running. As a result of the low-cost offer, the persistence of George Pool, and the record the company had established with its leased generators, Air Products beat out the competition.

The contract was signed on July 23, 1947. It called for Weirton to purchase a 400-ton-per-day oxygen generator from Air Products at an estimated cost of $1.5 million. The company was charging an astonishingly low fixed fee of only $75,000. Air Products was to be reimbursed monthly for all expenditures. In addition, it guaranteed that the unit would meet certain specifications when completed. If the plant failed to measure up, the company agreed to make all necessary alterations at its own cost, up to $500,000. It was a showcase contract which, Leonard Pool hoped, would lead to other more profitable contracts for tonnage installations. What really mattered was that he had moved his small and capital-poor firm into an important and technologically unfamiliar field without committing large sums of money. Once again, Pool was taking great risks and betting on the company's engineering staff. The firm's reputation rode on its ability to complete the project. The plant capacity was 65 times larger than any built by Air Products to date. It was a gamble that might pay off handsomely or might exhaust and bankrupt the company.

The schedule called for preliminary operating tests to start on July 1, 1949. The contract was one thing. The realities were another. The work went slowly and there were many unanticipated problems, especially with the heat exchangers. Clarence Schilling was the man on the spot in every sense. After several false starts, he devised an exchanger made of aluminum instead of copper. Aluminum, with its different thermal properties, promised fewer parts and easier manufacture. Tests seemed to bear out his choice; the aluminum heat exchanger was an improvement. However, the exchanger failed when installed and forced Air Products to negotiate changes in the contract. Schilling came through with a revised design and at last Air Products could finish the plant, test it, and receive on April 11, 1951 the coveted formal letter of acceptance. Weirton was a major risk and a difficult learning experience. The success, if less than glorious, did put the

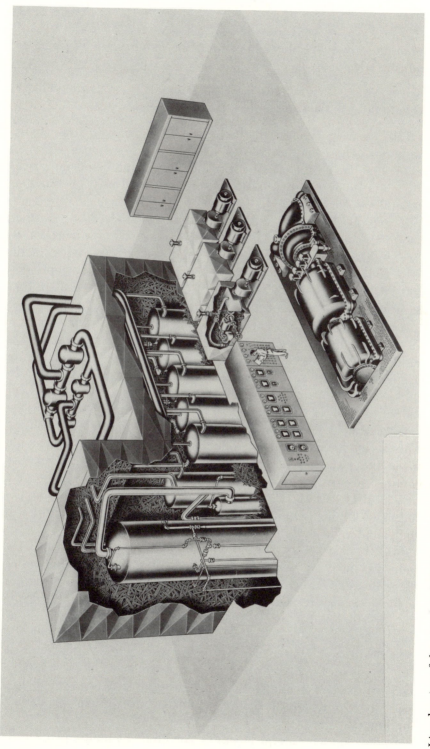

Line drawing of the completed Weirton tonnage plant (1951).

small, upstart Air Products in competition in a fresh field, facing the industry's leaders.

New Strategic Directions

Tonnage oxygen represented one new direction with strategic implications. Those implications had to do with sophisticated process technology, and with sales by a small engineering-based sales team to a few customers spread over a large geographical area. The situation was different in the cylinder gas business. Cylinder sales were labor-intensive, locally based, and depended on camaraderie and instinct, not on technical knowledge. A move in this second new direction by George and Leonard Pool rode on their prewar experience in the oxyacetylene gas business. While Leonard Pool was an entrepreneur and a dreamer, George was at heart a cylinder gas salesman. In time he would recruit an extensive cadre of salesmen as colleagues.

Air Products' first stab at the oxyacetylene business had come in 1944, when the company purchased an interest in Wolverine Gas Products, which distributed cylinder oxygen and acetylene gas in the Saginaw–Bay City area of Michigan. As part of the deal, Air Products sold Wolverine a small oxygen generator and agreed to loan gas cylinders as well as working capital.[16] This investment did not slake George and Leonard Pool's appetite for the cylinder gas business. This is not surprising given their backgrounds, but it is surprising given the way in which the gas market was collapsing. Domestic production of oxygen declined dramatically from 18.5 billion cubic feet in 1944 to 13.9 billion in 1945. The following year production fell to 10.9 billion cubic feet. As the market shrank, competition in the cylinder gas trade became fierce, and prices fell.

Still, Leonard and George Pool were determined to set up a cylinder gas business, which George would run. The outside members of the Board of Directors objected to the drain on the firm's resources, so the decision was rationalized as a backup for lease customers. While the directors and lease customers accepted the explanation, in actuality it was hardly possible to replace a generator's output with cylinder oxygen. On the single occasion when a leased generator did fail, the nearest cylinder plant was unable to meet the emergency.[17] The assurance of an emergency oxygen supply did, however, help to lease some units and to soothe the anxieties of certain members of the Board.

To develop its cylinder business, Air Products built a plant in the

Midwest. The site was chosen because of negotiations with the Studebaker Corporation, in South Bend, Indiana, for the supply of oxygen. Air Products won a contract from the automaker, and Leonard Pool recommended that the company locate its cylinder gas operation at Walkerton, Indiana, twenty miles southwest of South Bend. From there, the company could supply Studebaker in a cost-effective manner, and the Walkerton plant would serve as a base for entering the Chicago market for cylinder gases. The Walkerton plant, which began producing in 1947, was Air Products' first company-owned and -operated cylinder gas operation.

Leonard and George Pool also began groping their way toward vertical integration, along the lines of Linde and Air Reduction. The major demand for cylinder oxygen came from small welding shops. Linde and Air Reduction sold not only oxygen, but also oxyacetylene welding and cutting equipment. The Pools decided that since they were now trying to compete with the biggest concerns, they must adopt the same strategy.

In the summer of 1946, the Pools targeted for acquisition the K-G Welding and Cutting Company, Inc., a manufacturing firm headquartered in New York City. It was not a particularly attractive business. The company's market was narrow. Over 60 percent of sales were to distributors, the majority to five major customers. The company had been in the red from 1936 to 1943, but it had been profitable during the last two years of the war. Although K-G was successful immediately after its acquisition, the 1949 recession cut sales and produced a loss of $5,000. The company suffered from a number of problems, including a lack of outside salesmen. The most telling problem was revealed when Leonard Pool belatedly visited a K-G distributor in late 1949. He learned that K-G equipment was difficult to sell because the competitors' products had a superior finish and worked better. What was to be done?

Pool integrated Air Products and K-G operations. Air Products took over manufacturing, purchasing, invoicing, and payroll. As a former gas salesman, Leonard Pool understood salesmanship and the value of personal contact. Instead of depending on mail solicitations, Pool stressed face-to-face salesmanship as the key to obtaining new distributors. Drawing on the quality of engineering at Air Products, he had the Engineering Department redesign much of the K-G equipment line. He also hired Chester Delbridge,[18] who had been a salesman, then a district manager with the Air Reduction Company for over two decades. Boosting K-G sales became Delbridge's job. With

Leonard's encouragement, he transformed the firm's advertising and sales tactics, separated the purchasing and production departments, and established a program of acquiring distributorships. As a result, K-G's profitability returned.

With the purchase of K-G and the erection of the Walkerton facility, Air Products was firmly in the cylinder gas and welding equipment business. In 1947, the company, led by George Pool, also began buying existing gas businesses. One was the Parco Compressed Gas Company of Parkersburg, West Virginia, and a related company, Harris Calorific Sales Company, which made welding equipment and supplies. Both were acquired by way of exchange of common shares. Also that year, Air Products set up a cylinder gas operation at Iselin, New Jersey. Another but much smaller cylinder gas operation was started in Emmaus in 1947. The tests run on generators before they were shipped to customers supplied its oxygen.

Yet another strategic direction began to develop when Air Products entered the small argon and helium markets. Heliarc welding was a technique introduced by Linde at the end of World War II. It employed helium as a blanket to keep air away from the weld. Air Products purchased helium in cylinders and tank cars from the government's Bureau of Mines, had it shipped to its cylinder sales offices, and then resold it to local customers who used heliarc welding.

Cylinder gas operations placed a heavy burden on the company's already precarious finances. Fiscal 1946 and 1947 ended in losses. At the February 10, 1947 meeting of the Board of Directors, Leonard Pool presented a cash forecast for the three-month period ending June 30, 1947. He believed that $362,000 in cash outlays would be required by the cylinder gas business in that period, with almost a third of that going to just the New Jersey (Iselin) operation. Air Products had a compelling need for cash in the summer of 1947. There was insufficient money available to meet weekly payrolls and pay outstanding bills. It was absolutely critical, however, to keep this condition secret from employees and the outside world. Pool quietly disclosed the crisis to his brother George and to Anderson and Pavlis, asking for their help. By liquidating various assets, the four were able to come up with $125,000 to keep the company afloat. Pool recognized that this was a temporary stay. In order to achieve long-term success, the company would have to revamp its sales strategy.

By purchasing war surplus materials and by other economies, the company kept a tight rein on costs. Happily, it turned out that Air Products had entered the cylinder business just as oxygen sales were

The Parkersburg, West Virginia, cylinder gas district office in the 1950s. Note the cylinders in the building's rear.

beginning to recover from the postwar decline. From a low of $124,000 in fiscal 1947, cylinder gas sales shot up to $691,000 by fiscal 1948. But heavy start-up costs continued to devour revenues. Only in 1949 did the cylinder gas business show a profit, and it was fiscal 1950 before the strategy really began to prove itself. In that year sales amounted to $730,000, representing 30.2 percent of the firm's revenues and 25.8 percent of pretax profits. Air Products had 4 percent of the U.S. cylinder oxygen market. Although that share paled in comparison to Linde's 60 percent, the company had made some important strides toward industry-wide recognition.[19] George Pool's aggressive brand of salesmanship was having an effect even if Air Products' market share was small.

Looking Abroad

By 1950, domestic cylinder gas and leased plant operations were the major revenue sources. Overseas generator sales were in sharp decline. Nonetheless, Leonard Pool's appetite had been awakened to the possibilities that lay overseas. In 1950, he decided to respond to foreign shortages of exchange dollars. He would set up an overseas manufacturing capability, involving Air Products in the intricacies of technology transfer *to* rather than *from* Europe.

This further ramification of the company's opportunistic drive had its roots in the days immediately after World War II, when Will Dodge, the Board Chairman, had taken responsibility for the development of an Air Products overseas sales program. Dodge had a special office set up in New York. He was primarily interested in stimulating foreign sales by appointing distributors. Although most were not energetic sales agents, one of the distributors proved worthwhile.

In 1947, Sperry Gyroscope Company, Ltd., of England was granted the right to manufacture and sell non-tonnage Air Products generators in the British Isles, and the right to sell Air Products generators made in the United States in a sales territory comprised of the entire British Empire with the exception of Canada. On closing the contract, Air Products received a one-time payment of a $25,000 engineering fee. Sperry also agreed to pay Air Products a royalty of 7.5 percent and an engineering fee of 2.5 percent on all sales. A supplemental agreement of 1948 permitted Sperry to sell generators it manufactured, anywhere in the British Empire except Canada.

Leonard Pool recognized the potential advantages of the connection with Sperry. Exchange control problems would be avoided. Also, with lower European labor costs, Sperry ought to be able to offer generators at more competitive rates. Pool soon learned that it was not so easy. For one thing, the two companies had different perceptions. Patents were far more important to Sperry than to Pool, who told his company counsel and board member Jim Spencer in 1948: "It appears that the entire structure of the contract is based on certain patents and patent applications. . . . However, the know-how and techniques in general and the art which cannot be covered by patents are perhaps more valuable than the patents themselves."[20]

Pool was distinguishing between the accumulated experience and craft knowledge available to Air Products through Anderson, Schilling, and other engineers, and the formalized, law-oriented technology described by patents. Craft knowledge is geared to making technology actually *work* in an industrial setting. Patents and thermodynamic data do not assure a commercially viable generator. That was the lesson Pool himself had learned by having Frank Pavlis build his first generator. However, Sperry's focus was legal, not technological. The company had never before dealt with oxygen generators and was concerned that it be held free from any liability arising from Air Products' infringing on patents held by others.

The relationship with Sperry proved frustrating to both parties. In early 1950, Sperry made a bid on a British Air Ministry contract for five generators. Pool staunchly believed Air Products equipment was superior to that of the other bidders. Nonetheless, the contract was awarded to the British Oxygen Company, which had a virtual monopoly on the design and construction of air separation equipment in Britain. Pool now realized how tough it would be to crack the British market. He began to think that Sperry was not trying hard enough.

Sperry in turn was concluding that air separation equipment was not an appropriate field for it to be in. Its core business was the manufacture of fine precision devices (gyroscopes). Sperry decided to transfer its license to another company. In April 1950, Pool reviewed the prospects for the manufacture and sale of generators in Britain. One possibility was The Butterley Company. Butterley had been involved in engineering and mechanical construction for nearly two hundred years. The postwar nationalization (purchase by the British government) of Butterley's coal mines meant it had capital to invest.

E. Fitzwater Wright, Butterley's chairman, and Montagu Wright, its managing director, were enthusiastic. The Wrights and Pool soon began discussions about technology and, especially, patents. Pool, wiser from his experience with Sperry, worked to focus the meetings on the parochial aspects of technology transfer. He wanted to sell Butterley on the transfer of craft knowledge, of "know-how" and "art." Like Sperry, Butterley chose to focus first on its legal needs. It too wished to be held free from any liability which might arise out of building or selling Air Products' generators.

Pool was not deterred. He saw the negotiations as the start of an important venture. In addition to the transfer of drawings and personnel, Pool was transplanting, at least in principle, his leasing concept. He was also cultivating his first significant personal contact in a foreign business community. Pool especially liked "Monty" Wright. His Christmas gifts in 1950 to the Wright family included record albums of *South Pacific* and *Kiss Me Kate*, and much-coveted nylon stockings. All of Air Products' European operations would grow out of the Butterley–Air Products relationship.

Hustling for Business

The new approach to the flagging overseas business came at the same time as the revival of the U.S. military market. Although the surrender of Japan had brought all war-related orders to an end, another war, perhaps of global breadth, soon appeared imminent. In the words of Winston Churchill, an "Iron Curtain" descended over Europe. Tensions between East and West, NATO and Warsaw Pact, the United States and the Soviet Union, escalated. Those tensions suggested that there might soon be a revival in the military market for generators, at least for high altitude flight or for field maintenance and repairs. Air Products decided to search out those opportunities.

In World War II, George Pool had handled government sales. But he was now preoccupied with the growing cylinder gas operations. An obvious choice to replace him was Bill Thomas, who had served in the Navy program to develop oxygen masks and other equipment for high altitude flight during the war. When Thomas began looking for military orders, he confronted a considerable array of agencies: the Army Air Forces, the Army Corps of Engineers, the Navy, and the Treasury Department. Within a given bureaucracy, there were a number of offices each with its own programs and oxygen requirements. Chaos, not order, reigned.

Despite this welter of agencies, Air Products had earlier landed a few military orders in late 1945 and 1946. Spare parts for the Navy, the Army Air Forces, and the British Ministry of Supply had helped the firm survive, as had modifications of mobile units from an aircraft engine to an electric motor drive, for the Corps of Engineers and the Army Air Forces. By the end of 1946, however, military contracts had finally tapered off completely.

In 1948, things started to change. The creation of the National Defense Department and the rationalization of procurement practices provided the context in which Air Products landed a contract with the Navy for two generators. More significantly, during 1948 and 1949 the company became heavily involved in development work for the Navy and the newly organized Air Force. This development work provided another opportunity to enrich the firm's body of engineering know-how.

In 1948, the USS *Valley Forge* became the first aircraft carrier to be equipped with jets. Since jets fly at much higher altitudes than conventional aircraft, breathing oxygen is required for more of the flying time. Oxygen supplied to carriers in cylinders would no longer suffice. The Navy decided to proceed with development of shipboard liquid oxygen generating, storage, and charging equipment. In addition, the Navy wanted generators capable of supplying gaseous nitrogen, used as a flame arrestor gas for the fuel lines and similarly hazardous places.[21] The Navy awarded Air Products, along with rival Linde, contracts to develop an appropriate liquid oxygen generator. Other similar contracts followed, including work on a generating and charging plant and associated equipment, for pumping liquid oxygen and converting it into high pressure gas on submarines.

There was also development work available with the Air Force. Early in 1948, Washington had written to all Air Force bases around the world asking the number and condition of mobile generators and an assessment of the spare parts needed to put them in good shape. Bill Thomas was in close contact with the Army Air Forces at Wright (now Wright-Patterson) Field. Thomas learned that the Air Force was interested in the Air Products Type A-1 generator from World War II. By August 1948, the Supply Division, Ground Equipment Section, of Wright-Patterson was ready to order considerable numbers of A-1s.

The renewed focus on mobile generators also resulted in a study contract with the Army Corps of Engineers to consider possible fresh developments. A June 1948 report from Air Products detailed its ability to fulfill a wartime need for mobile oxygen and nitrogen generators with a rated hourly capacity of 70 pounds of liquid oxygen, 1,000 cubic feet of gaseous oxygen, and 200 cubic feet of high-purity nitrogen. The proposed generator was dubbed the Model A-2. The report indicated the minimum time required to produce a first mobile unit; identified the additional buildings, personnel, and equipment required to produce units at various rates, and recommended preparedness measures. Phase II of the A-2 development study was begun in April 1949. When the Korean War came, the A-2 would be an important production item for Air Products, as we shall see in the next chapter.

Development contracts, like that for the A-2, were fixed-fee agreements and not particularly profitable. But they were of fundamental importance, for they enabled the company to build its technical expertise and to hold its talented engineering group together. Development contracts were later to prove of the greatest significance to Air Products, as it gained additional expertise in tonnage oxygen technology. That expertise in turn would play a vital role in the firm's growth in the 1950s.

Revolt by the Board?

By 1950 the outlook for Air Products was significantly better than it had been only five years before. The company had cylinder gas operations in four districts located around Iselin (New Jersey), Emmaus, Parkersburg (West Virginia), and Walkerton (Indiana), as well as a modestly profitable welding equipment and supply business. While overseas sales of generators were declining, the company had signed an agreement to manufacture plants in England. Leased-plant revenues were growing. The Weirton tonnage project was almost finished. The firm had a permanent home in the Lehigh Valley. Air Products had also found short-term remedies for the financial problems arising from its move and from the capital-intensive nature of the leased-plant and cylinder gas businesses. The revival of military contracts was renewing a relationship with the government that lay at the heart of the firm's early years. Air Products was still a late entrant to the industrial gas business, but it now had an encouraging roster of projects. However, capital remained in desperately short supply as Leonard Pool aggressively sought to push forward on several fronts simultaneously.

By going public Air Products had fallen under the influence of outsiders, especially the representatives of Reynolds & Company.

The Air Products team in 1950 at the tenth anniversary celebration. From left to right: Don MacLeod, Mark Halsted, Clarence Schilling, Carl Anderson, George Pool, and Frank Pavlis. In front: Leonard Pool and Andrew Ross, former Deputy Chief, War Production Board, who joined Air Products briefly after the war as Director of Publicity and Advertising.

Investors had been drawn to the company by the novelty of Pool's concept of the leasing of on-site generators. The Board of Directors gave leased on-site generators priority over export and other requirements. However, Leonard Pool was not only a visionary but also an opportunist. The future of leasing was so uncertain that he was hungry for orders of any kind. Where necessary to get the order, the company sold rather than leased its generators, even though the outsiders on the Board were opposed to that policy. Even before the company finished the Weirton tonnage plant, the Air Products Board inconclusively debated the question of leasing versus selling the new tonnage generators at its January 12, 1949, meeting.

There was a persistent tension among members of the Board, partly because working capital remained tight and partly because of different concepts of what the firm's basic strategy should be. The Reynolds' directors were particularly upset over the amount of capital being devoured by the cylinder gas business. In January 1951, convinced that cylinder gas operations were consuming too much capital, one Reynolds representative went so far as to suggest selling one or more of the cylinder gas facilities to raise capital: Air Products should *not* follow the Linde model. Leonard Pool countered by reminding the Board of the study carried out by an outside consulting firm. The study emphasized how "It is our considered judgment that the company should . . . advance the retail sale of oxygen and other compressed gases to a program of major importance."[22]

The fight continued. Finally, Pool threatened to resign, and to take his brother, and Anderson and Pavlis, with him. Without them, the company would be leaderless. Their blend of entrepreneurial, sales, and engineering talents was the core of Air Products' operations. The outside members gave up. The revolt was over. Air Products would stay on the eclectic course that the Pools, Anderson, and Pavlis were charting through the troubled postwar years.

Notes

1. George Pool to Civilian Production Administration, 20 May 1946, APHO; Richmond E. Myers, *Lehigh Valley: The Unsuspected* (Easton, Penn.: Northampton County Historical and Genealogical Society, 1972), pp. 205–206; Karyl Lee Kibler Hall and Peter Dobkin Hall, *The Lehigh Valley* (Woodland Hills, Calif.: Windsor Press, 1982), p. 133; Preston A. Barba, *They Came to Emmaus* (Bethlehem, Penn.: Lehigh Litho, 1985), p. 220.

2. Mark Halsted to Leonard Pool, 9 April 1947, APHO.

3. Richard T. DeLamarter, *Big Blue: IBM's Use and Abuse of Power.* After the Justice Department's Antitrust Division took IBM to court, the consent decree stipulated that the firm also would offer its equipment for sale. United Shoe Machinery was another important example of a firm which had great success with its leasing strategy.

4. F.A. Willard to Thomas B. Butler, 10 February 1948, APHO.

5. The first Board of Directors consisted of Pool, his wife Dorothy, and Jim Spencer. Carl Anderson was added two weeks later.

6. In December 1945 there were five members of the Board: Leonard Pool, Carl Anderson, Jim Spencer, George Pool, and John Marshall. By November 1946 there were nine members, including five Air Products employees. The outside members were: Will Dodge, Herbert Grindal, Laurence Marks, and Frank Willard.

7. Frank Pavlis interview, 2 February 1988, APHO.

8. Hassell H. McClellan, "Air Products and Chemicals, Inc.," Harvard Business School Case Study, 4-375-370, 1975, p. 8.

9. *Business Week*, May 22, 1948.

10. "Dodge Accepts Post with Paris ECA Office," *N.Y. Oil, Paint & Drug Reporter*, n.p.; "Henry W. Dodge, Vice President of Mack Trucks," *Sunday Call-Chronicle* (July 10, 1949): 8.

11. J.D. Ratcliff, "The Oxygen Age is Just Ahead," *The Saturday Evening Post* (September 20, 1947): 70.

12. Charles R. Downs, "Impact of Tonnage Oxygen on American Chemical Industry," *Chemical Engineering* 55 (August 1948): 113–117, 121.

13. Air Reduction designed the plant but hired the Koppers Company to build it.

14. "Oxygen: Past, Present, and Prospects," *Chemical Engineering* 54 (January 1947): 130; C.C. Wright, "Current Status of Tonnage Oxygen," Report of Subcommittee on the Use of Oxygen in Gas Manufacture, American Gas Association, Conference, New York City, 24 May 1949, p. 9; Ratcliff, p. 70.

15. J. Strassburger, "Tonnage Oxygen: Versatile Air for Increasing Iron and Steel Output," *Steel*, 1948, pp. 149–161.

16. Initially, in 1944 Air Products acquired a 26 percent interest in Wolverine. By the end of 1946, it had acquired 61 percent of the shares.

17. Coverdale & Colpitts, "Business Survey of Air Products, Inc.," November 17, 1950, p. 53, APHO.

18. Delbridge had a B.A. in chemistry from Washington University and had taken courses at the Harvard Business School and the Massachusetts Institute of Technology.

19. Coverdale & Colpitts, pp. 12, 23.

20. Leonard Pool to Jim Spencer, 21 September 1948, APHO.

21. M.N. Amster, "Shipboard Oxygen-Nitrogen Generation Increases Independence of Carriers," *BuShips Journal* (September 1952): 31–32.

22. Coverdale & Colpitts, p. 66.

4

Air Products Comes of Age

For Air Products, the 1950s would be a decade of dramatic growth. In the private sector alone, the firm's revenues would increase over five times. More decisive would be the spurt in sales to the federal government from $200,000 in 1951 to $29 million in 1959. Military developments and the space race would multiply the demand for Air Products' engineering skills and fund the research that would make the company a major contender in low-temperature engineering.

Despite the importance of military contracts, Leonard Pool did not abandon the leased-plant business. It too became a major engine of growth when the company found a mechanism which not only financed its leasing activities, but also created a working capital fund. Equally important for the company's growth was the decision to begin selling specialized equipment to the chemical industry. As a result, Air Products became a process engineering firm, not just a manufacturer of oxygen generators. Salesmanship, risk taking, and a "can do" approach to novel engineering challenges remained central to the company's growth. That growth was greatly aided by the buoyancy of the American economy in general, and of the gas and chemical industries in particular. A company like Air Products, prepared to be aggressive and to take risks, could expect a larger share of a larger pie.

The Cold War Heats Up

The Korean War opened new markets for Air Products, markets the company was well positioned to serve. Bill Thomas' search for military contracts had already begun to pay off when the North Korean Army invaded South Korea in June 1950, and the United States became deeply involved in an Asian land war. The Air Force and the Army Corps of Engineers needed oxygen generators at air bases and at ordnance facilities for high-altitude flying, for cutting and welding, and for various medical uses. Generators also were needed aboard naval repair ships, carriers, and hospital ships.

The A-2 generator, designed with the help of military development contracts, was a two-ton-per-day generator that used switch-type heat exchangers and a centrifugal expander. The A-2 was capable of supplying both liquid and gaseous oxygen as well as low- and high-purity nitrogen. So heavy were the orders that Air Products required special assistance in acquiring aluminum, copper, rubber, nickel, and graphite, which came under wartime restrictions. The Air Force assured the firm priority for materials procurement and assisted in obtaining additional manufacturing space in the former Allentown Consolidated Vultee hangar. The cost of repairing and adapting the building was covered by a government-sponsored loan.[1]

With the Korean War, government contracts again became the largest part of the company's activity. Military business leaped from 7 percent of sales in 1951 to 71 percent in 1952. Although military business fell to 38 percent in 1954, orders continued to come in for mobile and shipboard units. From 1956 to the end of the decade, military procurement accounted for over half of total sales and reached a new high of 79 percent ($30 million) in 1958. By the late 1950s, it was the missile business that was providing the company with its most important government market. Through missile-related work, Air Products would become steadily more adept in the construction of ever-larger generators, designed to deliver oxygen in liquid rather than gaseous form.

Liquid Oxygen for Rockets

Air Products had been attentive to rocket technology and the potential market it might provide since the late 1940s. As early as 1946, Frank Pavlis had met with Captain Hilyer Gearing at the Naval Ammunition Depot outside Dover, New Jersey, to discuss liquid oxygen

Ed Lady testing a shipboard M-3 oxygen-nitrogen generator.

A mobile oxygen-nitrogen semitrailer built in 1955 and capable of supplying ten tons per day of liquid oxygen.

Plant #2, the former Convair hangar, in Allentown. The company airplane is sitting in the parking lot.

for rocket-engine tests. At the time the company faced a full roster of pressing problems on other fronts. Undaunted, Pavlis suggested to Leonard Pool that the company "contact all of the various private and government agencies with a view to our supplying a part of the liquid oxygen requirements by the use of our equipment."[2] Pool put Bill Thomas in charge of this work, as of other government-related initiatives.

Up till this time, the oxygen industry was essentially concerned with the uses of oxygen *gas*. Oxygen might be liquefied as part of the process of manufacture, but it was routinely transported and consumed as a gas. Linde had pioneered the American use of the technology necessary to handle the extremely low temperatures required if oxygen were to be stored and transported in the liquid state. Even though liquid transportation offered significant economies for bulk quantities of oxygen, other companies had been slow to follow Linde's lead. And, in the commercial market, the liquid was routinely regasified before being consumed.

With missiles it would be different. They would consume liquid oxygen in tonnage quantities, as a propellant. The criteria to be met by that liquid oxygen remained uncertain until 1949, when a federal commission established appropriate specifications. The necessary liquid oxygen would have to come from Linde, unless an alternative competitive source came into existence.

Leonard Pool and his colleagues sensed an opportunity. If the company could become a competitive source, then the know-how thus developed might also enable it to challenge Linde in the growing commercial market for "merchant" or bulk deliveries of liquid oxygen. Unfortunately, Air Products lacked the financial resources needed to undertake the necessary development work. However, it did possess a variety of contacts in the government and in law firms which handled government contracts. The New York law firm of Lincoln, Lungren, and McDaniel was retained to help draft proposals to the Department of Defense. As a result Air Products was awarded several development contracts to study the properties of gases converted to liquid form, at extremely low temperatures. These efforts provided the company with the enhanced data base which formed an essential resource for the subsequent engineering design of large-scale liquid oxygen plants.

By 1952 the Air Force had issued a development contract to Air Products for a fifty-ton-per-day liquid oxygen generator. The Navy contracted for a design of the same size, for the Bureau of Ships. Soon, at government expense, Air Products had mastered the art of making tonnage units producing high-purity (99.5 percent) liquid oxygen. Weirton had marked a beginning of Air Products' experience with tonnage plants, but it was military development contracts that enabled Air Products to move rapidly to the forefront of tonnage *liquid* technology. That move, in its turn, would mean that the company was no longer playing catch-up, but working at the leading edge of what was emerging as the central sector of the gas industry.

Edward Donley, now a sales engineer, was one great advocate of how the development of tonnage liquid oxygen generators for the military would also have commercial value. In 1952 he wrote to Carl Anderson regarding one military design contract: "We should endeavor to do this job, if at all possible, as the engineering know-how which is acquired will have a direct bearing on the proposed fifty-ton-per-day plant for Air Reduction. . . . "[3] This liquid oxygen plant for Air Reduction was itself a signal of how the whole industrial gas business was growing and changing. As part of that transformation, Air Reduction, the second largest U.S. industrial gas company, was switching from gaseous to liquid oxygen generators for its merchant gas business.[4] National Cylinder Gas Company also was switching to liquid oxygen. In 1953, Air Products sold tonnage liquid oxygen generators to National Cylinder and to Air Reduction, as well as associated equipment for storing, pumping, and transferring the liquid. At the same time, Air Products was selling twenty-five-ton-per-day liquid oxygen generators to the Marubeni-Iida Company, Ltd., of Japan, which purchased one in 1953 and others in 1956 and 1957.

By a natural sequence, a familiarity with military requirements thus led to a push into liquid tonnage technology. Here, as elsewhere in the company's history, development contracts from the federal government played a vital role. Because of them Air Products was able to become a significant operator of plants and a supplier of leading-edge technology in the civilian marketplace. Entrepreneurship and risk were leading to new markets and growing rewards.

Santa Susana

If civilian sales were encouraging by 1955, the military business in liquid tonnage plants was booming. Thanks to the experience gained through its development contracts, Air Products took a substantial share of this market. Production facilities were increased, through purchase and adaptation of an abandoned foundry in Wilkes-Barre.

Typical of the tonnage projects for the military was the contract to

The assembly area of plant #4 (Wilkes-Barre) around 1956, when Air Products was building a significant number of 75-ton-per-day plants for the government. Shown here is a cold box under construction.

provide liquid oxygen and nitrogen plants for the North American Propulsion Field Laboratory at Santa Susana, California. As initially planned, the Santa Susana facility was to produce 600 tons of liquid oxygen and 7.4 tons of liquid nitrogen daily at a warranted purity of 99.5 percent. The completed plant was to be on-stream by January 1, 1956, and to operate continuously at the rated capacity for thirty days.

Air Products was once again competing against Linde for a major project. The Air Force Air Materiel Command at Wright-Patterson Field asked for bids in March 1955. In April, the Air Force lowered the facility's rated capacity to 300 tons of liquid oxygen per day, but Santa Susana would still be a major undertaking for Air Products. Even before the Air Force announced the winner, Frank Pavlis urged the engineering and purchasing departments to prepare so that the tight deadline might be met. In spite of the risk of incurring costs without compensation, Pavlis was confident that Air Products would be named the successful contractor. If no work were done on the job until a final contractor was named, he argued, it would be impossible to meet the January 1, 1956, target date.[5]

Against Linde's well-established reputation, Air Products could muster two advantages. It proposed building the plants in multiple, seventy-five-ton-per-day units. Thus, if a unit went down, only a partial loss of production would result. Using the seventy-five-ton units also gave Air Products a cost advantage. The units could be prefabricated at Wilkes-Barre rather than building the whole plant from the ground up at the site, as proposed by Linde. The cost of the facility was also low because of Pool's willingness to make a small profit from the initial undertaking. He conceived the design and construction of the Santa Susana facility as a learning experience for Air Products and the federal government as well as a partnership between the two. In that sense, it would be like building the first (gaseous) tonnage plant for Weirton.

Pool's calculations and Pavlis' optimism were vindicated: Air Products won the largest military contract of its fifteen-year existence. On July 28, 1955, Leonard Pool announced this fact to his employees and prepared them for what would be a very tense race to meet the deadline. Because of the importance and complexity of the project, Carl Anderson was charged with the organization and management of construction, installation, and commissioning operations in the field. He would play that same role in what became a whole series of tonnage liquid oxygen plants for the Air Force. Anderson reported directly to Pool and was assisted at various times by a number of engineers, including Jay Fetterman, Phil Foust, and Bill Scharle, who acted as project manager.[6]

The signed contract called for installation of two seventy-five-ton-per-day units by January 1956, the third by April, and the fourth by July. It was agreed that the facility would not have to be 100 percent operational until August 1956. In addition to the tonnage facility, Air Products was to supply nine liquid oxygen storage tanks as well as buildings and ground installations, and to erect and test the facility through a cost-reimbursement contract. Originally, the government intended to operate the facility with military personnel. Sensing an opportunity, Air Products argued that a stable, highly trained operating and maintenance staff would provide more reliable results. This persuasive argument led to the award of an operating contract, which was subsequently renewed from time to time. Santa Susana was thus a government-owned, company-operated (GOCO) facility. This move would have important implications, helping to change the company from simply a manufacturing to a more diverse operation.

The project placed a major drain on the engineering staff. As Frank Pavlis pointed out, " . . . we are slanting all sections to do this job and in many cases at the expense of other orders that we should be working on."[7] To meet the needs of Santa Susana and other tonnage liquid oxygen projects, a branch office of draftsmen and designers was opened in Philadelphia under the supervision of Mark Miller. The demand for technical personnel became so acute that in the 1956 annual report Leonard Pool appealed to shareholders for help in locating engineers. The company also offered a bounty of $100 to employees recruiting an engineer or other technically trained individual.

Much of the field work had to be subcontracted. Lengthy delays became all too familiar. Anderson complained that "deliveries are getting worse day by day."[8] There were also union problems. A strike by members of the Teamsters union shut down the sources of ready-mixed concrete. In February 1956, Anderson was behind schedule by about ten days. In April, difficulties over the compressors slowed work even more. Finally, months after its deadline, the first unit produced liquid oxygen at 3:30 A.M. on Thursday, May 17, 1956, supplying about twenty tons per day. By May 30, Unit 1 was producing eighty-two tons per day of 99.7 percent liquid oxygen. The first benchmark had been reached.[9]

The erection of Santa Susana gave Air Products the experience and

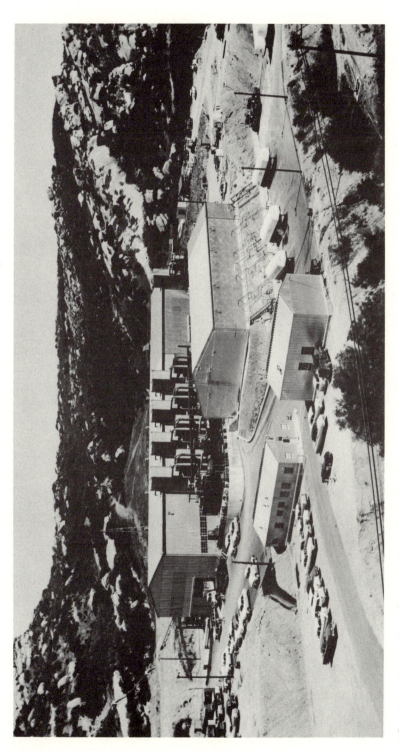

The Santa Susana plant, featuring four 75-ton-per-day oxygen generators. It was, as Leonard Pool told his employees, "the largest single contract in [the company's] history."

the reputation it needed to bid successfully on other military contracts for large plants, to be operated by Air Products' personnel. Seventy-five-ton-per-day units were selected as the preferred size. Air Products arrived at this size based on the maximal capacity of major equipment components which could be purchased "as is" from subcontractors. Units were grouped together on occasion to provide higher output, such as 150 tons (two units) per day at Patrick, Edwards, and Littleton air bases, and the 300 tons (four units) per day at Nimbus air base and at the Santa Susana project. Running these tonnage liquid plants for the military gave the company additional revenue spread over a long period, and also provided a training ground for technical staff. As Leonard Pool explained: "Taken together, this is a very big program, and of particular importance is the fact that we will get involved in operations on a much bigger scale than we have experienced previously."[10]

The military generators of World War II had not been operated by Air Products. Likewise, the operating responsibility for the domestic generators that were either leased or sold in the early postwar years lay with the customer. It was only in building generators to supply its own cylinder gas activities that Air Products began to operate generators in the field. In contrast, running tonnage liquid oxygen plants for the military was an activity carried out on such a scale by Air Products that the operations staff quickly numbered in excess of one hundred people.

Air Products' achievements for the Air Force were such that when the time came to renew the operating contracts (1958), the firm was approved as the sole source for running all Air Force liquid oxygen stations. The Air Force had good reasons to be satisfied: under this program the cost of its liquid oxygen had fallen from $65 to only $12.50 per ton.

The Three Bears

By the mid-fifties, the military market had become so large and such a significant part of Air Products' business that it began to reshape the firm and its strategy. Air Products had now developed the engineering expertise for very large projects and had learned how to manage these operations. A quite different demand for a liquefied gas for military use would further extend the firm's prowess in low-temperature processing. The gas was hydrogen.

It was clear by 1955 that U.S. rockets would have to be fueled by propellants with greater thrust per pound than traditional missile fuels if the rockets were to achieve orbital trajectory. The success of the Soviet Union in launching the *Sputnik* satellite in October 1957 drove home the message. However, the initial impetus to Air Products came from a somewhat different direction.

The Air Force had been experimenting with the idea of hydrogen-fueled aircraft for some time. Captain Jay Brill was in charge of meeting all liquid hydrogen requirements of Project "Suntan," aimed at developing a liquid hydrogen-fueled aircraft with performance superior to the U-2 spy plane. Liquefying hydrogen posed a variety of technical problems. The gas had to be of the highest purity, and it was, of course, capable of exploding violently in air.

The major obstacle to liquefying and storing hydrogen lies in the existence of two types of hydrogen molecules. In the orthohydrogen molecule, the two atoms of hydrogen spin in the same direction. In the parahydrogen molecule, they spin in opposite directions. Gaseous hydrogen is largely orthohydrogen. After liquefaction, the molecule undergoes a slow conversion to parahydrogen with an energy release which is considerable in comparison with the heat required to vaporize the liquid. As a result, liquefied orthohydrogen vaporizes entirely even if it is stored in a perfectly insulated container. To produce and store a stable liquefied hydrogen, a catalytic transformation from orthohydrogen to parahydrogen using ferric oxide is necessary during the cooling of the gas.[11]

In search of companies to solve these complex problems, Captain Brill visited Linde, Hydrocarbon Research, and Air Products in April 1956. Convinced that the necessary equipment could be built from existing technology, Brill awarded a consulting contract to the Arthur D. Little Company and also began to work on the problem with experts at the Bureau of Standards' Cryogenic Laboratory at Boulder, Colorado. In May, Brill contracted with Air Products to build and operate a plant at Painesville, Ohio, under the code name "Baby Bear." Lee Gaumer, a chemical engineer from Penn State who had worked at Du Pont and the Argonne National Laboratory before joining Air Products in 1952, was assigned the process engineering responsibility for this plant. He obtained valuable assistance from Peter VanderArend, previously with the Bureau of Standards, who was hired by Air Products. As a result of the Air Force contract, a liquefier was added to the Painesville plant. Whereas liquid hydrogen previously had been available only in "teaspoon" quantities, the Painesville plant, which became operational in May 1957, produced about 1,500 pounds a day for use in research related to Project Suntan.

One of the lessons that Air Products quickly learned was the importance of safety practices in handling liquid hydrogen. On April 24, 1958, there was an explosion and fire in the Baby Bear plant. The explosion was of such force that it ruptured the shell of the heat exchanger and started a series of small fires. The damage was limited and Air Products personnel were able to get the unit back into operation. The experience convinced management to give fresh thinking to the design of liquid hydrogen plants. Safety—already a watch word in other areas of the company's operations—was henceforth to become an urgent priority. Eventually it would become one of the selling points for Air Products' know-how in liquid hydrogen.

Baby Bear was followed by other contracts. The Air Force anticipated a large demand for liquid hydrogen at Pratt & Whitney's Florida missile-engine test center near West Palm Beach in the Everglades. United Aircraft[12] had given the federal government a tract of land for a liquid hydrogen facility, but the Air Force could not coax private industry into independent action. The military finally financed the plant's construction itself, at a cost of $6.2 million. After it was built, the Air Force decided that the plant should be operated by Air Products. Dubbed "Mama Bear," the facility was known locally (for security reasons) as the APIX fertilizer plant, an acronym for Air Products, Incorporated, Experimental. It began operation in the autumn of 1957 and had a daily capacity of five tons.

Even before Mama Bear was completed, the Air Force was planning a much larger hydrogen liquefaction plant to meet anticipated test needs at the Pratt & Whitney center. The Air Force gave a contract to Air Products in 1957 to build a second unit in the Everglades, a short distance away from Mama Bear. The facility, named "Papa Bear," cost $27 million and went into operation in January 1959. It had a daily capacity of thirty tons and was the world's largest. Although Project Suntan and the idea of a hydrogen-fueled aircraft had faded by the time they were finished, the two Everglades "Bears" were vital to the space program that followed. In fact, the complex was soon transferred from the Air Force to the National Aeronautics and Space Administration, to serve the latter's rocket-launch complex at Cape Canaveral, Florida.[13]

The three Bear projects carried Air Products into a wholly new realm of highly innovative engineering. For instance, the reciprocating gas-expansion engines and turbo-expanders used in large-scale

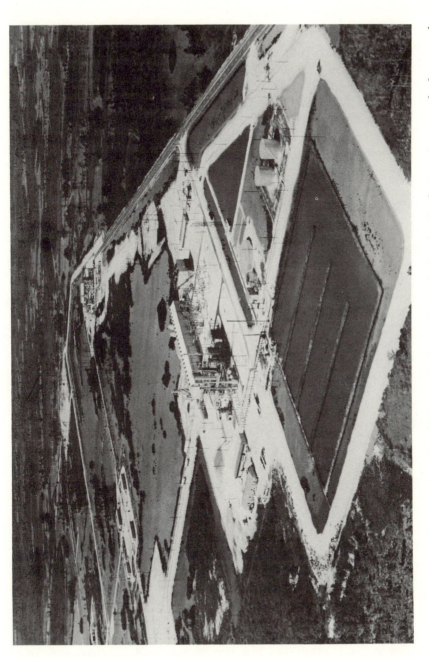

Aerial view of the Air Force tonnage liquid hydrogen facility at West Palm Beach, Florida. Papa Bear is in the foreground, while Mama Bear and storage tanks are visible in the distance.

air separation plants proved insufficient to the challenge of liquefying hydrogen for Papa Bear. The company developed high-speed turbo-expanders that gave high production at low cost. Also, more efficient insulating techniques were developed to minimize loss. The entire cold end of the facility was heavily vacuum insulated to eliminate product loss by vaporization. Air Products also developed special vacuum-insulated transfer lines to move the liquid hydrogen over several thousand feet with minimal losses.[14]

The Bear projects were a difficult technological challenge and their successful completion established Air Products as the nation's premier supplier of liquid hydrogen in tonnage quantities. Thus, when the Hamilton-Standard Division of United Aircraft started working on a proposal for a spaceship to travel to the moon and back using a liquid oxygen and liquid hydrogen fuel system, the company asked Air Products to work with them on a joint request for federal financing. Other military and commercial spinoffs would quickly follow in the fields of electronics and superconductivity, as well as a consultancy to the Atomic Energy Commission.

A New Lease on Leasing

Air Products benefited greatly from its military projects, through which it learned to develop new processes and operate them on a large scale. The initial excitement stirred by a military business worth more than a million dollars a month led Pool to pursue military contracts with great vigor. But the civilian economy remained important. Understandably, the leased-plant and cylinder gas businesses, and the sale of generators, were integral to the firm's strategy. But the leasing concept had to struggle against the advantages of generator ownership, as additional generator-manufacturing firms, particularly foreign-based firms, entered the American market.

Air Products, whether selling or leasing generators, faced competition from a variety of other companies, including such new entrants as the Joy Manufacturing Company of Michigan City, Indiana, and the Cambridge Corporation, which began selling oxygen plants in 1949. By 1952, the Air Products' salespeople charged with obtaining lease customers were also faced with competition from such overseas manufacturers of generators as Lindes Eismachinen of Germany, represented in the United States by the Blaw-Knox Company, and Air Liquide of France. The manufacturing costs of these European exporters were substantially lower than those of Air Products. The company found itself losing contracts. It was in this context that military development contracts for high-purity tonnage-liquid plants proved so timely, enabling the company to transform the size and caliber of the units that it could offer in the civilian marketplace.[15]

The existence of the leased-plant business concurrently with the growing number of military orders intensified the strain on Air Products' financial resources. The short-term loans which had been the source of capital for leased plants were becoming too burdensome. A fresh financing means had to be found. One break came in 1952, when Air Products arranged a revolving line of credit with the Tradesmen's National Bank of Philadelphia. But that was not enough. What the company really needed was long-term financing. The Board of Directors anxiously watched Linde shift its strategy from the *supply* of oxygen alone to one which included the *lease* of on-site oxygen plants in 1955. Imitation by Linde might be the sincerest form of flattery, but it was also a major threat. Many of Linde's new contracts were for massive plants making 500 or more tons per day,[16] and Linde could use its financial resources to offer long-term (fifteen-year) leases.

Leonard and George Pool experienced much frustration as they saw their giant competitor push into the on-site lease business, which they had pioneered. Air Products had negotiated its first long-term (fifteen-year) lease with Weirton Steel for two "E" series plants in 1954. But, handicapped by the lack of capital, the company could not aggressively pursue the use of long-term leases. Once Linde adopted the idea, however, Air Products—with or without financial capacity—simply had to respond in kind.

After an anxious search, the company was finally able to conclude a ten-year, serial-note loan agreement with Provident Mutual Life Insurance Company and Fidelity Mutual Life Insurance Company. The firm's short-term loans were paid off and its long-term loans reorganized in an indenture arrangement, in June 1956. Using Air Products' leased generators as collateral, the indenture established a revolving line of credit with a long-term pay-back. The indenture not only supported leased-plant activities, but also provided the credit capability needed to establish a general working capital fund. The signing of the indenture provided fresh incentives to the staff and officers of the corporation, particularly Jordan Gottshall who, as Treasurer, was given responsibility for keeping the company within the guidelines of the indenture.[17] Air Products could now respond to the imperative of competition on equal footing with Linde.

The indenture was critical to the financing of Air Products' contin-

The Jones & Laughlin Aliquippa facility (December 1957), showing storage tubes for gaseous oxygen in the foreground and two 115-ton-per-day oxygen generators in the background. This facility was Air Products' first fifteen-year lease of a tonnage plant and marked a new approach to the leased-plant business.

ued growth. It opened up fresh opportunities in the leased-plant business, especially for much larger, capital-intensive liquid plants. Air Products' leased-plant business shifted decisively toward a strategy focused on tonnage generators. The first such lease was with Jones & Laughlin for two 115-ton-per-day generators. That was quickly followed by a lease with the Granite City Steel Company for a 70-ton-per day plant. Tonnage oxygen plant contracts were also signed with the Acme Steel Company and Du Pont (New Johnsonville, Tennessee). As with the military GOCO plants, these tonnage generators would be operated by Air Products personnel, further boosting the firm's growing staff of operating technicians.

Air Products' changed strategy in the tonnage-plant business was a success. Income grew to nearly $5 million in 1960. Moreover, the vigorous construction of tonnage plants quickly opened the way to yet another radical change in company policy. The new policy, called "piggybacking," added excess gas or liquid capacity to those plants, as we shall see in Chapter 6.

Process Engineering for the Chemical Industry

Military contracts, new tonnage technologies, and financing through an indenture were not the only subjects to occupy Air Products in the 1950s. It was already apparent in the late forties that a growing number of chemical companies were interested in the purchase of large-scale air separation plants. This development did not escape Leonard Pool. The greatest promise, he believed, lay in the fertilizer business. Changes in American agricultural practices were triggering a huge demand for chemical fertilizers. At the same time, natural gas and by-product refinery gases were becoming important feedstocks for the chemical industry.[18]

Starting as early as 1948, Leonard Pool had his engineers carry out studies of how to provide gas equipment for the chemical industry. Experimental designs were made of plants to process natural gas, argon, nitrogen, and hydrogen. This was a substantial extension of the firm's engineering capabilities and, if successful, it would open new technological and sales frontiers for Air Products.

Company consultant Lee Twomey had been asked about removing nitrogen from natural gas, and Carl Anderson reported on the subject as early as the March 11, 1949 meeting of the Executive Committee of the Board. Those research and design efforts were intermittently pursued and eventually led to a 1956 contract with the Diamond

Alkali Company at Belle, West Virginia, for equipment to purify methane from a natural gas stream. They also put Air Products in an excellent position to enter the liquefied natural gas and helium recovery business, in due course. Leonard Pool also speculated that by-product refinery gases at low temperature could be a bountiful source of various gases with commercial applications, especially in the plastics field.

A far more successful strategy in the short term, however, was the effort to develop and sell tonnage oxygen-nitrogen generators to manufacturers of ammonia. In 1949, Pool had told the Engineering Department to start designing a tonnage plant capable of producing both oxygen and nitrogen. With the success of the Weirton plant behind him, he began the serious search for business. In the summer of 1952, Air Products entered into a $1.2 million contract with the Spencer Chemical Company to design and erect a 200-ton-per-day plant producing not only oxygen, but also nitrogen for the manufacture of ammonia. The plant was finished in the spring of 1954. The quality of the engineering work moved the Spencer Chemical Company to write a letter commending Air Products' work. (This effort also underlined the slow change in status of nitrogen from an unwanted by-product in air separation, to a useful gas in its own right and, by the 1980s, to the leading industrial gas. Indeed, by 1990, nitrogen was second only to sulfuric acid as the leading chemical.)

A second contract, dating from September 1952, was with Foster-Wheeler, Inc., to build a 225-ton-per-day oxygen-nitrogen generator for the W.R. Grace Company's ammonia synthesis operation. As these two contracts signalled, Air Products was finding a profitable niche in the chemical industry. At the same time, Pool pushed for further broadening of the range of plants the company was offering the synthetic ammonia industry. Air Products engineers next developed hydrogen purification equipment,[19] which dovetailed well with the sale of generators since ammonia synthesis requires hydrogen as well as nitrogen. Air Products sold two nitrogen and two hydrogen purification units, with capacities large enough to synthesize 235 tons of ammonia per day, to C.F. Braun & Company of Alhambra, California, in 1954. Braun installed the plants outside Los Angeles for Brea Chemicals, Inc., a subsidiary of the Union Oil Company. Air Products also sold "packages" of air separation and hydrogen purification equipment for synthesizing ammonia to the Girdler Corporation (for Northern Chemical Industries), the Lummus Company (for Gonzales Chemical), Phillips Chemical Company, and the Sun Oil Company.

The 200-ton-per-day oxygen-nitrogen plant (completed 1954) Air Products built for the Spencer Chemical Company, at Vicksburg, Mississippi. It signalled the firm's entry into the business of supplying ammonia manufacturers with gas processing equipment.

The effort to sell gas-processing equipment to the chemical industry also led to sales of tonnage oxygen plants in the petrochemicals area. In 1956, an 80-ton-per-day oxygen generator was sold to the Dow Chemical Company for its Freeport, Texas, plant. Then came the sale in 1957 of a 350-ton-per-day oxygen generator to the Celanese Corporation of America at Bishop, Texas. That plant's output replaced air in the oxidation of hydrocarbons for the production of acetic acid and other organic chemicals. The fact that Air Products equipment was increasingly being used to produce "building block chemicals" for the chemical industry foreshadowed the subsequent move "from cryogenics to chemicals," as the publicity of the company was to phrase it.

Other areas besides the chemical industry also benefited from Air Products' enhanced capabilities. George Pool quickly saw the implications of the firm's new hydrogen know-how for the cylinder gas business, and built up sales in this area. Argon too was gaining in commercial value. Its most important use was initially as a shielding gas in welding. Both Linde and Air Reduction had their own brands of argon-consuming welding equipment. By the mid-1950s, argon had become a major industrial gas, in demand for the electronics industry, for the production of titanium and zirconium, and for annealing purposes.

Air Products was determined to enter the booming argon market, so in 1953 Clarence Schilling carried out experimental work in the field of argon purification. The Air Products process involved combining crude argon (which contains a percentage of oxygen and nitrogen) with hydrogen over a catalyst to remove the oxygen, then removing the nitrogen in a cryogenic distillation column. This research led to tentative negotiations in 1955 for the purchase of crude argon from Jones & Laughlin. The following year, Air Products reached an agreement for the erection of a three-million-cubic-feet-per-month argon purification plant at Jones & Laughlin's Aliquippa plant. That was the start of, and only one aspect of, the company's business in argon purification equipment. Much of that equipment was sold in tandem with tonnage oxygen plants to steel companies. Equipment was also purchased, starting in 1955, by such Air Products customers as the National Cylinder Gas Company, the Burdett Oxygen Company, and the Marubeni-Iida Company, Ltd., of Japan. The firm's entry into the argon purification field placed it in an ideal situation to obtain a contract in 1958 to supply argon recovery and purification equipment to Universal Cyclops Steel Company, in Pittsburgh, for an "In-Fab" room handling very reactive metals like titanium, zirconium, columbium, tantalum, molybdenum, and tungsten. This was the first application of its kind.

The Technological Supermarket

The designing of large-scale, low-temperature, gas-processing equipment for the chemical and steel industries, and of tonnage oxygen and hydrogen plants for the military, stretched the firm's technological base. Air Products was transforming itself from a small company that made oxygen generators into a major designer, maker, and seller of a broad range of gas and cryogenic processing equipment. Pool and his colleagues were accomplishing the difficult feat of changing the scope and increasing the scale of their business, as the industrial gas field itself changed around them.

In seeking fresh ideas, the firm increased its attention to Europe. There, technology was available for a price. Air Products systematically began exploring the Continent for new processes. The company also was committed to manufacturing in Europe and thereby taking advantage of lower wage rates.

The 1951 agreement with Butterley provided a base from which to explore European technological developments. Air Products engineers made annual trips to England and to the Continent. In late 1954, for example, Ed Donley made a two-month visit. He was accompanied by Ed Lady, who had joined Air Products after previously working as an engineer at Union Carbide. Lady had been a student of S. C. Collins at MIT and was knowledgeable about research on cryogenics and air separation. Donley and Lady investigated industrial and academic facilities in Germany, Belgium, France, Holland, Italy, and England. They were particularly interested in ammonia and coke oven gas recovery plants, and their trip led to a licensing agreement.

In early 1955, through Donley's negotiations, Air Products acquired a license from N.V. Stamicarbon in the Netherlands for the production of ammonia from coke-oven gas. This experience led Pool and his colleagues to believe that the European countries should be tapped more systematically for their technology. In 1956, Air Products hired Lajos von Szeszich to act as its European consultant. Von Szeszich, who had a doctorate in engineering and extensive industrial experience, reported directly to Leonard Pool. The peripatetic consultant (and eventual Air Products employee) wrote numerous and lengthy reports on European developments in coal gasification equipment; desulfurization of coke oven gas; heat exchangers for tonnage plants; ethylene separation processes; and even processes for making heavy water for nuclear reactors. These reports and the experience of "shopping" for new technologies provided Air Products with a window on a variety of opportunities for diversification, opportunities that would continue to transform the company into the 1960s.

Accomplishments

By 1957, diversification had begun to transform Air Products. It was now involved in multimillion-dollar projects and had net sales of $34 million. Two-thirds of its business was with the federal government. The sales figures disguised the fact that civilian and government projects were symbiotic, each contributing to the firm's acquisition of new levels of scientific and engineering expertise. One example of this symbiosis was the application of hydrogen purification technology, developed for the civilian anhydrous ammonia industry, to the military's liquid hydrogen project. Another example was tonnage liquid oxygen, a technology Air Products developed for the military, then sold in the civilian sector.

Meanwhile, Air Products' generator sales, leasing, and cylinder gas businesses continued to grow. George and Leonard Pool, in conjunction with company salesmen, truck drivers, and other field personnel, plugged away at the cylinder gas market. In the fifties George steadily built up a small sales team to sell cylinder gases and welding equipment. The firm's engineers also helped keep the organization moving ahead, through innovative design. Under Leonard Pool's direction, Air Products continued to undertake more complex projects, diversifying into the liquefaction of gases in tonnage quantities and into the development of equipment and processes using feedstocks other than air. By 1957, Air Products was a much larger company. It continued to be a highly competitive, risk-taking enterprise, with a culture that reflected the importance of both engineering and salesmanship in company strategy.

Notes

1. "Emmaus Firm to Take Over Convair Hangar for War Goods Manufacture," *Evening Chronicle*, 5 May 1951, pp. 11, 18; "Air Products Firm

Leases Convair Hangar to Produce Military Oxygen Generators," *Sunday Call-Chronicle*, 6 May 1951, pp. 5, 7.

2. Frank Pavlis to Leonard Pool et al. "New Developments in Oxygen Production and Use," 1946, APHO.

3. Ed Donley to Carl Anderson, 25 October 1952, APHO.

4. John A. Hill, President of Air Reduction. Digest of speech to New York Society of Security Analysts, 21 March 1949, APHO.

5. Frank Pavlis to P. Foust, "300 T/D California Liquid Oxygen Station," 26 April 1955; Frank Pavlis to J. Fetterman, "300 T/D Liquid Oxygen Station, California," 20 April 1955, APHO.

6. Bill (William) Scharle joined Air Products in 1951 after completing his B.S. and M.S. degrees in chemical engineering at Villanova and Lehigh Universities, respectively.

7. Frank Pavlis to Leonard Pool, 18 August 1955, APHO.

8. Carl Anderson to Donald Marshall, 16 December 1955, APHO.

9. Nitrogen production, however, was not ready until the week of June 8, 1956, when 5.5 tons per day of liquid nitrogen was first produced.

10. Leonard Pool to Carl Anderson, 22 May 1956, APHO.

11. Peter C. VanderArend, "Liquid Hydrogen Fuel for Rockets," *New York Herald Tribune*, 25 October 1959, section 11, p. 1; "Technology Newsletter," *Chemical Week* (30 November 1957): 61.

12. United Technologies Corporation since 1975.

13. John L. Sloop, *Liquid Hydrogen as a Propulsion Fuel, 1945–1959*, (Washington, D.C.: NASA, 1978), pp. 160–163.

14. VanderArend, p. 1; Sloop, pp. 161–162.

15. Minutes of Board of Directors Meeting, 17 June 1952, APHO.

16. Union Carbide and Carbon Corporation, *Annual Report for the Year 1955*, p. 23; Union Carbide and Carbon Corporation, *Annual Report for the Year 1957*, p. 26.

17. Jordan Gotshall was an auditor for Arthur Anderson before joining Air Products in 1949.

18. Peter Spitz, *Petrochemicals: The Rise of an Industry* (New York: John Wiley & Sons, 1988), pp. 157–164.

19. Also called "liquid nitrogen wash units," because they used liquid nitrogen to purify the hydrogen.

5

The Technological
Enterprise and Its Culture

Air Products has always had engineering as a root of its growth. Initially growth came through diversification in the equipment the company built, moving from generators supplying only oxygen to those producing a variety of gases; from plants supplying gaseous oxygen to those delivering liquid oxygen and other liquefied gases; and from air separation units to gas purification systems. Later, growth came through other, linked endeavors: the move to a sale-of-gas orientation in the company's core business; the designing and operating of chemical plants; and the application of the company's skills to environmental and energy systems. What remained constant was the way in which the culture of Air Products was shaped by a dual stress on process engineering and on sales.

Leonard Pool's Values

In the company's early days Leonard Pool frequently made a sale and then returned to the office and challenged his engineers, led by Anderson, Pavlis, and Schilling, to devise a novel solution that would meet the contract's specifications. Sales set the direction and pace for technical change. Pool had enormous faith in his engineers. He assumed that if he could sell a project, then his engineers could certainly turn the project into reality.

Leonard Pool approached business in a highly personal manner. Like most good salesmen, he wanted to deal with his customers, his managers, and his shop floor employees on a face-to-face basis. Then he could size up the men and women with whom he was dealing and wherever possible convey to them the enthusiasm he felt for what they were jointly trying to accomplish.

Joint effort was the key to success and Air Products was from its early years a tightly knit "family" undertaking. Air Products was family in the literal sense. There were three Pools—Leonard, George and Dorothy—in crucial roles. But the boundaries of this "family" extended further, embracing Anderson, Pavlis, and other key employees. Leonard Pool was the father, the authority figure, and he did not expect to see his power challenged. In this brand of paternalistic business, Pool fully expected to take care of those who shared his dreams and efforts. His sense of community reached down to the shop floor and out into the community and the world. He felt a deep sense of responsibility for those with whom he labored and lived.

Pool's sense of responsibility was the motivation, for example, behind his encouragement of employees to help "the destitute people of Austria" in 1948. Pool himself was sending old clothing: "If any of you folks would like to join me by contributing any clothes that you have discarded, I would appreciate it very much, no matter how old they may be, if you would bring them to the plant and leave them in my office. I will see that they are forwarded to Austria. We Americans are certainly lucky to have warm clothing, enough food, and warm houses. If we possibly can, let's give a little bit to the less fortunate."[1] Again, when Hungarian refugees came to the Lehigh Valley in 1957, Air Products organized various services to integrate them into local life. The firm employed interpreters to teach them how to shop in supermarkets, and hired refugees when it could.

Locally, Air Products donated significantly to the Allentown Hospital, Ceder Crest College, and Lehigh University, and for many years Pool's message to students appeared in the Emmaus High School yearbook: "We salute you and look to the time when some of you grads will join us, and our staff will be refreshed by your skills, your pep and your forward vision. Sic 'em and good luck!"[2]

Scarred by his own childhood experiences, Leonard Pool hoped to be able to provide a full measure of security for his fellow workers. Mind you, they had to work hard, as he did. He demanded one hundred percent effort. But with those who worked hard and were loyal to the Air Products family, he was willing to share the profits of their successful joint endeavor. His goal was to pay his coworkers

Employees in front of plant #1 (Emmaus), December 1948.

well, to keep them on the job, and to help them realize their capabilities.

He expected employees to be flexible, heedless of status and rules when a job had to be done. Bureaucracy and organization charts were foreign to Leonard Pool. As he liked to say, "The job is the boss!" You should do whatever had to be done to complete the job successfully—on time, under budget, and to the full satisfaction of the customer. Pool could be a fierce opponent when he encountered workers or managers more concerned about rules or their standing in the firm than they were about the job at hand. Business to Pool was a series of discrete challenges: challenges in finding opportunity; challenges in making sales; challenges to innovate in process technology; challenges to meet deadlines; challenges to stay within budgets that were extremely tight as the firm sought to break into new markets; and challenges to meet the customer's expectations.

The Hard Realities of Labor Policy

While Leonard Pool was a very determined and successful businessman, he found it difficult to implement his values and realize his goals in a world that was often harsh and unyielding. Nowhere was this more evident than in labor relations, and especially in Pool's dealings with organized labor. Air Products' involvement with unions began at Chattanooga, and was shaped by the labor unrest that hit many businesses as World War II came to a close. The end of the war signaled the termination of wage, price, and rent controls. Peace also brought inflation, unemployment for many, and shortages of important consumer goods.

During the first full year after the war nearly five million workers struck at one time or another, and nationwide stoppages hit such key industries as steel, railways, coalmining, and meatpacking. At Chattanooga, after protracted hearings before the National Labor Relations Board, two of the Air Products unions struck and picketed the plant. Pool's sense of family was affronted, as was his desire to control an organization he saw as his personal property. That desire was evident, for instance, in his effort to maintain control of the bulletin boards, an important means of communication. The International Union of Operating Engineers (IUOE), local 910, wanted Air Products to have no jurisdiction over bulletin boards, which the union saw as an extension of the workers' right to free speech. Pool, who wanted to approve all items before they were posted, went to the expense of installing locked bulletin boards. That censorship irritated union members, as did his desire to ban the solicitation of union membership on company time.

Initially, the IUOE demanded a closed shop. Pool, who was against unions as a matter of principle, insisted on an open shop. The IUOE negotiators tried to compromise by offering to settle for a union shop, that is, one in which contracts would apply to all employees, whether union or not. The company would be permitted to hire non-union employees, with the understanding that they would join the union within a certain period. For Pool that was ceding too much control. He wanted to set wages as he saw fit, according to his personal appraisal of the worker's value to the business. He refused the demand for a union shop, but he too was forced to compromise. The final contract called for maintenance of membership, which required that a worker keep his union membership current as a condition of employment.

Conflicts such as those experienced by Air Products at Chattanooga were typical of the traditional adversary relationship between labor and management. The system presumed a lack of cooperation between workers and managers as they each struggled to achieve their own best interests. It was assumed that this was a zero-sum game: what the employer lost, the worker gained, and vice versa.

Pool's Philosophy

What became known as "Pool's Philosophy" was one man's attempt to articulate a better way in employee-management relations. When Air Products left Chattanooga, Pool's hope was to avoid labor unrest. He knew quite clearly that he wanted to be the one who controlled the shop floor in Emmaus. As he put it in 1947:

I learned the value of intelligent selection in the employment of people the hard way, at Chattanooga. The mistakes I made concerning the employment of people there would have surely bankrupted the company if we had stayed at that location, and indeed was one of the principal motives for getting away from Chattanooga.[3]

What Pool proposed was essentially a tradeoff: from his employees, he demanded loyalty and the conscientious and meritorious execution of their duties. He was especially concerned with the quantity and the quality of production. As he wrote to Dick Turner, "it was generally recognized that our Chattanooga operations averaged about fifty percent efficient and, in some instances, as little as twenty-five percent."[4] In exchange for greater efficiency, Air Products promised employees fair wages, job security, a good benefits package, and a sense of not being "just another number."

By 1950 many firms had organized "company unions" that provided the form but not the substance of independent union representation. Others were developing various benefit plans, including health-care and retirement programs, that attempted to shift workers' loyalties from the union to the company. That was the route chosen by Leonard Pool: "an improved procedure was devised and given to [Bill] Reiterman[5] to administer, and I believe the results have already shown in our plant. We have an above average class of employee."[6]

"Pool's Philosophy" did not prevent the growth of unions at Air Products. Indeed, in that regard, the Lehigh Valley in the 1950s and 1960s turned out to be a more difficult environment than such southern climes as Chattanooga. It proved difficult to convert Pool's general sentiments into acceptable practices. Differences in wages for similar work upset some shop workers. The company introduced job evaluations, according to a system applied by the company's Industrial Consultant, Fred Salmon. As Pool explained to his shop workers, "Your job has been evaluated. You receive a rate of pay which was arrived at by careful thought and study. You benefit by these things because no favoritism is shown to any job or any man."[7] Of course this system looked different from the bottom than it did from the top, and not all were satisfied with the results.

Air Products wages were set at par with those offered by Lehigh Valley businesses of a similar size. Pool also promised his employees job security. This goal proved more elusive than fair wages:

> Your company will make every attempt to provide continuous employment. Despite this fact, sometimes (we hope not) it may be necessary to temporarily lay off a worker. If this becomes necessary, the workers who were employed for the longest period will be laid off last, except in the case of those with special skills, who are necessary to continue production. The leaders of the various departments will be the last to be laid off.[8]

Such sentiments were all very well, but on occasion shop workers as well as technical personnel were abruptly fired. Indeed, Pool earned

The shop at Emmaus (plant #1), October 1952.

a reputation for firing people as quickly as he hired them, and that necessarily bred a sense of insecurity.

An equally serious source of insecurity was the firm's shaky financial position. The late 1940s was a particularly difficult period. In early 1947, the Board of Directors had unanimously voted itself a pay cut, and after the national recession of 1949 began, Leonard Pool noted that, "it becomes more and more necessary to tighten our belts in view of current business conditions." He called on "loyal" employees to be careful about wasting material in the office, in the shop, and while driving trucks, and to "take good care of our equipment, whether it be a typewriter, a machine tool in the shop, or the truck you are driving. Another important thing is that we all accomplish our tasks in the shortest reasonable time, whether your work is an engineering problem, typing a letter, operating a lathe, doing assembly or testing in the factory, or delivering gas."[9]

Management carefully watched every outlay no matter how large or small. Expense accounts were a frequent target of cost cutting. Long-distance telephone calls were discouraged. Employees were asked to consider using air mail or the telegraph service instead. Frank Pavlis kept a careful eye on costs. "Penny pinching" became a part of company lore. In 1949, for example, Pavlis wrote a memo concerning an employee's expense account charges: "I suggest that you use the luncheon meeting in preference to a dinner meeting because of its greater value and lesser expense."[10]

In these circumstances, the company simply could not afford to employ hourly workers who were not immediately needed. Layoffs were frequent and painful, and not consistent with Pool's Philosophy. Nor did the situation change as government contracts mounted. Although net sales increased dramatically, Air Products was continually short of working capital. A recurring need for cash resulted in more belt tightening and Black Fridays (payday), when large numbers of employees were laid off, then later rehired. The biggest and last Black Friday hit in 1960.

Because most of the government orders were done under cost-plus-fixed-fee contracts, Air Products did not receive payment until it presented invoices for amounts already spent. Hence the shortage of cash. In order to raise cash quickly, on two occasions in the late 1950s, Pavlis (Financial Vice President at the time) and Lee Holt, the new legal counsel to the company, took the Lehigh Valley train to Manhattan, sold shares to brokerage firms, and returned the same evening with money needed to pay employees. Another stratagem was for the

Assistant Treasurer to go every Friday morning to Middletown, Pennsylvania, where the government's accounts payable were handled. There he visited and made friends with the Payable Manager, occasionally playing golf with him or bringing him a bottle of whiskey, to make sure that the Air Products invoices were moved to the top of the pile. The Assistant Treasurer would return to headquarters on Friday afternoon with a check in hand, deposit it, and the firm would meet its payroll. Air Products employees scarcely enjoyed the economic security that Pool lauded.[11]

They did, however, have certain other advantages. The company provided its employees with good benefits. In addition to six paid holidays per year, workers at Emmaus received one week of vacation after one year of service and two weeks after two years on the job. Air Products also provided a loan service, as well as a profit-sharing plan which gave certain employees a portion of the company's annual profits. "This policy makes each one of you, in effect, in business for yourself," Pool declared.[12] The company also offered an insurance plan with "benefits far in excess of those demanded by convention." Air Products paid 50 percent of the cost of employee group life insurance, group hospitalization, and health and accident insurance. Having proper medical and hospital care was a strong concern for Pool, who was convinced that his own family had not had suitable treatment.

Another aspect of assuring good working conditions was the provision of a grievance procedure. If a worker did not feel satisfied with how the foreman or the factory superintendent handled his complaint, he was encouraged to see the production manager, then the personnel director, who was to act as a mediator between the production manager, the factory superintendent, and the employee. If all else failed, employees were invited to present their grievances to Leonard Pool himself. Of course, a certain temerity was required to take advantage of this latter procedure.

An important facet of "Pool's Philosophy" was creating a feeling among employees that they were "something more than an insignificant cog in a large wheel. . . . "[13] Air Products tried to instill in its employees a sense of belonging to an important, exciting venture. Pool wanted them to share his enthusiasm for the enterprise. He made special provisions when an employee had a death or birth in the immediate family. He wrote letters of congratulation and consolation, and took a personal interest in his employees and their families. He visited the shop and talked with his workers, most of whom he knew on a first-name basis. Pool saw his employees as a valuable resource. He had always pushed individuals, emotionally and intellectually, often with the positive result of better job performance. However, one negative consequence was the inconsistent treatment of employees.

As the company grew, Pool slowly acknowledged the need to develop more uniform procedures. The real development of staff training and consistent attitudes toward workers came only as the firm grew to a far larger size, in the years after 1957. Career planning, the creation of adequate legal and financial departments, and more orderly administration also were tasks for the years after 1957. By then, Pool increasingly found himself facing issues that he could no longer resolve unaided, even should he wish to. At the same time, the experience and judgment of such early colleagues as Anderson, Donley, and Pavlis had greatly matured, while the company finally possessed the resources to hire seasoned professionals in such fields as law and human relations. But, in the early, bumpy days "Pool's Philosophy" did serve as a vision of cooperative endeavor.

Safety and Quality

Like "Pool's Philosophy," safety entered the company's attitudes virtually from the firm's beginning. It was Carl Anderson who sought to make safety part of the culture. His concern was typified by an event that took place during the move to Emmaus. Anderson asked Dick Turner if he had inspected the shop for safety. Turner replied that he felt it would be better to wait until things were organized before focusing on safety. Anderson, however, insisted that the shop be inspected and that nothing be operated before a safety check was made.

In 1947 Carl Anderson wrote Bill Reiterman to call his attention to unsafe practices in the shop, and to what had to be done to protect employees as well as equipment from accident and damage. Anderson stressed that everyone should be briefed on regulations concerning the manufacture and use of oxygen. "I know that this is a practice that you are now following, but this is a word of warning that we must not fail in this important function."[14] Every new employee was handed a safety pamphlet, given an individual talk, and tested on his or her knowledge of oxygen and acetylene safety practices. Any questions missed on the test were reviewed.

In each department, certain individuals wore "a safety man's badge." They formed the Safety Committee, which met every week.

Various recommendations came out of those meetings. Posters were placed in strategic spots about the plant, and Pool urged workers to participate in the safety programs. However, as Frank Pavlis pointed out, "it is so easy to neglect such items until someone has been injured."[15] Too often the posters and meetings were not strong enough inducements to make the effort successful. The entrepreneurial stress of pioneering in new processes and meeting tight deadlines took its toll. In 1951, for instance, the accident record was such that the company's insurance carrier refused to renew its policy.

Safety would remain a continuing concern, and took on still greater importance, in the late 1950s, as Air Products moved into the leasing of tonnage plants and into plant operations. There was particular concern about the purity and safe handling of hydrogen. The Hindenburg disaster was still remembered, as well as the Baby Bear incident. At the temperature at which hydrogen liquefies, all other substances save helium become solids. Air could condense or freeze and form potentially explosive local mixtures or plug up liquefaction equipment and transfer lines. Frozen gases also could obstruct the operation of rocket engines and might create severe explosive hazards if any oxidizing materials were included.[16] Consequently, Air Products spent a lot of time and effort on safety. As Bill Scharle later recalled, "Leonard, Ed Donley, Anderson and others were extremely committed to the safety aspects."[17]

Closely related to the safety issue was the question of quality. At Air Products, Carl Anderson was "Mr. Quality." He demanded the best of everyone. The Anderson approach was that there was only one way to do a project and that was the right way. Part of doing the job right was making it look right. The aesthetics of design had their place along with the economics of design. Quality engineering had to be reconciled with the need for low-cost production. The best answer lay in process innovation as when, through the use of Anderson's liquid oxygen pump on the World War II mobile generators, the firm brought down the cost of producing oxygen.[18]

The Complexities of the Culture

The culture that had emerged at Air Products by 1957 was a relatively homogenous one, but it had its complexities. In a few short years, buy outs, further diversification, and continued growth would introduce far greater complexities. But in the 1950s, the demographic and geographic extent of the company was still limited. Most of the

An annual tradition: Leonard Pool throws out the first ball.

relatively small number of employees worked in Emmaus, Allentown, or Wilkes-Barre. Shop, field, and office workers alike shared certain values and traditions. There was the annual Christmas party as well as the company picnic and its perennial games, dancing, and Pennsylvania Dutch humor. Shop workers organized baseball games, a bowling league, and other sports activities. Worker contributions and the vending machine fund helped finance these events. Each year at the beginning of the baseball season, Leonard Pool threw out the first ball. Another early tradition was the distribution of turkeys to all employees just before Christmas. That tradition lasted until 1957, when the cost and the number of employees had gotten so large that Pool dropped the practice.

Despite the essential unity of the company culture, there were variations that emerged out of functional and locational differences. There was, for example, a distinct shop culture. The surnames of the shop workers reflected the local prevalence of the Pennsylvania Dutch. Characteristic names in 1947 were Kline, Knappenberger, Koppenheffer, Stoudt, Schmoyer, Meitzler, and Stroh. The number of shop workers grew as the number and size of military contracts increased and as additional manufacturing facilities were added in Wilkes-Barre.

There was also a distinct culture among the cylinder salesmen. Cylinder gas sales personnel were located in the field, in contrast to those responsible for selling generators and obtaining generator leases, who were based at company headquarters. Cylinder salespeople and the production and distribution personnel, including plant operators, truck drivers, and office employees, were locals. These men were individuals whose education was limited. Both Pools, of course, had been in gas sales in the thirties.

The slowly growing cylinder gas operation gave employment to an increasing number of "route salesmen." In George Pool, they had an inspirational leader. George's own disdain for the more conceptual approach of the company's engineers typified an attitude born of his own experience as a cylinder gas salesman. As Pavlis recalled: "George was always active on the industrial gas side, had really almost taken pride in his aloofness and, as one of the industrial gas people, always referred to the Engineering Department as 'that damn Engineering Department.' It was never 'our Engineering Department.' He was always its antagonist. George never took any interest in finances or management in general. He was a peddler and loved it."[19]

Cylinder gas sales were not centered on technology, but on people, the customer. In sales, formulas did not make sense. The atmosphere was open and informal, traits that were necessary in order to make the sale or keep the account. George Pool's cylinder sales force was totally committed to winning accounts and virtually refused to concede a loss. Pool believed that the watchwords of a good salesman were opportunity and initiative and he encouraged a practice which eventually came to be known as "door stepping": being in the potential buyer's office or presence every day until the order was awarded. "Some fellows," he said, "have that eagerness in their eyes and you can just see that if they are given the opportunity that they'll grab the ball and run to beat the band."[20]

The cylinder salesmen employed by Air Products learned to bring a tenacity to their work, to bring home the coveted contracts that would make the company's strategies succeed. That tenacity was cultivated at sales meetings where George Pool, Chester Delbridge, and Art Steele worked hard to develop the special combination of perseverance, persuasion, and pluck that quickly typified the group.

Salesmen had to distinguish the company's cylinder gas products from those of the competition. The gases sold by Air Products and other industrial gas firms were, after all, identical. If the tenacity of Air Products personnel was not enough, the sales force explained how air plants worked, how customer systems functioned, and introduced to the customers the people—from plant operators to truck drivers—who managed cylinder sales locally. Sales were supported by a competent production and distribution staff. George and Leonard Pool impressed on truck drivers the importance of cleanliness, public appearance, and other quality and safety matters.

The sale and leasing of generators was a far more complex and technical pursuit than the sale of cylinder gases. Consequently, in this area of sales, most personnel were trained as engineers. Success required an understanding of cost estimates and of how to prepare a bid. Generator sales teams combined expertise in salesmanship, engineering, and cost estimation, with a deep knowledge of the customer's needs. It was not unusual for generator sales and leasing personnel to move back and forth between engineering and sales.[21]

The success of the firm's efforts in generator placement rested on the talents of sales and engineering staff, and there was room at the top of the corporate ladder for engineers versed in both sales and process technology. It was from among the engineers that Air Products drew most of its management team. Frank Pavlis, though trained as a chemical engineer, found himself increasingly involved with fi-

The engineers of Air Products, Emmaus, 1948. From left to right: Jay Fetterman, Phil Foust, (unidentified), Len Volland, Mr. Gelly (from The Butterley Company), Clarence Schilling, and Carl Anderson. Squatting in front is Jack Graeffe.

nancial questions. It was Pavlis, for instance, who drew up the first lease agreements and who later became Financial Vice President. Carl Anderson and Clarence Schilling were also Vice Presidents. In fact, the fast route up the corporate ladder was to combine college education with exposure to both engineering and sales. Ed Donley, an engineering graduate, rose through the ranks as a sales engineer, then as a sales manager, before becoming a vice president, then President. A somewhat similar route was taken by the two Presidents who followed him, Dexter Baker and Frank Ryan.

The engineering staff employed by the firm was also on the rise. It was the engineering side of the company culture that would dominate management into the 1980s. In the late fifties, two-thirds of all employees with college degrees had engineering degrees. About one in three employees with college degrees had majored in chemical engineering, roughly twice the number with degrees in business administration, accounting, economics, and law combined. Leonard Pool was the most influential individual at Air Products, and he was strongly influenced by engineers and the engineering culture with its emphasis on problem solving, quality control, and technical expertise.

The Engineering Department lay at the heart of Air Products. As the firm grew, so the Engineering Department became larger and more complex, a mark of the variety of functions performed. In 1955, the company had over 150 engineers. At the head of all engineering at Air Products was Carl Anderson, with his extensive practical experience in generator design. His position of importance and prominence allowed Anderson to maintain engineering excellence as an intrinsic and lasting characteristic of Air Products.

The Engineering Department was composed of Process, Design, and Project Engineering. Project Engineering was responsible for the management of a specific project from receipt of the order through process design, manufacturing, construction, start-up, and initial operation. Process Engineering, organized in 1952 along with the Tool Design Department, applied basic cryogenic data and knowledge to specific projects, selecting the one cycle to use out of a large number of possible and available cycles. Design Engineers transformed the basic cycle selected by the process engineers into detailed equipment designs suitable for manufacturing. Because technically challenging projects like the Weirton tonnage plant and the Bear family units were so complex, design engineers built scale models, which, for example, helped to plan the complex piping of the plant.

The Air Products Engineering Department, Plant #2 (former Vultee Hangar), June 1953.

The Standards Department aimed to eliminate unnecessary variety and duplication, to promote the use of the most up-to-date materials and methods, and to incorporate the latest safety practices and designs. Standardizing components helped to reduce inventories. The code numbers assigned to each part and component became a common technical language throughout the company. The Standards Department was concerned with such components as driers, heat exchangers, and distillation columns, which were manufactured internally. Standards were also prepared for raw materials and finished components supplied by subcontractors, and for the selection of materials, drafting room practices, and equipment.

The Department of the Chief Engineer was the section of Engineering where the best of Air Products' engineers were to be found. They were Leonard Pool's troubleshooters. They spent much of their time working out the problems associated with the company's most intricate, advanced engineering projects. If a Project, Process, or Design Engineer had a problem, the Department of the Chief Engineer resolved it. The Chief Engineer was Clarence Schilling, who had solved the problems of the Weirton tonnage plant and many more of the firm's technically complex projects. His Department was staffed by the senior engineers, like Carroll Claitor, Assistant Chief Engineer. Claitor, who had joined Air Products in 1955, had extensive chemical and mechanical engineering experience with the Elliott Company, where he had helped to develop the Elliott oxygen generator.

There was also a Construction Department, which oversaw the erection and start-up of plants in the field. Its genesis was the Bear projects and tonnage liquid oxygen plants erected for the military.

The Beginnings of R&D

The increasing complexity of the Engineering Department reflected the growing complexity, scale, and variety of the work being done by the firm. This same transition was taking place in that part of the engineering operations dedicated to research and development. Years before the inauguration of a formal Research and Development Department in 1952, in fact from the company's founding, Air Products' engineers had carried out experiments. There was, however, no distinct category of company activity considered to involve experimentation. Betterment orders was an umbrella term that covered a wide range of developmental, design, and experimental work. During

World War II, the company engineers had filled many betterment orders. For example, in 1942 they had worked on an experimental electrolytic cell. In the following year, they experimented on a special oxygen valve, a packed column, a mobile generator, a liquid oxygen vaporizer, a vacuum bottle, and a machine for making purifier-tower curls. Other such betterment orders involved improving tools and equipment for in-house use.

After World War II, this informal style of experimental work continued. Probably the most important postwar betterment order was that issued on July 6, 1946, for an experimental heat exchanger: studies aimed at the Weirton tonnage contract, which would have far-reaching implications for the company's future, had reached the experimental stage. A few years later, a similar order was logged for a report on the fabrication of mobile oxygen generators for the U.S. Army. Thus began years of military research and development work.

The Testing Department was the locus of many of the experimental programs. Although Testing was primarily responsible for the quality of the company's products, it also conducted experiments, as was the case in 1950, when Air Products was developing a shipboard oxygen-nitrogen generator for the Navy. Internal research was supplemented by private consultants such as Lee Twomey and Judson Swearingen, the Director of the Petroleum Division at Southwest Research Institute. In addition to his consulting services, Swearingen sold Air Products his patented rotary expanders, a vital component in large tonnage plants. The firm also had research agreements with private and public laboratories, including the Bureau of Mines; the Bureau of Standards' Cryogenic Engineering Laboratory (Boulder, Colorado); the Southwest Research Institute (San Antonio, Texas); the Anthracite Institute (Wilkes-Barre, Pennsylvania); Lehigh University (Bethlehem, Pennsylvania); Rice Institute (Houston, Texas); and Ebasco Industries, Inc.

In 1952, experimentation by the Engineering Department and by the outside consultants and laboratories was supplemented with the formal creation of a research and development laboratory. By this time Air Products' military business had driven the financial wolf away from the door; working capital was still tight, but the firm was on a far more secure footing than had been the case in the late 1940s. Government-funded research was increasing, and the prospects for more of that type of work were excellent. Linde and Air Reduction already had extensive R&D facilities, and these were the models for Leonard Pool's strategy. However, what prompted Pool to action was a patent infringement case.

Patents

In 1949, at the annual meeting of the Independent Oxygen Manufacturers' Association, Carl Anderson learned that a competitor, Superior Air Products, claimed to have invented a liquid oxygen pump which appeared to be identical to his. After Pool and Anderson discussed the matter and consulted with both Jim Shanley, the firm's patent attorney, and the Air Products Board of Directors, the company filed suit for infringement of Anderson's patent.

The district court gave Leonard Pool what he wanted, a protected position in the design and manufacture of liquid oxygen pumps. The victory came just as the Weirton tonnage plant was successfully completed. Leonard Pool received the formal letter of acceptance from Weirton on April 11, 1951. Riding on a wave of technical victories, he was elated. Aware of the pending acceptance letter Pool wrote to Charles Oakes, the president of the Pennsylvania Power and Light Company. Oakes had been part of the group of businessmen who worked to encourage Air Products to locate in the Lehigh Valley (electric power was of central importance in the production of industrial gases). Leonard Pool valued highly his relationship with Oakes. Likewise, Oakes liked Leonard, worked hard on Air Products' behalf, and took a special interest in helping Pool to articulate his plans for the future.

Pool outlined the position of the company and suggested the direction in which he thought it made sense to move:

> While I recognize that I am a very prejudiced judge, it appears to me that if the engineering skill and talent, and the sales ability, and, in general, the management of Air Products were applied to other fields, for example, other branches of the chemical industry or the oil industry, it would be probable that the results of operation would be more attractive than our meager showing.[22]

Oakes encouraged Pool to push the company in the direction of designing and selling equipment to the chemical and petroleum industries. Such a move highlighted the need for a more systematic approach to research and development. However, the euphoria of April 1951 did not immediately lead to the creation of a research organization.

The catalyst for change came in 1952. Dissatisfied with the ruling of the District Court, Superior Air Products took the patent case to the U.S. Court of Appeals, which was less sympathetic to the patent holder. The judge there declared Anderson's patent invalid "for lack of invention" and reversed the judgment of the lower court. This was a blow to Anderson personally and to Air Products.

Pool knew he had to act. He decided to pursue a more organized policy of seeking patent protection and promoting research. As he wrote on June 3, 1952: "It is my view that we should do everything possible to attain a strong patent position . . . I think we should be aggressive about obtaining patent coverage wherever possible. . . . Perhaps a semi-annual review concerning our patent position might be valuable."[23] At the same time, Pool committed Air Products to creating its own research facility:

> Starting first with the backbone of our company, the Engineering/Manufacturing Division, probably the most important development, which will have far-reaching effects on the entire company, [is] the establishment of a basic Research and Development Department. . . . Not only are present product improvements anticipated from the department, but also the development . . . of new products and uses of gas and related products. It is hoped that diversification of manufacturing activities will result, further stabilizing our economic and growth structure.[24]

The plan was to have the lab not only protect the firm's position but also chart a growth path by developing new products. Here as elsewhere, hope and reality were to prove farther apart than Leonard Pool desired.

The results of the more aggressive patent policy were quickly visible. The number of patents issued to employees increased dramatically in 1953. Pool instituted a Patent Committee to review the company's situation periodically. The committee included Pool himself, as well as Anderson, Schilling, Pavlis, and Donley. Working with Jim Shanley, Pool developed an employee patent agreement that established company ownership of employee inventions for six months after termination of employment. In 1957, to encourage employees to patent inventions, Air Products began to pay them $50 when an application was filed and an additional $100 when the patent was granted. Four such awards were made the first year.

Institutionalizing R&D

The initial step in organizing an R&D laboratory came with the appointment in 1952 of a scientist to head the operation. The choice reflected Pool's strategy of diversification. By selling air separation and hydrogen purification equipment for the synthesis of ammonia to chemical companies, like the Spencer Chemical Company and the W. R. Grace Company, Air Products sought to promote an entirely new line of business. Hence Pool's initial choice of Research Director, Otto Stern, who had a Ph.D. in chemistry (1921) from the University of Vienna and extensive experience managing fertilizer, acid, and other chemical plants. When Pool saw that Stern's research agenda lacked any short-term pay off, he quickly replaced him. Clyde McKinley had a similar background but a different style. After earning an M.S. and an Sc.D. in chemical engineering from the University of Michigan, McKinley had gained experience as an industrial research chemist. During World War II, he had worked in General Aniline & Film's research laboratory and later he had been a research administrator in that company's lab, pilot plant, and semiworks.

In March 1953, Air Products broke the ground for the Research Laboratory that management hoped would lead the way. At the same time, the Testing Department and the Engineering Department were expanded in a $200,000 program at the Emmaus and Allentown plants. Because research was conceived as an adjunct to engineering, some of Anderson's functions and administrative duties were assigned to McKinley. Moreover, while McKinley was director of both research and development, Len Volland in Engineering was in charge of certain development work and special projects, and worked closely with Schilling on low-temperature R&D.

These changes assured that engineering, research, and development would be coordinated; in fact, the distinction between research and development was blurred in practice. Many of the pioneers of industrial research in the United States—General Electric, AT&T, RCA, Kodak, and Du Pont—had separated research from engineering and development more clearly, in an effort to promote basic, scientific modes of innovation. Air Products followed a different path. The company's products at this time—oxygen, nitrogen, and argon—were simple chemicals, not amenable to the sort of basic research applied to polymers at companies like Du Pont or Rohm and Haas. Also, Air Products was still a late-entrant intent on catching up with leaders in the industrial gas business. Adapting and improving available technology was its best strategy. Consequently, research would be directed at improving processes rather than creating new products. Lowering the cost of making and operating generators and developing new gas uses and new processing equipment took precedence.

Leonard Pool actively supported the research program. As Clyde McKinley recalled, "I think he was by far the strongest single person in making sure that funds were available, that research was done, and that people were accomplishing things."[25] Research expenditures rose. By 1958, the budget for research amounted to $463,655. In addition, large sums of money flowed from the development contracts with the military.

For a while, Pool tried to get ideas from the salesmen for research projects during monthly meetings. He constantly maintained pressure to prove that the research ventures were worthwhile and that the right problems were being worked on. Initially, the R&D program included a Research Council, consisting of three or four university professors who met periodically to discuss possible projects and to review those under way. When the council failed to generate immediately useful ideas, Air Products implemented a committee plan more consistent with its emphasis on research tied tightly to developmental engineering.

Regular meetings were held between the Research and Development and the Engineering departments. As Pool explained to McKinley in 1958:

> [your duty] is to establish and maintain contacts with Clarence Schilling, Carroll Claitor, Robert Latimer, Joe Cost, and others in the company and to draw out from them concepts that may result in technical breakthroughs. You should coalesce the suggestions that are transmitted by members of our Engineering Department, and these ideas together with the contribution made by personnel of Research and Development should be the basis of a vigorous R&D program conducted on an urgent basis.[26]

Much of the department's work was scientifically mundane but vital to the business. Of particular importance was the effort to enhance the efficiency of distillation columns, where an improvement of 2 to 4 percent could translate into savings of $100,000 per unit on larger tonnage plants. McKinley divided the activities of the Research and Development Department into three areas: (1) Research, which was closely related to process cycles and to the chemical relationships and the thermodynamic characteristics of the substances handled by plants in the field; (2) Development, which worked on new equipment and improvements in components for Air Products plants; and (3) Technical Services, which were provided to the company as a whole. Technical Services was, in effect, an institutional means of plugging the Research and Development Department into all of the operations of the company.

McKinley started by preparing a Technical Data Book. He had quickly seen that each process designer had his own information on the characteristics of gases at low temperature. One had a chemical engineer's handbook, another a handbook of chemistry and physics, another a government publication. They all gave different figures for the enthalpy, heat transfer coefficients, and physical properties of gases at low temperatures. The result was that two people designing the same generator would come up with different designs because of the variation in thermodynamic data used. McKinley decided to provide Air Products' engineering with uniform technical data.

At this juncture, the company's familiarity with development contracts from the federal government proved relevant. As we have seen earlier, Air Products won major contracts to conduct research on the physical properties of gases at cryogenic temperatures. An important benefit of these contracts, in addition to the data collected, was that they permitted a buildup of research staff in an area vital to the company's business.

McKinley focused the Research Section on four areas: (1) the adsorption, concentration, purification, and separation of gases; (2) the physical and chemical properties of gases and liquids at low temperatures; (3) fundamental heat transfer studies for cryogenic equipment insulation and the investigation of the performance of heat and mass-transfer equipment; and (4) special applications of cryogenics, the use of low temperatures for high-intensity magnetic fields, and the generation of extremely low temperatures by mechanical means for cooling special electronic sensing devices. This work led to the improvement of Air Products' process technology. A good example was the effort directed by C. T. Hsu, a Ph.D. in chemical engineering from the University of Pennsylvania. He conducted adsorption studies which led to fresh techniques and new knowledge of such adsorbents as silica gel; this in turn led to the use of smaller, more efficient driers and separation chambers for the removal of impurities.

McKinley integrated the firm's concern for safety into his department. As Air Products gained experience in operating tonnage plants for the military and commercial markets, safety fitted naturally into the business of R&D. The Process Safety Group in Technical Services, headed by Frank Himmelberger, developed new safety equipment. One example was the batch sampler, a pressure cylinder that prepared a fluid for analysis and for delivery to the laboratory. A major advantage of the sampler was its ruggedly constructed features. Another product was a continuous total hydrocarbon analyzer for monitoring the air intake stream of a separation plant for dangerous impurities such as acetylene, methane, and ethane. Development of the hydrocarbon analyzer grew out of an accident that occurred in 1956 to ammonia synthesis equipment Air Products had installed and sold to the Sun Oil Company at Marcus Hook, Pennsylvania. So successful was the hydrocarbon analyzer that it was adopted at Air Products and throughout the industry. As commercial tonnage plant operations mushroomed, the Process Safety Group was removed from Technical Services and organized as a separate Safety Department. The department's functions were expanded to include all facets of safety within the company. Air Products was thus well positioned to deal with, to learn from, and to move on after the explosion in its Baby Bear liquid hydrogen project.

As the Research and Development Department expanded its work, it began to contribute to the company's growth and diversification. In this and other ways, Air Products was maturing in the 1950s, achieving significant organizational capabilities that would carry the firm forward after its early leaders had passed the torch. Technical Services included a Diversification Group, headed by Jacob Geist, a Ph.D. in chemical engineering from the University of Michigan. The Diversification Group examined technologies that Air Products might want to pursue as the basis for entering new fields of activity. Diversification worked closely with a new Market Research Group. Starting in 1957, for example, it studied possibilities in chemicals and in the field of cooling, storing, and transporting liquid natural gas from Venezuela to England and Germany.

Into the Future

In 1950, in the midst of the first wave of military development and production contracts, Leonard Pool had plotted a fresh course for Air Products. It would sell processing equipment to the chemical industry. That fresh course and the increasingly sophisticated low-temperature plants being designed for the military raised the level of engineering activities at Air Products. His decision to establish a Research and Development Department, prompted by a patent infringement suit, also helped shape the firm. As an important center of technical creativity, the R&D Department was one marker of the growing internal differentiation of Air Products.

That differentiation was not accomplished easily, and owed little to the application of management theories or to a stress on organization charts. As Pool had tried to make clear to the Sperry Gyroscope Company and to The Butterley Company, formalities mattered far less to him than what people knew and could achieve. Pool was acutely aware that Air Products was only as good as its people. Throughout the 1950s, he actively sought to push the firm forward and to seize fresh opportunities. His entrepreneurial talents and their interaction with the Engineering and Sales departments shaped both the development of the firm's business and the evolution of its culture.

The late 1950s were to mark a watershed in the company's history. Over the preceding decade, Air Products had gone from a troubled enterprise fending off bankruptcy to an institution with substantial resources. A three-month strike in 1958 was one signal of the need to devote attention to those structural and organizational issues Pool preferred to duck. And in a number of other ways that year proved the harbinger of an entirely new set of challenges through which Air Products would be transformed into a far larger and still more diversified corporation. The future was just beginning.

Notes

1. Leonard Pool to Air Products Employees, 31 March 1948, APHO.
2. *The Tattler*, Emmaus High School Yearbook, 1947 to 1953, APHO.
3. Leonard Pool to Chester Price, 17 January 1947, APHO.
4. Leonard Pool to R.E. Turner, 1946, APHO.
5. William F. Reiterman succeeded Dick Turner as Personnel Director.
6. Leonard Pool to Chester Price, 17 January 1947, APHO.
7. API Employee News, 14 February 1947, APHO.
8. Leonard Pool to "Employees of Air Products Production Department," 24 January 1947, APHO.
9. Leonard Pool to Air Products Employees, 13 January 1949, APHO.
10. Frank Pavlis to P.F. McEnaney, 2 May 1949, APHO.
11. Lee Holt interview, 11 August 1988, APHO.
12. Leonard Pool, Speech to Shop Workers, 3 March 1947, APHO.

13. R.C. Kerr, "Air Products and the Man in the Shop," undated [ca. 1947] paper written for Leonard Pool, APHO.

14. Carl Anderson to Bill Reiterman, 3 April 1947, APHO.

15. Frank Pavlis to Bill Reiterman, 30 April 1947, APHO.

16. Peter C. VanderArend, "Liquid Hydrogen Fuel for Rockets," *New York Herald Tribune* (October 25, 1959), Section 11, p. 9.

17. Bill Scharle interview, 30 March 1988, APHO.

18. Ed Donley to Carl Anderson, 9 December 1986; Dex Baker to Carl Anderson, 14 October 1986, APHO.

19. Frank Pavlis interview, 2 February 1988.

20. George Pool, "The Future of the Cylinder Gas Division," speech given to an Air Products Cylinder Gas Division meeting, 31 October 1952, APHO.

21. Clyde McKinley interview, 10 March 1988; Lee Gaumer, comments at APCI History Advisory Meeting, 23 October 1989, APHO.

22. Leonard Pool to Charles Oakes, 10 April 1951, APHO.

23. Leonard Pool to Carl Anderson, 3 June 1952, APHO.

24. Leonard Pool, Newsletter, 22 December 1952, APHO.

25. Clyde McKinley interview, 10 March 1988, APHO.

26. Leonard Pool to Clyde McKinley, 26 November 1958, APHO. Joe Cost joined Air Products in 1953, after working for the Elliott Company and conducting research at the University of Delaware and Ohio State University. Robert Latimore joined Air Products from Linde, in 1958.

PART III

THE MODERN FIRM EMERGES

By 1958, Air Products was a business with substantial technical resources, and a strong track record. It was still very much Leonard Pool's creation, a family enterprise that had implemented a series of successful business strategies and acquired a strong position in several important markets. It was also a company grappling with the transition from late entrant in an established field to early and major player in newly emerging technologies. The managers of a much-enlarged Air Products found themselves struggling to exploit the opportunities offered by the enhanced scale of the firm's operations, and by the scope of markets that were now both national and international. Those managers began to sense the need for better means of exercising administrative control. They were also learning how to make decisive contributions to the manner in which Air Products innovated and the growth path it followed.

During the sixties and seventies, these patterns of development would be much extended (Table 6). Financial, legal, and human resources issues would take on a greater importance. The internal organization of the firm would become an important issue, successfully addressed by Ed Donley. An enlarged company could no longer depend on one charismatic figure to call all the shots. While Leonard Pool would exercise a veto over strategic decisions until his death in 1975, the company's managers and their divisions would generate more and more of the ideas about how and in what directions the business should grow. Their plans would be especially important because the corporation would use its strong credit capacity to finance new ventures. The change of the company name, to Air Products and Chemicals, Inc. (APCI), symbolized the widening scope of its ambitions.

Table 6
Air Products Sales and Profits, 1957–1978

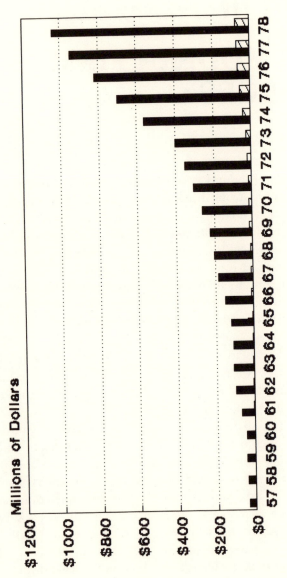

Millions of Dollars

6

Charting a New Course

In the late 1950s, Air Products was still experiencing occasional financial troubles. There were Black Friday layoffs, a three-month strike, and an aborted stock offering. But these setbacks proved temporary. By 1962 the company had crossed a major watershed in its history. Sales exceeded $100 million for the first time. The stock was listed on the New York Stock Exchange, and Leonard Pool appeared on the cover of *Business Week*.[1]

Along with these visible symbols of success came a changed corporate name, registration, and strategy for growth. In 1961 the company shifted its charter from Michigan to Delaware, a state more attuned to the requirements of corporations, and the name of the firm was changed to Air Products and Chemicals, Inc. The new name was chosen as the result of a company-wide contest. The winner was Leonard Pool! The company also adopted a new corporate logo, a stylized version of the alchemist's symbol for air. The company's home remained in the Lehigh Valley, where operations were slowly being centralized on a "green-field" site in Trexlertown, outside of Allentown. In 1958, the first elements of the new corporate center were opened, an office building and a large fabricating and machine shop.

These developments reflected deeper changes in structure and strategy: Legal, financial, and human resource issues began to receive more careful attention. In technology and in sales, the company played fresh tunes on the by-now familiar themes of expansion and diversification, pushing the growth of its industrial gas business in the United States and overseas and diversifying in a substantial man-

Leonard Pool on the cover of *Business Week*, July 30, 1960. Air Products was featured earlier that year in the March issue of *Fortune* magazine in an article titled "Pool's Fight for Air." The two articles acknowledged Air Products' arrival in the American business community. (Reprinted from *Business Week* by special permission, copyright © 1960 by McGraw-Hill, Inc.)

ner into chemicals. While the sale of capital goods to military and space agencies had been the company's major source of revenue in the 1950s, by the mid-sixties this line of business had yielded pride of place to enterprises based on the sale of consumable products. Air Products was more and more a company engaged in the production and sale of chemical products, primarily gases. Along the way, the corporation became less of a one-man show and began to change into a professionally managed firm. Gradually—and as yet incompletely— the system was becoming the boss.

Organizing for an Enlarged Scale of Operation

A major event which helped to force the systematization of Air Products' operations was a three-month strike in the summer of 1958. The shop employees refused to work after their contract expired. The company felt under severe pressure, for the strike coincided with a national recession. The company and the union aired their grievances in the local press. Harassment and minor damage to automobiles turned into more violent acts. An Air Products gas truck was set on fire, and incidents of vandalism occurred at the homes of Leonard Pool and another employee. Workers rejected a settlement that would have lowered the pay rates of some employees. Only with the intervention of the Federal Mediation and Conciliation Service did the strike come to an end. The settlement included a two-year contract that granted pay raises as well as improved insurance and vacation programs.[2]

The strike and the recession cost the company dearly. Pretax income declined by 20 percent in 1958 and fell again in 1959. An offering of common stock was cancelled. Instead, a ten-year note, convertible into stock, was negotiated with an institutional investor.[3] The 1958 strike was a watershed, dividing the family firm from the more formally organized modern corporation. Both labor and management learned enough from the confrontation to avoid another strike for sixteen years. Immediately after the strike, the company set about restructuring its manufacturing and personnel operations.

The organization of the shop and the high costs of manufacturing had been matters of concern since the move to Emmaus. On March 3, 1947 Pool had declared "our first difficulty at present is the high cost of manufacturing our products."[4] Ten years later, despite the efforts of Mark Halsted, who headed the shop, this problem had not been solved. Orders had been lost because shop overheads were too high. Halsted's forte had been putting out fires rather than organizing. In the fifties, the company had even gone so far as to seek overseas contractors for generator parts. The strike brought home to Pool and his colleagues the need to correct the situation.

George Hartnett, the General Works Manager at Babcock and Wilcox in Barberton, Ohio, was recruited and given the task of re-structuring the shop. Hartnett found that Air Products was function-ing more as a specialty job-shop than as a general manufacturer of generators. The shop was relatively small and the work required a high degree of skill and know-how, from engineering to manufacturing techniques, and from quality control to metallurgy. Much of the know-how had been developed within the company by trial and error. The shop also lacked stability and an established routine. It was not un-common for a manager to hold a position for a month or two, then be transferred to another function as a new assignment developed. Managers were pulled in several directions at once and did not have the time to concentrate on making operations more efficient.

The shop formed part of the Production Department, which also handled the generation of cylinder gases in the field. A first step was to separate gas generation from manufacturing. Another obvious move was to add to existing skills by hiring people who possessed special knowledge—as Hank Mason did in metallurgy. Hartnett thought that the people running the shop lacked the broad general knowledge needed to manage in a systematic fashion. To cut costs, he needed to make sure that material and drawings arrived in a timely way; production quotas had to be established and achieved; work in the shop could no longer constantly be interrupted for rush orders.

All work was still done on a job-order basis. Whether a job consisted of a betterment order, construction of a single, unique generator, or a batch of standardized models, the job was assigned an order number, under which all labor costs and parts were added as the job moved through the shop. "The job was the boss." This system was flexible: when a crisis hit, management could pull workers from several jobs to a high-priority task. But, as Hartnett knew, crisis management was neither orderly nor efficient in the manufacture, assembly, and testing of generators.

As restructured by Hartnett, the newly named Manufacturing De-partment was able to lower unit costs through more efficient and systematic production. The price that was paid was the ceding of a certain amount of control by Leonard Pool. No longer could he insist that all hands respond to opportunity as he perceived it. With the reorganization of the shop, there was a new unspoken dictum: "The system is the boss." That was the theme of other changes taking place at Air Products.

Only months before the 1958 strike, Jim (James) Boyce had been hired to manage the company's modest labor relations, the central activity of the Personnel Department. In 1960, he was appointed Director of Labor Relations, and he continued to head up the employee-relations function for over twenty-five years. He brought seven years' experience in personnel administration and labor relations to the job, plus a degree in management from New York University.

Boyce began building an organization, gradually increasing his staff to meet the human resources tasks facing the enlarged company in a new era. First and foremost, he sought to hire exceptional people. From the start, Leonard Pool had stressed the compelling need to aim for the "top of the class," and had set the example by hiring Frank Pavlis and Carl Anderson. The initial core of exceptionally talented and dedicated employees helped in the task of attracting more high-caliber people over the years. Managers came to see it as part of their job to bring good people into Air Products and became committed to spending time in Allentown and on college campuses, interviewing and selling the still relatively unknown company as a place with a future.

Through the 1960s, Jim Boyce's department expanded to encompass employee benefits, professional recruiting, performance evaluation, wage systems, job standards, equal opportunity, training, and personnel development. Ed Strobel was instrumental in developing the emerging function of employee benefits. Dick Waterbury headed up the field industrial-relations group with Ray Stevenson. Meanwhile, in the Allentown area, Everett Mills and Dayton Pryor led the constant effort to seek out highly qualified professional candidates from every source.

As sales doubled from $100 to $200 million in the mid-sixties, employee relations policies and systems were developed to anticipate the needs of a rapidly expanding work force and a company that was going global. More broadly, the Employee Relations Department proved to be central to a gradual change in the perceptions of labor and management, in which a union-based conflictual relationship was replaced by company-based cooperation.

This change was greatly fostered by Lee (Leon) Holt, whose initial task was the creation of a law department. After graduating from the University of Pennsylvania Law School, Holt worked for a law firm and in the oil industry, before joining Air Products in 1957. In addition to organizing the Law Department, he designed new pension plans, handled relations with the Board of Directors, and quietly and continuously sought to emphasize the importance of human resources to the company. By 1978, Holt had risen to become Vice Chairman and Chief Administrative Officer of the company.

Donald Shire was also brought on board in 1957. Shire was hired mainly to handle the company's government-contract business. Since the first government contracts of the forties, Air Products had relied exclusively on outside lawyers. Shire, a graduate of Boston University's School of Law, later became Corporate Secretary and Assistant General Counsel, Vice President of Energy and Materials, Vice President of Human Resources (the name for the much-expanded successor of the original Personnel Department), and then Senior Vice President of Human Resources and Administration, succeeding Lee Holt, in mid-1990. In these various ways the importance of people, the company's basic resource, received more serious and systematic attention than had been possible in the first hungry decades of the company's life. And Jim Boyce, Lee Holt, and Don Shire were important instigators of that quiet revolution.

Remaking the On-site Concept

As the company altered its managerial style following the 1958 strike, it also embarked on an important shift in strategy. Air Products decided to change its trail-blazing leased-plant concept, at the very time when Linde had begun to imitate it. Supplying oxygen—"selling milk"—had been the tradition around which the early industrial gas companies had organized. Pool's original idea—"to keep the cow and sell the milk"—involved the use of on-site generators. As time went on, on-site plants steadily increased in size, while Air Products increased its share of a growing market for merchant gases. New ideas about how to handle the demand for gas began to seem appropriate. It was no longer a case of selling small, fluctuating quantities of "milk" but rather of dealing with customers who desired great quantities of the substance on a regular basis. In response to this change in the market, Air Products shifted its core business from one of leasing on-site equipment to one of direct selling of huge quantities of gases. Supply contracts became the order of the day.

The new idea came to Air Products with Lee Holt. Holt had previously worked on natural gas contracts for a group known as Pan

American Petroleum and Transport Company. Given his background, he found Air Products' leased-plant business rather unusual. Why did the company lease out plants that the customers then operated? Why not simply own and operate the tonnage plants, he suggested, and enter into "take-or-pay" contracts to supply gas? Arrangements of this kind provided that customers would be committed to certain minimum monthly expenditures, regardless of their actual needs. The agreements were routine in the interstate transportation of natural gas. The indenture, which had financed the construction of the company's leased plants, could be modified to cover company-owned plants with secure, long-term supply contracts to reliable customers.

Air Products had built up experience in tonnage plant operations through its military contracts. Holt suggested that the company take the next logical step. It would build and own tonnage plants on or near the customer's site, then sell the gases produced on a long-term, take-or-pay basis. The customer would pay a base charge regardless of whether or not any gas was consumed. Steel companies proved willing to accept this arrangement, because their basic oxygen furnaces and converters required huge quantities of oxygen to be regularly available, on demand. The typical steel mill did not have the talent necessary for safe operation of a tonnage oxygen generator. In addition, steel companies locked into labor agreements that mandated their use of highly paid workers and generous staffing ratios could see other attractions in this new style of contract.

The changed strategy quickly proved successful. The strategy brought with it powerful incentives to reduce labor costs and increase generator efficiency, since all running costs were now the direct responsibility of Air Products. One immediate consequence was that the Research and Development Department constructed an experimental 12-ton-per-day automated plant at its Iselin gas branch, to produce gaseous nitrogen and oxygen, liquid nitrogen and oxygen, and crude argon. The amount authorized for the project, $138,850, was larger than any other R&D project in 1958. The plant proved a success. Its automated controls enabled Air Products to save on labor and energy costs. The technology was applied to other air separation plants, even to those in the 100- to 300-ton-per-day range. This innovation, coupled with the new arrangements of the take-or-pay contracts and financing through the indenture, was to prove decisive to Air Products' ability to compete in the domestic tonnage market.

Don Cummings,[5] aided in steel mill sales by his mentor Art Steele, and by Jack Stewart,[6] quickly built up large tonnage orders with Jones

& Laughlin at Cleveland (two 250-ton-per-day units) and Pittsburgh (two 170-ton-per-day units), Weirton Steel (two 325-ton-per-day units), Granite City Steel (one 170-ton-per-day unit), and Bethlehem Steel at Sparrows Point (one 350-ton-per-day oxygen-nitrogen unit) in the brief space of twelve months. This flow of large orders put extraordinary demands on the Engineering Department, and on the Treasurer and the legal staff.

Treasurer Jordan Gottshall kept an eye on every contract, to keep financially on track. Lee Holt, bringing to bear his broad range of experience and aided by Don Shire, went over each contract to make sure that the company was not promising something it could not deliver. Once the order was won, the Law Department assumed increased responsibility for actual contract negotiations. Also, Shire and Gottshall reviewed the contracts to ensure that Air Products could finance the plant under the indenture.

The indenture proved crucial in supporting the expanding on-site activities. The rapid flow of contracts meant that capital needs went through the roof. Coming out of an extremely cash-poor period, company managers were concerned about the excessive amount of capital being spent. However, Leonard Pool knew when he was on a roll. He urged everyone not to worry. There would be no problem getting the money, thanks to the indenture. "Just go out and get the orders," he told them, as he "set loose the tigers" of sales.

The complexity of large tonnage generators demanded extensive plant-operating skills. The experience that Air Products had acquired with large-scale plants for the military proved crucial in operating tonnage generators for the civilian market. A key part of this new on-site story lay with the development of the Operations Department.

Plant operations had been under the purview of Don MacLeod, until his untimely death in an airplane accident in 1956. Mark Halsted took over this responsibility, and became head of a new Operations Department in 1958. He was briefly assisted by Burle Wobker, who came from Phillips Petroleum, where he had substantial experience in operations. Halsted created the Operations Department from the bottom up. In just three years, the department more than quadrupled to keep pace with the booming on-site business. Halsted pulled people from the shops, people who had tested the plants and knew their peculiar quirks. He also organized safety engineers in each region as well as in the central office, further ingraining safety as a value in the company culture.

The new strategy refocused on-site operations from the leasing of equipment to the sale of industrial gases in tonnage quantities. Conceptually, on-site and merchant gas sales activities were now the same: in each case customers were supplied with gases by Air Products, from its own plant. However, out of necessity, the two activities were organizationally quite different. On-site sales of gases in huge quantities required laborious engineering and financial calculations and years of working with the customer. The sales, design, and process engineering staffs responsible were centralized at company headquarters as the Cryogenic Systems Division. In contrast, merchant sales involved smaller amounts, on short-term contracts, to many more customers. Salesmanship was less closely connected with engineering or with the head office. Nonetheless, Air Products created synergies between the on-site and merchant businesses through its innovative use of piggybacking. All the large-scale tonnage plants being built for the steel industry at this time were provided with additional liquid oxygen capacity to serve the local merchant market. Piggybacking proved a highly effective way of supporting the company's aggressive, if belated, bid to become a supplier of bulk quantities of industrial gases in merchant markets.

Into the Merchant Gas Business

By the mid-fifties, Air Products had discovered that many of its small customers were beginning to want oxygen, argon, hydrogen, and nitrogen in increasingly large amounts. Those amounts became too great to be handled economically in standard cylinders, but too small to be supplied by on-site tonnage generators. The middle range between cylinder and tonnage quantities had at one time seemed the natural market for Pool's leasing concept. But it became clear that there were other, far more rewarding routes to this emerging merchant gas market. Tube trailers, tankers, and other wheeled transport could convey substantial amounts of a growing number of gases in a liquid state.

Air Products had little merchant gas business as late as 1957. Its rivals, especially Linde, had long been building up their capabilities in the distribution of liquid. Air Reduction and National Cylinder Gas had followed the leader, even purchasing generators from Air Products. Despite the high cost, some of the larger independent industrial gas companies had also converted to liquid technology in the 1950s.[7] Clearly, the merchant market was too important for Air Products to neglect.

Entry into the merchant gas business involved purchasing trucks, such as this liquid oxygen truck parked in front of Air Products' corporate headquarters in Trexlertown.

Pool and his colleagues soon devised a two-front campaign as they played catch-up in the merchant gas field. The first and less risky venture grew out of the company's on-site endeavors. That was piggybacking, which meant providing capacity at a plant in excess of that dedicated to the on-site customer. Piggybacking made Air Products a low-cost producer in merchant gas and gave it the opportunity to acquire a large market share very quickly. On-site tonnage plants built in the sixties were routinely equipped with piggybacked merchant capacity.[8]

Air Products' second major step came with the decision to install its own "stand-alone" liquid oxygen plants to serve the merchant market. The initial proposal was to erect a seventy-five-ton-per-day plant of the same design as those the company had built and operated for the Air Force. Such a move would tie up a significant amount of capital and would subject the company to new risks. A decline in demand might leave Air Products with expensive, unused capacity. However, the profitability of the large liquid oxygen plants Air Products operated for the government was clear.

In 1958, Ed Donley and others researched the cost of installing a single seventy-five-ton-per-day liquid oxygen generator at Creighton, near Pittsburgh, where the steel industry gave rise to a large merchant demand for industrial gases. Their report suggested that the firm could undercut Linde's liquid oxygen price. They pressed Leonard Pool to undertake the project. A Creighton plant might also serve as a backup source for the tonnage plants the company was erecting for its steel customers. Pool agreed to discuss the proposal with Donley, Pavlis, Anderson, and his brother George, at his home one Sunday morning. After looking at the figures for an hour or two, Leonard said, "OK, let's go ahead and do it. Send someone out to get the land and we will do it." The group reexamined the figures over lunch, and then, as they were preparing to leave, Pool told them to install two such generators. The Creighton installations were rapidly followed by another stand-alone plant in Delaware City, Delaware.

These generators, the additional product from piggyback capacity, and the new types of on-site supply contracts revolutionized the tonnage and merchant gas businesses, significantly lowering costs. Air Products was able to cut deeply into markets previously dominated by the industry's largest producers. The company's capital needs increased sharply, as did the risks that came with this new style of business. But the company believed the opportunities justified both

Liquid oxygen storage tanks at the Cleveland facility, holding piggybacked surplus sold in the merchant market.

The Creighton facility near Pittsburgh: Air Products' first stand-alone tonnage liquid oxygen plant for the merchant market.

costs and risks. Profitability would follow if the efficiency of the plants was kept at a high level, and the distribution system improved.

Many of the smaller, independent gas companies in existence in 1960 found that the changes in the merchant gas business were a considerable threat to their livelihood. To acquire their own liquid oxygen technology was scarcely a viable option. A small liquid plant required an investment of about $1 million, in addition to outlays for equipment to transport, store, and deliver liquid. In order to finance the conversion to this newer technology, many independents had to go public or sell out to a larger company.[9] Air Products sensed an additional opportunity.

By 1960, the company was in an excellent position to push ahead with strengthening its distribution network. Profits were up, as was the value of Air Products' stock. George Pool, Don Cummings, and Jack Stewart led the move into southern and midwestern markets. Air Products acquired the Southern Oxygen Company in July 1961, by the issuance of 190,220 shares of common stock. Southern Oxygen was headquartered in Bladensburg, Maryland, and served twelve states ranging from Pennsylvania in the north to Florida in the south and Tennessee in the west. It produced and distributed oxygen, acetylene, nitrogen, hydrogen, argon, and medical gases, as well as related equipment. The company was integrated into the Air Products organization as the Southern Oxygen Division. Southern's Chairman, Robert Swope, and President, Robert McMillan, joined the Air Products Board.[10]

The expansion into the South continued: Air Products bought Miami (Florida) Oxygen Service, Inc.; Chattanooga (Tennessee) Welding Supply Company, Inc.; and Sun Coast (Florida) Oxygen Service, Inc.; three small firms specializing in industrial and medical gases and welding supplies. Next, it bought the Delta Oxygen Company, Inc., a much larger company. Delta served portions of Tennessee, Arkansas, Kentucky, and Mississippi not served by Southern Oxygen. Air Products rounded out this regional expansion by purchasing the Keenan Welding Supplies Company, which manufactured and distributed industrial gases and cutting and welding equipment in parts of Alabama, Florida, and Georgia.[11]

In December 1961, Air Products moved into the lucrative Texas and Oklahoma markets by purchasing the Hill Industrial Gas Company of Dallas. Air Products had previously strengthened its position in the Midwest by acquiring Compressed Gases of Ohio, Inc., and

Steele Gases of Illinois. It also purchased the Acme Welding Supply Company of Kansas City, Missouri. The company moved into Nebraska, Iowa, and South Dakota with the acquisition of The Balbach Company, another manufacturer and distributor of industrial gases.[12]

Somewhat over half the volume of the acquired companies was in oxygen, acetylene, and nitrogen gas. The remainder was in cutting and welding equipment and supplies, and medical gases. The acquisitions were financed through cash and stock. As Lee Holt observed, Air Products stock was "selling at thirty- sometimes forty-times earnings. We were using Chinese currency to buy these companies, and we were buying them at ten times earnings."[13]

These companies provided Air Products with the sales force and established customers it needed to penetrate rural and small-town cylinder gas markets. Air Products continued to expand its merchant gas business, too. Significant fractions of the cylinder gas business of the companies acquired were ripe for conversion to liquid-delivery technology. George Pool was the crucial player, when it came to integrating the newly acquired gas companies into a single Air Products sales force. Don Cummings and Jack Stewart, now Vice Presidents, helped with the many organizational issues.

Unlike its competitors, Air Products did not maintain separate cylinder and merchant sales organizations. George Pool ran the two operations as one (the Industrial Gas Division, or IGD), and reaped the benefits of his organizational approach. In the 1960s, he restructured his sales organization from the ground up, with branch, district, and regional offices. The company established distribution centers in New York, Pennsylvania, Virginia, Kentucky, Florida, Mississippi, Missouri, Oklahoma, Iowa, Minnesota, Michigan, and Indiana. There were sixty-five distribution outlets by 1963 and the network continued to expand through the end of the decade. Production and sales were decentralized into the field, leaving wide discretionary powers (but not budgetary power) in the hands of the local managers.

Pittsburgh was the first regional office because of the steel industry and its market potential. Jack Blanton became the Regional Manager, overseeing sales districts in Pittsburgh, Parkersburg, and Cleveland. Michael Cashman was recruited to be the Pittsburgh District Manager.[14] In 1961, Lanny Patten became the first engineer to transfer from Allentown into the new sales organization at Pittsburgh.[15] Patten, and several others brought in, later moved on to positions of increasing responsibility within the company. Their ranks included Hap Wagner, and Frank Ryan.[16] Cashman was transferred to manage a new eastern region office in Philadelphia, in 1962. There he recruited Pat Dyer, who later became a major figure in the firm's industrial gas operations.[17]

The new recruits to IGD lacked experience, and the experienced employees knew mainly cylinder sales, so everyone had to learn the merchant gas business together. The company's efforts in the merchant gas sector enjoyed the ambivalent blessing of having only a small business base to defend. Air Products could send its sales tigers to attack without fear of losing previously held territory. Their quarry was hard to run to ground, however, mainly because few merchant accounts had ever heard of Air Products. The sales force tried to deal with this problem by casting the company as a small underdog, up against entrenched competition. The sales effort required a campaign to win an account, as opposed to getting an order in one call. Air Products' aggressive salesmen made good use of the company's story, describing how breakthroughs in technology, and creative financing, had provided the opportunity to share cost savings with customers.

One big break came early in 1962 out of the Pittsburgh office, where Frank Ryan had replaced Mike Cashman as District Manager. Ryan and Lanny Patten quarterbacked negotiations with the Westinghouse Corporation. Although negotiated in Pittsburgh, the Westinghouse contract included supply for plants across the country, giving additional impetus to George Pool's colleagues as they scurried to learn the merchant gas business.

The tremendous challenges and the rapid growth of the 1960s created an uncommon esprit de corps among the sales, distribution, and production employees. It also made for unique sales personalities. Jack Blanton was quick and fiery tempered. Mike Cashman, a superior salesman, was long remembered for his version of the Air Products story, which he told with glowing eloquence, and which became the "authorized" version of the company's rise.

Stories aside, Air Products had to compete by providing better service at lower prices. It was through piggybacking that Air Products entered the growing California market. In 1963, Jack Stewart drove a major marketing effort, organized by Frank Ryan and Pat Dyer, to penetrate California. They sent ten people from the company's field sales group to northern California for a two-week market survey to determine the potential for merchant sales. Supplies would come from a plant to be built for the Libby-Owens-Ford Corporation in Lathrop, California. Cummings had negotiated the deal at the company's office in Toledo, Ohio. Libby-Owens-Ford had second thoughts after receiving a letter of intent which seemed quite different from the original oral agreement. Don Shire, of the Law Department, was sent out to repair the damage and push through the altered proposal or otherwise to negotiate a solution. Shire tailored a new contract that was acceptable to both parties and put the West Coast operation back on track. This was the beginning of the company's push into California, which later in the sixties included a major plant at El Segundo in the south and a Silicon Valley pipeline complex in the north.

The merchant gas business would be profitable and a source of growth for years to come. It would help swing the firm away from being a producer and lessor of equipment to being a producer of gases for sale. This same transition was especially marked in the defense and space markets. In the 1950s, generator sales had provided the bulk of the company's sales and profits. In the 1960s, gas sales would play a major role.

The Defense and Space Markets

When the Soviets launched *Sputnik* in October 1957, Americans were shocked. The United States quickly accelerated its missile programs. For Air Products, that meant a shift of emphasis from defense to space sales, and from equipment to product sales. The firm still sold five-, twenty-, and fifty-ton-per-day oxygen-nitrogen generators to the Corps of Engineers; skid-mounted units and liquid oxygen assemblies to the Bureau of Ships; semitrailers to Army Ordnance; generators to the Navy Bureau of Aeronautics; and a range of plants to the Air Force. But after *Sputnik*, Air Products' new opportunities were primarily in the burgeoning space industry, where the emphasis was on the supply of gases, not equipment.[18]

The leaders of the American rocket-testing programs quickly began to look for more powerful propellants and oxidants. One oxidant considered was fluorine, which could be consumed in combination with hydrogen. Bill Thomas and Ed Donley seized the opportunity to enter this field in the hope of long-term contracts. Because the government wanted fluorine in a liquid state, the company would be able to make good use of its expertise in low-temperature technologies. Unfortunately, fluorine has two major disadvantages. It is toxic to virtually all living things, and corrosive to most materials. It has to be stored in liquid form, without loss from vaporization. Production and delivery of liquid fluorine posed a severe technical and safety challenge.[19]

The Air Force was interested in fluorine for the intercontinental ballistic missiles being developed by Rocketdyne (North American Aviation) and by Bell Aircraft. When the initial experiments were favorable, the Air Force pushed forward with its liquid fluorine program. Air Products, which served Rocketdyne with liquid oxygen from the Santa Susana facility, developed the technical capability to generate, liquefy, store, and deliver fluorine. Rocketdyne was favorably impressed with the Air Products system. For a time Air Products worked closely with the Air Force on this new oxidant. Eventually, both the military and the National Aeronautics and Space Administration decided not to pursue a fluorine-oxidized missile. By that time, the company had positioned itself to exploit the civilian market that would develop for fluorine in the 1960s. Here as elsewhere, development work for the federal government led to technological innovations that could not have been anticipated when the contracts were undertaken.[20]

Meanwhile, Air Products was looking for other ways to capitalize on its ability to handle complex technical problems in cryogenic engineering. The experience of designing, constructing, and operating the liquid hydrogen Bear plants had established Air Products' expertise in cryogenics. One way to exploit that knowledge was in Project Rover, the joint Air Force and Atomic Energy Commission (AEC) attempt to develop a nuclear-powered aircraft-propulsion system cooled with liquid hydrogen. In July 1958, Ed Donley visited the Los Alamos Scientific Laboratory (made famous by the atomic bomb) to explore the possibility of Air Products' becoming the cryogenic consultant on the project. The firm was asked to comment on the AEC's plans. This report and the subsequent contract negotiations were successful, positioning Air Products to do about $5 million worth of consulting. Eventually this undertaking was discontinued, but again the firm was able to build its engineering and research ability in a growth area of high-tech development.

The same results could be seen in other areas of military business using specialized cryogenic equipment. In this period, the company's other military research-and-development contracts averaged about $1 million annually. With these funds, the Research and Development Department developed a number of specialized cryogenic devices for research in advanced chemistry, physics, astronomy, and related fields. Some of these small-scale cryogenic refrigeration systems using liquid helium, hydrogen, or neon found commercial markets in the electronics and defense industries.

The space program also offered fresh opportunities for the supply of liquid hydrogen. In June 1960, Linde began supplying the National Aeronautics and Space Administration (NASA) with liquid hydrogen from its own Torrance, California, six-ton-per-day facility.[21] Even as the Linde plant was going on-stream, NASA was determining that its California-Nevada region had a much larger requirement for liquid hydrogen than Linde could supply. The agency discussed plans and possible specifications for a contract with which to meet the antici- pated demand. NASA decided that it had to reassert its oft-ignored policy of not building or operating a facility that commercial busi- nesses could and would, if required.[22] One pressing reason was that, at this time, NASA lacked the capital funds to build its own plant.

NASA issued a call for bids. Air Products, which was awarded the contract in December 1961, was one of four companies submitting bids.[23] Winning this contract was an important victory for Air Prod- ucts. Now, in addition to being the dominant liquid hydrogen supplier in the East, it would share the West Coast NASA market equally with Linde. Air Products built a 32½-ton-per-day liquid hydrogen facility at Long Beach, near Los Angeles, California, that started production in January 1963. Because the NASA contract only required 30 tons per day, the facility's piggybacked capacity allowed the company to compete with Linde in the civilian, merchant liquid hydrogen market in the West.[24]

Liquefied Natural Gas and Helium

Although the company had shifted its emphasis from sales of equip- ment to sales of gases, Air Products was far from being out of the business of making and selling plants. Designing new equipment provided one means of diversifying into fresh areas, and management was correspondingly on the lookout for new markets for equipment. Relying on the know-how gained in the research and process-design work of the early 1950s, the firm branched out in two new directions, natural gas liquefaction and helium extraction. The two processes were technically related, as both entailed cooling natural gas. One, however, was an immediate success, while the other appeared at first to be a failure. The success was in helium. The apparent failure was the attempt to enter the liquefied natural gas business.

When Air Products began to consider involving itself in the liq- uefied natural gas market in the early 1950s, a major disaster which had nothing to do with the company was still in the public's memory.

On October 20, 1944, an insulated storage container had ruptured, releasing 1.1 million gallons of liquefied natural gas in Cleveland, Ohio.[25] The gas had vaporized and ignited, destroying a large portion of the area around the plant and killing and injuring many people. This terrible accident ensured that for many years development of this industry would have to take place overseas. Leonard Pool believed that such development would certainly occur, and that one day there would be a worldwide market in natural gas.

One attractive idea was to transport liquefied natural gas from South America to Europe, where demand for fuel was high. Carl Anderson and other Air Products engineers had studied the characteristics of natural gas at low temperatures as part of an effort to learn how to strip the nitrogen from it. Based on that research, Air Products began negotiating with the Shell Company in Venezuela for the purchase of liquefied natural gas and for the creation of a joint venture. Pool's idea was to form a company which would refine and liquefy natural gas in Venezuela and transport it to Europe.

Before committing the firm to the project, however, Pool commissioned a marketing report by Jack Geist, McKinley's assistant and head of the Diversification Group in the Research and Development Department. The report examined the possibilities for shipping liquefied gas from Venezuela to Germany or the U.K., from Iran to Italy, from New Guinea to Australia, from Algeria to Western Europe, and from Borneo to Japan. Geist recommended against this program because there were so many uncertainties about European gas prices. Air Products abandoned the idea for the time being, but in the 1960s the firm would return to this business and would cash in on the technical knowledge it had already acquired.

Meanwhile, the research and engineering work on liquefied natural gas placed Air Products in a decisive position to exploit a new market developing in helium extraction and purification equipment. Like much of the company's work at this time, the sale of helium equipment was tied to a government market. The Bureau of Mines was the country's sole producer of helium because of a government monopoly instituted during World War I. Relations between the Bureau and Air Products began shortly after World War II, when the company began purchasing helium for resale from the Bureau of Mines. In 1952 the two parties entered into a one-year cooperative research venture to study coal gasification and purification at the Bureau's synthesis gas branch at Morgantown, West Virginia.

The Bureau of Mines was also increasingly interested in removing nitrogen from natural gas, at its Amarillo, Texas, helium facility. The Bureau hoped to improve the thermal content of the gas, and sell it commercially. In 1956 Air Products obtained a preliminary contract for the nitrogen removal plant. Because of a rapid rise in helium demand, the Bureau shifted its focus to the task of designing a much larger helium recovery plant. Located at Keyes, Oklahoma, the plant was to process about 70 million cubic feet of natural gas per day. The gas had an exceedingly high helium content (almost 2 percent) and would thus produce 300 million cubic feet per year of 99.995 percent pure helium.

Even though Air Products did not have a contract in hand, it began preliminary engineering design and process work in order to position itself. The same strategy had been used in winning the Santa Susana contract. Bill Thomas negotiated with the Bureau, and he came away with a contract to build three helium separation units. The Bureau officially dedicated the Keyes facility on October 10, 1959.

The Keyes project left Air Products in an excellent position when the government decided to privatize the helium industry. In 1959 President Dwight Eisenhower signed the Helium Conservation Bill, which ended the Bureau of Mines' monopoly and provided federal funding to private companies which would strip and store the gas. The program involved building helium recovery plants on natural gas pipelines. Andy Mellen and other sales engineers of the Cryogenic Systems Division sold plants to Northern Natural Gas, Phillips Petroleum, and Cities Service. Subsidized by the federal government, these companies stripped the helium from their natural gas and stored it in wells or other underground areas for later purification. Air Products provided over 80 percent of the equipment used in this program.[26]

Designing and building the program's heat exchangers posed some difficult problems. The equipment had to process very large amounts of natural gas. The Keyes heat exchangers had handled 70 million cubic feet of gas per day. The Helium Conservation Program exchangers, by contrast, treated up to 500 million cubic feet of gas each day. It would have been impossible to use standard copper coil winding, which would have been colossal and inordinately expensive. Lee Gaumer in the Cryogenic Systems Division proposed building the heat exchangers out of aluminum, a lighter and less expensive metal. Because they were so large, up to eight feet in diameter and sixty feet long, the new aluminum exchangers were difficult to construct. George Hartnett oversaw this work, and his team mastered the prob-

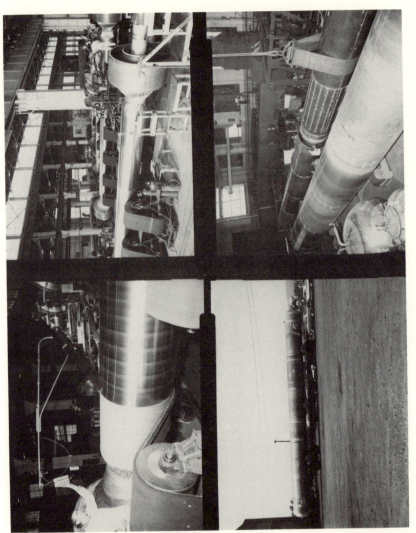

Construction of the massive heat exchangers for the Helium Conservation Program. Their fabrication was an unprecedented manufacturing challenge, and its mastery gave Air Products a significant engineering edge.

lems of designing and manufacturing these large-scale exchangers. Later, those exchangers provided Air Products with a technological edge when the firm finally entered the international market for liquefied natural gas equipment. By then, too, helium had become a major industrial gas. For Air Products, that meant a growing merchant gas market and, later in the decade, the construction of the largest commercial pure helium plant in the nation.

Air Products Limited

While the industrial gas business was being transformed, Air Products was also becoming a multinational corporation. As it did so, the company necessarily became less a one-man show and more a modern, managerial firm. The Atlantic Ocean made it impossible for Leonard Pool to exercise day-to-day control. He had to rely on others to manage and to perform the entrepreneurial function overseas. Pool had the final say, the power to approve or disapprove any decision. But the initiative for corporate action came from those on the spot.

At the same time, it was Pool himself who pushed the initiatives whereby Air Products moved from having a British licensee (Butterley), through participating in a joint venture, to running a wholly-owned subsidiary, Air Products Limited. While Pool and Ed Donley were in Europe in 1956, they had discussed the formation of a joint venture in industrial gases with Butterley's E. F. Wright. The selling point was the importance of keeping up with technological change. As technologies not covered by the licensing agreement came along, they argued, it would be imperative to exploit them, using Butterley capital and Air Products technical and managerial expertise. A joint venture would enable Air Products' expertise in tonnage and liquid technologies, for instance, to be married to Butterley capital. The Butterley board was initially doubtful but, aware of severe problems with its own contracts for tonnage plants, it approved the new agreement in April 1957.

Leonard and Dorothy Pool journeyed to England later that year. There they joined Dexter Baker, a sales engineer, the chosen administrator for this new and very important joint venture. Baker, a Lehigh University engineering graduate, had joined Air Products in 1952. By 1957 he had extensive experience in sales, especially in leasing tonnage plants to the chemical industry. He arrived in the United Kingdom by airplane for his new assignment carrying two bottles of peach brandy and a recording of *My Fair Lady* for Mr.

Column trays being made by Hughes & Lancaster (a subsidiary of Butterley) for a (metric) 269-ton-per-day plant. Left to right: H. R. Newman (Hughes & Lancaster), Leonard Pool, and G. R. Weetman (Hughes & Lancaster).

Wright. One Butterley representative said he was "very much impressed with your Dexter Baker and I don't think we could have had either a better or nicer chap to deal with."[27] Good relations with Butterley soon proved to be highly important in keeping the venture afloat.

As Baker pushed forward with what had now become Air Products (Great Britain) Ltd., (APGB), he quickly discovered that Pool's original concepts of how the business would develop had to be altered to fit the realities of European markets. It was no easy task to buck Pool, who was full of advice and expected monthly reports from him. But as Baker learned, Air Products' American air separation technology could not be effectively applied to the European market. In the United States in the 1950s and 1960s, electric power, the major plant operating charge, was plentiful, inexpensive, and declining in cost each year. As a result, American designs featured safety, operating flexibility, reliability, and low capital cost, not necessarily lowest power cost. In Europe, electric power was expensive and supplies somewhat uncertain. Sophisticated buyers, confident of their plant operating knowledge, insisted on efficient, low-power-consumption plants. Initially, as Baker reported, contracts were lost to British Oxygen and Lindes Eismachinen. Baker wanted to offer the market a more efficient plant for a premium price. He advised: "our customers will pay more for a superior plant."[28]

As a consequence of Baker's repeated entreaties, Pool set Air Products' engineers to work. Under the leadership of Jack Graeffe, they soon made the transition from "split-cycle" air separation plants, which utilized pebble-bed regenerators and liquid oxygen pumps, to low-pressure air separation plants, which utilize aluminum plate-fin heat exchangers and centrifugal gaseous oxygen compressors. The immediate result was to enable APGB to build European plants that would be both energy efficient and safe. Air Products was also able to switch to these new low-pressure plant designs in the United States. When energy costs escalated in the seventies, Air Products would benefit greatly from this innovation—an innovation arising from Baker's urgent proposals.

APGB was meanwhile working on a number of important contracts. The two most demanding were contracts won by Butterley, which its Board knew were in trouble when the joint venture was launched. The contracts were for a 200-ton-per-day high-purity oxygen plant for Stewarts and Lloyds at Corby, heralded in the English press as the first tonnage oxygen plant to be owned and operated by a steel company, and an oxygen-nitrogen plant of somewhat larger capacity for I.C.I. at Billingham. Initially, there was trouble with the Corby regenerators, in which the aluminum tubes had to be replaced with copper equipment. From the point of view of Stewarts and Lloyds, this change "at once brought the whole structure of the design of the plants into question."[29] Even with the copper tubes, the plant failed, at first, to produce oxygen. After APGB was unable to meet three deadlines, Leonard Pool joined Dex Baker and Clarence Schilling in a meeting with E.F. Wright and two other Butterley executives. The situation had become critical. Stewarts and Lloyds was turning to the British Oxygen Company for oxygen and wanted indemnification of the expense. Air Products claimed that the problems were not peculiar to its plants but were endemic to all similar units.

These problems, and an explosion at the company's I.C.I. plant, strengthened Pool's determination to take full control of the company. Accompanied by Baker and Frank Pavlis, he met several times with Butterley's management in London. Pool stressed likely future needs for frequent capital inputs to develop on-site and merchant operations. Butterley, aware of investment opportunities in its own brick business, reluctantly agreed to sell. Pavlis spent a year in England sorting out the subsidiary's fiscal affairs, arranging financing for future on-site projects, and recruiting Austin Walker, an astute accountant from Scotland, as Financial Director. Dex Baker guided through a name change to Air Products Limited (APL) and strengthened his organization by bringing over George Hartnett as Deputy Managing Director. Baker then spent six months back in the United States to learn the merchant gas business, which he intended to develop in England.

The subsidiary's next major step was to move into the merchant market. Dex Baker turned APL toward the strategy being employed in the United States: by owning rather than leasing plants, APL could use its excess capacity to generate low-cost gas for the merchant business. Again, Air Products was fortunate in its timing. A British Monopolies Commission ruling was opening up the market previously controlled by the British Oxygen Company. Baker had already sold argon and excess oxygen from one of his customer's tonnage plants. He had also entered the hydrogen business, using the by-product from a caustic chlorine works in the English Midlands to obtain hydrogen.

Baker pushed ahead quickly. He maneuvered into the growing nitrogen business by building a 150-ton-per-day nitrogen plant for the Esso Petroleum Company at Fawley. As a result of that successful plant, Baker reported that he was getting requests from "almost all of the government departments," including the Admiralty, the Atomic Energy Authority, the National Coal Board, and British Railways, for nitrogen generators. Winning fifteen-year tonnage gas supply contracts with two smaller steel companies in Wales and a third one in the English Midlands, Baker was able to piggyback extra low-cost liquid capacity for sale in these areas. A further step came in 1963 with the purchase of Saturn Industrial Gases (for which Anderson had worked, long ago). Baker closed the inefficient Saturn plants and used excess liquid oxygen capacity from his tonnage generators to supply customers. Liquidating Saturn's real estate almost paid for the acquisition, giving Baker the kind of success he needed to convince Pool and his colleagues to support Baker's ambitious plans for the continental European market.

The Move into Chemicals

The transformation into a multinational corporation was paralleled by Air Products' diversification into chemicals. In 1960, the company created a Chemicals Division. While it had been selling air separation and gas purification equipment to the chemical industry since the early 1950s, it was now going to manufacture and sell "regular" chemicals as well as industrial gases. This diversification would involve new technologies, and markets in which the company had no experience. The decision was risky.

Consciously or not, the firm's management was copying the strategy adopted by gas industry giants Union Carbide, Linde's parent company, Air Reduction, and Chemetron (the name of National Cylinder Gas, after 1958). Frank Pavlis recalled that, in the 1950s, "Leonard was always interested in chemicals, and I found to my regret many times discussing how oxygen could be used in various oxidation reactions and how that would be great in chemicals. I found that he wanted to do it right away and I was not prepared to do that. He was a dangerous man to talk to in a dreaming fashion because he wanted to run with the ideas. You had to be careful."[30]

By 1960, the situation had changed. Ed Donley argued that the company would need investment opportunities for the cash now being generated by the on-site business, and Pavlis agreed. As Donley later noted, "my idea from the beginning was that we ought to go into chemicals because our strength was engineering skill. If the industrial gas business was generating cash we could not absorb, then industrial chemicals would be something where we could use some of the same skills."[31] In industrial gases, Air Products was busy turning a joint venture into a wholly-owned subsidiary, Air Products Limited. In chemicals, an unfamiliar field, somewhat different strategies were called for.

Leonard Pool explored several possibilities including the purchase of Gonzales Chemical Company, which he declined. Eventually he found the opportunity that he was seeking, through Gordon Kiddoo.[32] Kiddoo was hired at Air Products as General Sales Manager of the Cryogenic Systems Division, which had a unit devoted exclusively to the sale of gas processing equipment to the chemical industry. Kiddoo was charged with developing new equipment markets. In the process, he found an opportunity to make and sell oxo-alcohols.

In July, 1961, Air Products entered into a joint arrangement with the Tidewater Oil Company to produce oxo-alcohols. The two firms created a 50–50 joint venture to produce several types of oxo-alcohols used in the manufacture of plasticizers, chemical softeners, vinyl resins, plastics, and synthetic detergents. The oxo-alcohol installation, which obtained its raw material from the Tidewater refinery at Delaware City, Delaware, started production in October 1962. Most of the output was sold under long-term contract to Reichhold Chemicals, Inc.

A more formidable step in the development of a chemicals business came through the acquisition of the Houdry Process Corporation of Philadelphia, Pennsylvania. By this time, Air Products had some familiarity with the oil refining and petrochemical world. It was George Pool who learned from a broker friend in Philadelphia that Houdry was available.[33] The main business of Houdry, a subsidiary of the Sun Oil Company, was in process catalysts, used in refining petroleum. Houdry sold its catalysts domestically and overseas, to more than 100 plants either operating or under construction in ten countries.

The directors of Houdry and Air Products entered into an agreement in November 1961. Management of the oxo-alcohol venture was turned over to Houdry's Gene Sidoroff. Air Products also gained a patent department and a research laboratory. In the mid-sixties, the patent department, under Max Klevitt, was relocated to the Lehigh Valley and integrated into Lee Holt's law department. Houdry's R&D lab remained at Linwood, Pennsylvania. Out of that laboratory had come a number of chemical processes and products that made Houdry a highly profitable venture.

The Houdry R&D laboratory at Linwood, Pennsylvania.

Table 7
Catalytic Sales and Operating Profit, 1961–1982

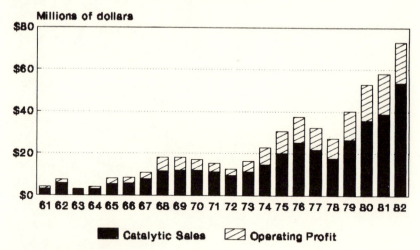

Operating profit is defined as profit
before interest expense and income tax.

As a further bonus, Air Products acquired the Catalytic Construction Company, a Houdry subsidiary (Table 7). Organized in 1946 and headquartered in Philadelphia, Catalytic undertook engineering and construction work for the petroleum, chemical, defense, and space industries. Under its head and organizer, Alan Knight, the company was also the industry leader in contract maintenance, which involved providing management, supervision, and skilled labor for over fifty refineries, and petrochemical and other plants. There was considerable potential for synergisms between Catalytic and its new parent company, which had started its own operating engineering branch a few years earlier. Nonetheless, Air Products maintained Catalytic as well as Houdry as separate operations.

The company had now grown into its new name—Air Products and Chemicals—and was well situated for a major phase of expansion at home and overseas. Cash-rich and confident, the firm was prepared to move forward on several fronts. Dex Baker was eager to increase the merchant gas business in England and to establish a foothold on the European continent. In the United States, George Pool's merchant gas operations were also in an excellent competitive position due to low-cost production and an enlarged distribution system. Chemicals too seemed to call for new investments and to present great opportunities for profitable growth. Like many other American companies during those prosperous years, Air Products would push forward aggressively to exploit all of the opportunities its managers could envisage. The entire nation would follow a similar path, confident that it could meet every challenge whether at home or overseas.

Notes

1. *Business Week*, 30 July 1960.

2. "Approval of 2-Year Pact Ends Air Products Strike," *The Morning Call*, 19 September 1958, p. 5; "Man Fined for Air Products Vandalism," *The Morning Call*, 7 October 1958, p. 16.

3. Air Products negotiated the ten-year note with the Trustees of the Savings and Profit Sharing Pension Fund of Sears, Roebuck and Co. Employees. It was later converted to common stock. Minutebook, Board of Directors, 16 September 1958.

4. Leonard Pool, address to shop workers, 3 March 1947, APHO.

5. Donald Cummings graduated with a B.S. in mechanical engineering from Yale University. He gained valuable experience in the steel industry working for Jones & Laughlin in Pittsburgh before joining Air Products in April 1964.

6. John Stewart earned his B.S.M.E. from Carnegie Institute of Technology in 1950 and then served as the Assistant to the President at Industrial Nucleonics Corporation in Columbus, Ohio. He joined Air Products as a sales engineer in 1956.

7. Auerbach Report, pp. 26–29.

8. "The Industrial Gas Industry," Report by William Blair & Company, 16 September 1976, pp. 10–18, APHO.

9. Lee Holt interview, 11 August 1988, APHO.

10. "Southern Oxygen Growth and Operations Reviewed," *The Cold Box* (August-September 1961): 3–7.

11. Air Products and Chemicals, Inc., "Listing Application to New York Stock Exchange," 25 September 1961, APHO.

12. Air Products also added production capacity for the manufacture of welding supplies and equipment with the purchase of the Black Manufacturing Company of New Jersey, a manufacturer of welding supplies and equipment.

13. Lee Holt interview, 11 August 1988, APHO.

14. Michael Cushman had an M.B.A. from the Harvard Business School. He joined Air Products in 1960, after working for Air Reduction as a salesman.

15. Lanny Patten earned a B.S. in industrial engineering from Iowa State University in 1956. After service in the Air Force, he joined Air Products in 1960.

16. Frank Ryan joined Air Products in 1957. He graduated with a B.S.

in chemical engineering from Villanova University in 1953 and served as a meteorologist for the Navy before coming to Air Products. Harold Wagner earned a B.S. degree from Stanford University in 1958 and an M.B.A. from Harvard University in 1963. From 1958 to 1961 he served as an officer in the Strategic Air Command, USAF. He was recruited by Leonard Pool after completing his Harvard degree.

17. Patrick Dyer graduated from the U.S. Military Academy at West Point in 1954. In 1959 he received an M.B.A. from the Harvard Business School and began working with the Humble Oil & Refining Company. Dyer joined the company in July 1963 as Cashman's assistant.

18. Jane Van Nimmen and Leonard Bruno, *NASA Historical Data Book*, vol. 1, (Washington, D.C.: NASA, 1988), pp. 3–4.

19. John D. Clark, *Ignition! An Informal History of Liquid Rocket Propellants* (New Brunswick, N.J.: Rutgers University Press, 1972), pp. 109–112.

20. Ed Donley to Leonard Pool, "Weekly Report," 28 July 1958, APHO.

21. Union Carbide and Carbon Corporation, *Annual Report*, 1960, p. 21.

22. Ernest Brackett to Mr. Siepert, August 2, 1960, "Procurement Plan for Liquid Hydrogen"; Brackett to Robert Seamans, 8 September 1960, "Procurement Plan for Liquid Hydrogen," NASA History Office.

23. "NASA to Purchase Additional Liquid Hydrogen," NASA News Release No. 61-285, 22 December 1961.

24. Ibid.; Union Carbide and Carbon Corporation, *Annual Report*, 1958, p. 23.

25. Arlon R. Tussing and Connie C. Barlow, *The Natural Gas Industry: Evolution, Structure and Economics* (Cambridge, Mass.: Ballinger, 1984), p. 63.

26. William Deaton, "The U.S. Helium Conservation Program," *Cryogenic Engineering News* 1 (July 1966): 20–22; W.H. Thomas to Edward Donley, July 29, 1959; W.H. Thomas to Gordon Kiddoo, 9 December 1959, APHO. Andy (Arthur) Mellen joined Air Products in 1960 as a sales engineer. He received a B.S. in chemical engineering from Cornell University.

27. M.F.M. Wright to Leonard Pool, 17 September 1957, APHO.

28. Dexter Baker to Leonard Pool, 12 February 1958, APHO.

29. M.F.M. Wright to Leonard Pool, 7 October 1957, APHO.

30. Frank Pavlis interview, 2 February 1988, APHO.

31. Edward Donley interview, 11 December 1987, APHO.

32. Gordon Kiddoo was a graduate of Cornell and MIT and came to Air Products from the National Research Corporation in Cambridge, Mass. "Gordon Kiddoo Assumes Post," *The Cold Box* (September–October 1959).

33. Lee Holt interview, 11 August 1988, APHO.

7

Investing in the Future

Air Products was in an ideal position to take advantage of the economic expansion that occurred in the United States during the 1960s. Renamed, restructured, rechartered, diversified, and run increasingly by professional managers, the company had cash to invest, a risk-taking style to display, and a high level of technical expertise to sell. The general economic expansion included an extraordinary increase in the demand for industrial gases, from several quarters. As the nation's space programs grew, Air Products was there to provide them with the gases, the engineering talent, and the equipment they needed. In the private, domestic market, the company was quick to satisfy new demands for specialty gases and to expand the market for its familiar low-cost products. Chemicals, too, provided a fresh area in which to experiment, to make mistakes, and to grow.

The company passed some important sales milestones. In 1962 total revenue had exceeded $100 million; in 1968 it passed $200 million. Success wiped away the memory that only a decade before cash had been so short that large-scale layoffs had been necessary. A much larger firm was now primarily a producer of consumables. Industrial gases sold in the tonnage, merchant, and cylinder markets and related cutting and welding apparatus accounted for 70 percent or more of Air Products' revenues in the 1960s. The largest contributors to sales were the on-site tonnage plants, which accounted for about 80 percent of the company's productive capacity.

The pace of Air Products' growth is reflected in the fact that, at the end of fiscal 1965, the capacity of all company-run air separation plants totaled about 7,000-tons-per-day; yet generators then under construction would add about 6,800-tons-per-day to that total. The new emphasis on the massive supply of consumables (gases) was evident in government sales, which were now, for the most part, sales of rocket fuels for the nation's space programs. The private industrial gas business was changing, too. Steel manufacturers were making increased use of oxygen and other gases, as were companies in the fast-growing electronics industry. The market for specialty gases also began to take off.[1]

Technology remained central to Air Products' corporate strategy. Systems to make, liquefy, purify, and mix both large quantities and special small lots of industrial gases were designed by the company's Cryogenic Systems Division (CSD). CSD in turn relied on Research and Development to gather data on the characteristics of gases and gas mixtures. Research continued to be primarily market oriented, task specific, directed to cost cutting and safety, and geared to the immediate needs of the company's engineers. Applied R&D, a branch of the Industrial Gas Division, discovered new gas uses which boosted merchant sales. The more basic research favored at the company's Houdry subsidiary also yielded a series of new products.

The main business of Air Products was no longer in leased or even on-site oxygen generators. More and more, management perceived oxygen plants as merely one of several forms of investment opportunity. As government sales increased sharply, as nitrogen, hydrogen, and other gases came to the fore, Air Products' share of the merchant and cylinder markets grew, and as Houdry proved highly profitable, company earnings and the undistributed surplus increased dramatically. The flow of cash, together with the credit capacity provided by the indenture, meant that management was able to explore additional areas in which to invest.

Leonard Pool, adventurous as always, speculated about opportunities Air Products might find in real estate. That and other radical moves were not pursued. Instead, the firm entered the agricultural chemicals business. This investment presented Air Products with marketing challenges that proved more strenuous than anticipated. The company had become accustomed to dealing primarily with a few large customers: the government or a large steel or automobile or chemical plant. In agricultural chemicals, Air Products flirted with the retail business before retrenching to its more familiar modes.

The Merchant and Tonnage Businesses

Throughout the decade, the bulk of Air Products' gas business was in the private sector. Both tonnage (on-site) and merchant demand for industrial gases grew at a very vigorous rate. Chemicals and glass-making accounted for an increasing share of sales. The rise of the electronics industry spurred demand. While the steel industry remained the chief customer, its requirements were shifting.

In the steel industry oxygen was still king. The 1960s saw a trend toward a new steelmaking furnace, the basic oxygen furnace (BOF). The consumption of oxygen per ton of steel produced was considerably higher in the BOF than in the open-hearth furnace, which had provided the major demand for oxygen in the 1950s. In addition, companies began to make steel by "blowing" molten iron and scrap with oxygen in a special vessel called a converter. Nine oxygen converters were scheduled to come on-stream in 1963 and 1964 alone. These and other changes raised oxygen consumption in steelmaking over 140 percent from 1960 to 1965. Air Products' market share for on-site oxygen grew from 5 to 20 percent in the same period.[2] Production of tonnage plants soared accordingly.

The steel industry was also a growing consumer of nitrogen, which was made by the same on-site tonnage plants that supplied oxygen. Nitrogen, once an unwanted by-product, was steadily becoming a valuable gas in its own right. One reason was the decision throughout the industry to replace natural gas with a mixture of nitrogen (95 percent) and hydrogen (5 percent) when annealing steel. Annealing is a process in which steel is heated then cooled in a controlled atmosphere to relieve internal stresses, improve formability and machinability, and provide uniform physical properties. By the mid-sixties, Air Products was selling about 25 percent of the nitrogen used in this process.

The introduction of the float-glass method of making plate glass opened up another market for on-site nitrogen. Air Products had an inconsequential share of that market in 1965 but, thanks to its aggressive salesmanship, the firm was providing about half the nitrogen for float-glass facilities by the end of the decade.[3] Another significant use of on-site nitrogen was in the electronics industry. Helium was the gas initially used to provide a protective atmosphere in which to grow silicon and germanium crystals. Those crystals enabled the electronics industry to move from vacuum tubes to solid-state transistors and other semiconductor devices. As the electronics industry developed, the idea of replacing helium with lower-priced argon and nitrogen became attractive, and opened up a market for increasing amounts of those gases. Nitrogen is also a cheap and effective gas with which to "purge" a work area of unwanted contaminants, a concern of ever-greater importance as electronics companies moved toward the miniaturization of components. In 1965, Air Products began to supply several customers in Silicon Valley, the semiconductor manufacturing area near San Francisco, by pipelines from an automated nitrogen plant at Santa Clara, California.[4]

Air Products faced tough competition in the on-site market from Air Reduction and from Linde, which now had a decade of experience. On-site customers were first and foremost steel companies like Allegheny Ludlum, Armco, Bethlehem, Granite City, Jones & Laughlin, U.S. Steel, and Weirton. In the chemical industry, major customers included Du Pont, Monsanto, Rohm and Haas, and Wyandotte Chemicals. In the military market, the largest liquid oxygen consumer was NASA. The commitment of President John Kennedy to land an American on the moon by the end of the decade spurred demand for liquid oxygen, which Air Products provided under long-term supply contracts. The company also retained important operating and supply contracts for Strategic Air Command bases.

In 1964, Air Products began construction of a 900-ton-per-day oxygen generator at Bethlehem Steel's Sparrows Point plant in Maryland, with piggybacked capacity for the merchant market.[5] At the time, it was the firm's largest industrial gas plant. Sparrows Point was triple the size of Santa Susana, built less than a decade before, and almost three thousand times larger than the original generator that Frank Pavlis had built just a quarter of a century earlier. The changes in scale reflected the transformations affecting the whole field of industrial gases, and the extraordinary rise of Air Products as a player in that field.

By now, the bulk of Air Products' productive capacity consisted of on-site plants whose output was secured under long-term, take-or-pay contracts. These plants used the low-pressure, energy-efficient cycle developed as a consequence of Dex Baker's exhortations to improve generator design. The Operations Department played a vital role in the running of the increasing number of ever-larger plants. Mark Halsted, aided by Bill Scharle and Walt Rector, was responsible for the necessary discipline in this flourishing activity, which enjoyed the best operating performance in the industry. In subsequent years,

Air Products' 900-ton-per-day facility at Bethlehem Steel's Sparrows Point, Maryland, works, in 1966. It was the largest air separation plant built by Air Products up to that time.

Hugh Wynn and then Chris Lloyd succeeded Halsted as the department assumed responsibility for more than 180 oxygen units.[6]

The merchant oxygen market was also undergoing tremendous expansion, the rate of growth being about *twice* that of the tonnage business.[7] In the 1960s, liquid nitrogen, delivered in bulk quantities by trucks, also became an important merchant commodity. A 1966 industry survey found that most of the eighty-four commercial plants producing liquid oxygen also were producing liquid nitrogen. The growth of merchant liquid nitrogen sales was linked to nitrogen's uses in the freezing of food.[8]

Air Products quickly seized growing portions of these expanding markets. To exploit the opportunities before it, Air Products undertook an ambitious plan to enlarge its merchant capacity by 70 percent. As a result, the firm brought record capacity on-stream in 1970, thanks to an investment of more than $30 million. Many of the smaller on-site generators leased by Air Products in the 1940s and 1950s were replaced in the 1960s by merchant deliveries of liquid oxygen.

Even more important for the growth of Air Products' merchant business was the sale of hydrogen. Traditionally, hydrogen had been a gas obtained from chemical sources, then used in the production of methanol or ammonia, and in the hydrogenation of edible fats and oils. However, merchant demand was rapidly growing in electronics, and in other industries, for hydrogen as a non-reactive atmosphere. Thanks to the earlier efforts of George Pool, Air Products was in an excellent position to supply merchant quantities of gaseous, high-purity hydrogen. Hydrogen sales accounted for a significant portion of Air Products' merchant market growth.[9]

Argon and helium represented far smaller markets than hydrogen, nitrogen, or oxygen, because of the scarcity of supply. Nonetheless, they provided further keys to the growth of merchant sales during the 1960s. Argon sales were tied to the metalworking industries, where it was used in welding aluminum, stainless steel, and titanium. In order to supply the metal industries, Air Products designed a new tonnage oxygen-nitrogen-argon cycle, with liquid capacity piggybacked for the merchant market. One such plant was built near Chicago and another near San Francisco. Already by 1965, Air Products was the second largest seller of merchant argon, behind industry leader Air Reduction. In 1969 one of the largest pure argon facilities in the world was designed and built by the company at Middletown, Ohio.[10]

Air Products Unlimited

While Air Products was deepening its position in most domestic regional gas markets, Air Products Limited (APL), the British subsidiary, was expanding onto the Continent and beyond.

Air Products was the pioneer of American entry into the international gas market. As John MacLean, General Manager of Gas Products at Linde, noted: "In 1960, a major transition of our business to its current status as a worldwide industry began, when the Air Products Company . . . expanded from its then large American base and began a major thrust into England. This was the first American company to make a move into the home country of one of the major powers in the industry."[11] By 1965, APL had achieved a substantial minority share, almost 20 percent, of the British gas market. The subsidiary also sold generators throughout the world. APL accounted for around 15 percent of the parent company's total sales.[12]

Dex Baker and his sales force used APL as a base for penetrating merchant gas markets in the Benelux countries, and in France, Germany, and South Africa. Crucial to this phase of expansion was Air Products' ability to sell generating capacity to the steel industry and to piggyback for the merchant market. Abroad—as at home—this kept down costs and opened a passageway into large markets dominated by the European gas giants. The home office had not planned this expansion and at times put roadblocks in its way. It was a case of entrepreneurship being bred within the company as Baker and his colleagues sought to exploit the opportunities that emerged.

Especially important to the firm's penetration of the Continent was the plant it built in Belgium. APL learned that Sidmar, a large steel company, was planning to build a sizable basic oxygen operation. The plant would need 400 metric tons-per-day of oxygen on a long-term basis. John Hinchley, in charge of the sales effort, "door-stepped" by making fifty-six trips (accompanied by engineers and other sales personnel) to Brussels and the plant site over a period of thirty months. By early summer 1964, Sidmar was close to awarding the contract.

In an attempt to dissuade the company from selecting Air Products, a competitor cautioned Sidmar about Air Products' generators which, the competitor claimed, had a substandard record in Italy, where deliveries were late and plants failed to produce the specified quantities. Sidmar demanded an explanation; Hinchley replied by inviting a delegation to Italy to inspect the plants, talk to the operators and owners, and draw its own conclusions. The Sidmar detachment discovered that the Italians were more than satisfied with their generators and pleased with their relations with Air Products. Sidmar quickly awarded a twenty-year supply contract.

Excited about this success and the potential of Continental merchant gas markets, Baker decided to open sales offices in Paris, Brussels, and Dusseldorf. Managers were selected and offices located. The office rental agreements required approval from America. Headquarters viewed the proposal as premature.[13] The request was denied. Senior management in the United States continued to be more pessimistic than Baker and his colleagues about opportunities in Continental Europe.

Disappointed but undeterred, Baker pressed on with marketing efforts. Within weeks of the Sidmar contract, he and his colleagues had in hand a similar agreement with a steel works in the Ruhr Valley. This agreement materialized after John Grieger, a salesman, learned that Rheinstahl Hüttenwerke, A.G., a prominent German steel producer, planned to expand its basic oxygen capacity and needed 400 metric tons-per-day on a twenty-year contract basis. Rheinstahl Hüttenwerke was not as firmly tied to the established giants of the German oxygen industry—Lindes Eismachinen, Adolf Messer, and Knapsack Gresheim—as were other major steel companies. When Grieger won this order there was much rejoicing. George Hartnett remembered how "coming quickly on the heels of the success in Belgium, the new German contract gave Air Products a permanent presence in two of the major industrial centers in Europe."[14] Baker's optimism was beginning to look like realism.

This was especially so after the Sidmar contract paid off in an unexpected manner. Air Products was now well known to the Société Générale de Belgique, (SGB) S.A., the giant Belgian investment group which owned Sidmar. SGB and APL began to discuss a joint venture and decided to move into the sale of merchant gases in the Benelux region. In 1964, Air Products and SGB jointly organized a venture called Air Products, S.A., headquartered in Brussels. Air Products, S.A. added 200 metric tons-per-day of liquid capacity to the Sidmar plant to provide the low-cost supply needed for merchant sales.

That same year, Air Products created a wholly owned subsidiary, Air Products G.m.b.H., headquartered in Dusseldorf. The Rheinstahl Hüttenwerke generator was piggybacked with another 200 metric tons-per-day of liquid capacity to supply merchant product for this new subsidiary. As 1965 began, Baker's sales force had created a secure foothold in the Continental tonnage and merchant markets.

The Dusseldorf and Brussels offices were convinced that they could duplicate the success Air Products had enjoyed in carving out a strong position in the United States. For instance, Air Products, S.A., entered the Netherlands in 1967 by incorporating a wholly owned subsidiary called Air Products Nederland, N.V. The Dutch venture was especially profitable because of that country's rich industrial base. Air Products Nederland was soon able to announce plans to construct one of the largest industrial gas facilities in Europe, at Rotterdam. It included plants to supply tonnage oxygen and nitrogen as well as to process steam for local industries. With the Air Products banner firmly planted in Germany, Belgium, and Holland, it was time to move into France, the third largest market in Europe after England and Germany. The French industrial gas market was dominated by Air Liquide, the largest gas company in the world. To cope with this stiff competition, Air Products located its French headquarters in Paris but focused its marketing efforts on southern France, where Air Liquide had only minor operations.

APL also provided a base for expansion outside Europe. In late 1962, APL learned that the Iron and Steel Corporation of South Africa (ISCOR) was asking for bids on a 200-ton-per-day, low-pressure oxygen generator for its steel mill near Johannesburg. Peter Clifton, the APL sales manager, and John Hinchley received from ISCOR complete specifications for the plant, which had to be built primarily with local products and services. The contract, moreover, had to be on a fixed-price basis, including field installation. That condition posed a real problem, since the head office of Air Products had a flat, corporate-wide prohibition against bidding any fixed-price construction contracts. APL pushed ahead, helped by the fact that one of the potential contractors was a local branch of Babcock & Wilcox. George Hartnett, Deputy Managing Director of APL, had worked for Babcock & Wilcox in the United States. He was able to use his personal ties to good advantage. Hartnett succeeded in persuading Babcock & Wilcox to submit a fixed price for the overall installation. He then used the agreement to pressure the reluctant home office into accepting a fixed-price bid.

Just as ISCOR prepared to make a decision on the bids, a competitor offered to carry out Air Products' part of the design for £25,000 less than the Air Products price, sight unseen. ISCOR rejected this grandstand offer, observing wryly that the competitor had paid the company a high compliment. Air Products installed the plant on time, under budget, and within the specifications for performance. Several repeat orders were to come from ISCOR over the years. In 1969, ISCOR, Air Products, and Babcock & Wilcox joined forces to organize Air Products South Africa (APSAP), headquartered in Pretoria. This joint venture operated ISCOR's tonnage plants and sold industrial gases, using the same piggybacking technique perfected in the U.S. market.[15]

When Dexter Baker returned to the United States in 1967, he continued to support the company's expansion overseas. Indeed, he could now press for a more enthusiastic approach from within headquarters; he was, for example, able to launch Air Products' gas and plant sales in Puerto Rico and to help point toward Asia.

On June 26, 1968, Air Products incorporated Air Products of Puerto Rico, Inc., in the state of Delaware. This subsidiary owned and operated a 1,000-ton-per-day nitrogen plant, furnished pipeline oxygen and nitrogen to several petrochemical operations, and served merchant gas markets along the island's southern coast. The Asian market was more difficult to penetrate, although Air Products had acquired a minority equity position in Asiatic Oxygen, Limited, of India as early as 1963. The most attractive market was Japan, which had a growing steel industry. In 1970, the company finally created a wholly owned subsidiary, Air Products Pacific, Inc., headquartered in Tokyo. The subsidiary's aim was to provide marketing services for Air Products.

If the company's presence in the industrial gas markets of the Pacific Rim was negligible in the sixties, that was equally true of its American competitors. In contrast, its European record put Air Products ahead of those competitors and proved invaluable when the time came to go global.

Houdry

The overseas and domestic gas businesses were not alone in their buoyancy. Air Products' recently acquired Houdry subsidiary proved to be an important money-maker.

Houdry was a company built on basic research, and on the success of its founder's experimentation. In 1961, at the time of its acquisition, Houdry had several chemical processes under development. Typical was the Litol process, the only single-step method of purifying by-product coke-oven benzene, as well as toluene and xylene, for use in chemical processing. After building the first commercial works at Bethlehem Steel's Sparrows Point plant, Houdry licensed the process overseas in Australia and Great Britain.

Houdry also developed the Pyrotol process for producing benzene from liquid by-product hydrocarbons created in manufacturing ethylene. By 1970, about 20 percent of the benzene produced in Japan was processed under Houdry licenses. Pyrotol also was licensed to a number of communist countries, including the People's Republic of China. Houdry experienced similar success licensing its Catadiene process, which produced both diolefins (such as butadiene and isoprene, two of the ingredients of synthetic rubber), and mono-olefins, such as butylene.

The single greatest Houdry success, and its largest profit producer, was Dabco, a catalyst used in the production of polyurethane. Polyurethane foam is cheap and can be produced with a moderate consumption of power—a factor which would become of great importance when the costs of power rose dramatically during the energy crisis of the seventies. Dabco was discovered at Houdry's research lab, as Thomas Gresham, an organic chemist with wide industrial experience, became the head of the lab. Dabco was rapidly developed, and put into production in 1962, at Houdry's Paulsboro plant. Dabco quickly became the world's most widely used polyurethane catalyst. In 1968 alone, it was used to produce over one billion pounds of polyurethane. About 50 percent of Dabco sales were overseas. To meet this demand, Houdry established supply depots around the world. As sales in Japan grew, Houdry began to manufacture in that country through a joint venture with the Sankyo Air Products Company, Ltd. Dabco marked an important accomplishment: this was the first time that Air Products was the world leader in an important chemicals market.[16]

Good Things from R&D

As Air Products enjoyed success at home and overseas, its revenues provided the firm with a financial capacity that had been lacking in earlier decades. In the 1960s, the company strategy was still the deferral of immediate profits for long-term growth. Federal tax laws favored capital gains, and investors were seeking stock that delivered those gains. Air Products thus sought new opportunities for investment.

Don Cummings and Jack Stewart were among those who had advocated a greater attention to R&D by the Industrial Gas Division. Their hope was that Air Products could emulate what research had done for Linde's reputation in the steel industry. Linde had grown in part by originating fresh uses for oxygen in steelmaking, and its salespeople could attract customers by describing the firm's successes. The Linde innovations focused on new oxygen-consuming equipment and incremental improvements of existing equipment. At first, Air Products' Applied Research and Development (AR&D) Department focused on the Linde strategy of stimulating larger oxygen sales in the steel industry. But the real contribution of AR&D at Air Products was to come later and in a quite different area.

The Applied Research and Development Department was created in 1959, placed in the Industrial Gas Division, and headed by Ed Kurzinski, who had been a Division Head for Linde's Development Laboratories. Kurzinski oversaw the development of Air Products' oxy-fuel lance. The lance burned natural gas and oxygen for refining steel. Air Products also investigated the use of the lance in non-ferrous refining furnaces.

Kurzinski was soon replaced by Dwight Brown, a chemical engineering graduate of Rensselaer Polytechnic Institute who had wide experience in the steel and chemical industries. Brown launched AR&D into its most important work, focused on nitrogen applications. Out of that work came Cryo-Guard, a liquid nitrogen system for truck refrigeration. Mechanical refrigeration units frequently failed to maintain the temperatures required for transporting frozen foods, particularly where many stops had to be made. Cryo-Guard provided competition for mechanical refrigeration units as well as for Linde, which had tested its own liquid nitrogen frozen-food truck as early as 1960.[17] Cryo-Guard also competed against liquid carbon dioxide systems manufactured by several large corporations. Even so, Cryo-Guard found its market niche and sales began to grow. Customers included major truck and trailer fleets making local and long-haul deliveries of frozen and perishable foods. Air Products also developed similar systems for rail and marine shipping.[18]

The use of liquid nitrogen in food transport proved modest in comparison to food freezing, which became the largest market for merchant liquid nitrogen. Here, too, nitrogen competed for market share with carbon dioxide and mechanical freezing systems. In 1965, Air Products introduced its Cryo-Quick system for freezing food, which offered several advantages. Liquid nitrogen enabled the pro-

Developed in 1961, the Oxy-Fuel Lance was the first result of the new Applied Research and Development Department. Its oxygen–natural gas flame speeded up scrap meltdown and refining in open-hearth furnaces. The two foremost onlookers are (l–r) Leonard Pool and Ed Kurzinski, Director of Applied R&D.

ducer to freeze single items rather than blocks of food, while minimizing dehydration and largely eliminating the mushy texture typical
of slower methods of freezing. Shrimp, avocados, citrus fruits, and
quality meats were among the items successfully frozen in Air Products' laboratories. The food was taste-tested by the company's own
employees, some of whom still recall being asked to eat the "experiments."

Cryo-Quick became a market leader. Commercial installations used
the process for freezing meats, seafood, bakery products, and vege-
tables. By 1970 there were more than 100 customers, many with
overseas units in the United Kingdom, Canada, Germany, Belgium,
Holland, France, Israel, Japan, and South Africa.[19]

One major market emerged in the late 1960s from discussions that
took place with a small Philadelphia meat purveyor, H. Lotman and
Son, about freezing hamburger patties. From this modest start,
pushed on by Lanny Patten, Jack Speary, and Tom Sills, a large-scale
use of Cryo-Quick rapidly developed. Lotman's company became a
principal supplier of hamburger patties to McDonald's. The first production site near Philadelphia grew to seven freezer lines each processing 3,000 or more pounds of beef per hour. Liquid nitrogen
consumption often exceeded 200 tankloads a month, an unprecedented amount to be supplied by truck. Large consumers like Lotman
drove the merchant liquid-nitrogen market to new heights. They also
swelled Air Products' sales of gases and equipment, leading to on-
site generation of liquid nitrogen for food production.

In 1967, Air Products introduced another AR&D development,
Cryo-Trim, a process that removed excess material from molded rubber parts after cooling them in liquid nitrogen to make the excess
brittle and able to be broken off mechanically. This technology proved
less labor-intensive and more cost-effective than other methods. The
company soon had more than two dozen Cryo-Trim installations in
commercial operation, an important share of yet another market.

Less spectacular and less visible to the public eye was the success
of the Advanced Products Department (APD), managed by Bill Snow.
That department too was formed in 1959, this time as an outgrowth
of cryogenic research funded by the government. The initial products
of APD were customized equipment for laboratory research in advanced chemistry, physics, astronomy, and related fields. In the early
1960s, APD began manufacturing miniature heat exchangers for cooling infrared sensors used in military applications, such as night-vision
devices or missile-guidance systems. These heat exchangers were

A Cryo-Quick unit freezing hamburger patties for McDonald's. In the sixties, the frozen food industry became a leading consumer of liquid nitrogen.

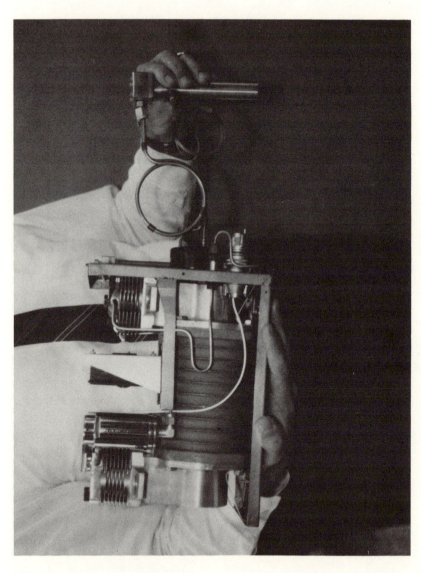

A compact cryogenic cooler manufactured by the Advanced Products Department in the early 1960s and used in a variety of military and laboratory applications.

used in the Sidewinder, Maverick, and Chaparral missiles. APD also brought out a new type of helium refrigerator that could be used in "cryopumping" or creating a vacuum by condensing or adsorbing gas molecules on the surface of cooled panels. Cryopumps were used in the electronics industry, where high vacuums are required.[20]

Air Products also organized a Specialty Gases Department in 1963, under Bill Eggers. Specialty gases and gas mixtures were defined as those of an ultrahigh purity or special composition, sold in cylinder quantities. While sales volumes were small, unit selling prices were high. Like APD, the Specialty Gases Department grew out of government-funded research. The Specialty Gas Department combined government-funded fluorine research with the company's small trade in xenon, krypton, and gas blends. Thanks to that research, Air Products had developed substantial expertise in high-energy chemicals, such as nitrogen trifluoride.[21] It used that knowledge to good effect in the 1960s, particularly in the production of sulfur hexafluoride, the company's first success in specialty gases. In 1963, Air Products started commercial fluorine and sulfur hexafluoride production with one production cell at Emmaus. Sulfur hexafluoride was used by electrical utilities as a dielectric in circuit breakers. The earlier fluorine research carried out for the military had finally started to pay off.

Air Products began to produce and market a broad range of specialty gases. Those gases were increasingly employed in electronic, medical, chemical process, research, instrument calibration, and other applications. By 1965, more than 2,000 customers purchased Air Products' specialty gases. The next year the number of customers grew to over 5,000. In addition, the company sold a complete line of equipment and related sensing and measuring devices. In terms of total sales and production volume, fluorine and fluorine-based chemicals were the company's most important specialty gases.

In his characteristically aggressive way, Leonard Pool had pushed for this new activity, even as IGD was occupied with all its acquisitions and with its expanding merchant gas operations.

Liquefied Natural Gas

While the Specialty Gases, Advanced Products, and Applied Research and Development Departments all represented conscious efforts to leverage research and technology into growth opportunities, not all research successes were planned. Serendipity was certainly at work in the case of liquefied natural gas (LNG). Air Products had failed to turn its exploratory research into a viable LNG venture in the late 1950s and had abandoned the project. When the opportunity finally arose to enter the LNG business, the company was able to take advantage of additional research undertaken by employees on their own initiative. It was another example of entrepreneurship being bred within the company, this time in the Cryogenic Systems Division.

In the 1960s, European demand fostered a growing market for LNG equipment. The unstable natural gas prices which had deterred the enterprise in the 1950s were replaced by briskly rising prices and growing consumption. As a result, worldwide interest in LNG increased sharply. Air Products had a decisive edge in this market because of its earlier work.

The company's several technologies overlapped and interacted creatively in the natural gas business. While supplying aluminum heat exchangers for the Helium Conservation Program, Lee Gaumer and Chuck Newton in the Cryogenic Systems Division had developed the Multi-Component Refrigeration (MCR) system. In the MCR system, helium-rich natural gas ran through a distillation column, which separated out the helium. The column (a so-called flash column) consisted of a series of stages. In each stage, the pressure was lowered, some helium recovered, and the remaining liquid passed to the next stage. At the end of the flash column, the helium-stripped liquid was returned from the column to a heat exchanger, where it cooled incoming natural gas. In order to use the helium technology for the commercial liquefaction of natural gas, Gaumer had to find the gas mixture with the right characteristics to replace the helium-stripped natural gas used for cooling. He tackled the problem in his spare time with the help of friends within the company.

Gaumer obtained the necessary thermodynamic and other research data from the R&D Department. The work involved numerous and tedious manipulations of mathematical equations, which fortunately could be carried out on the department's newly acquired computer. Without the computer, Gaumer later concluded, it would have been impractical to do these calculations.

Through the efforts of Gaumer and others, the company had the technology in hand when the first opportunity for a contract in the LNG field arose. That happened in 1964, when Air Products received an inquiry from Esso. The giant oil company wanted to ship Libyan natural gas to Europe and had been working for several years with

Air Liquide, studying various plant sizes and configurations, the economics, finances, and manufacturing techniques necessary to build a facility. Esso was worried about the project, because it involved a new technology. Esso decided to build the project itself unless Air Liquide or Air Products could offer a savings of 20 percent. Certain that the contract would go to Air Liquide, Esso nevertheless invited Air Products to bid because of its track record in the design and construction of low-temperature, tonnage generators.

When Esso opened the bids, they were surprised. Air Liquide proposed building the plant from the ground up in the Libyan desert, where labor was in short supply and construction problems likely to be difficult. Air Products, by contrast, planned to manufacture the equipment in the United States, at Wilkes-Barre, and assemble it at the site. Moreover, the Air Products facility would be 20 percent more efficient. Air Products won the bid. The company was in the LNG equipment business, but shortly it would pay a huge price for breaking into this market. There were enormous cost overruns on the contract, in the shop and on the site. Ultimately, several million dollars were lost on the deal.[22] Such an experience was truly painful.

When the possibility of a second LNG contract emerged, Air Products brought George Hartnett back from Europe to help prevent another such disaster. He and Lee Gaumer saved the day by devising a novel technique for manufacturing the huge LNG heat exchangers. This second contract was with Shell, which wanted to build an LNG facility in Brunei on the island of Borneo. A sales team including Hartnett, Gaumer, Bruce Ambler, and Jack Pryor won the order for a plant to come on line in 1972. For the job, the world's largest LNG plant, Gaumer invented a propane pre-cooled process, which remains the industry standard. That was Gaumer's third patent in this field.[23]

The key to the company's success was the intellectual curiosity and persistence of one of its principal engineers. The whole episode also illustrates the continuing importance of the kind of development work being carried out in Clyde McKinley's R&D Department. Air Products had an edge over the competition because of its thermodynamic data and its prefabricated units. The firm was able to parlay this edge into a series of profitable contracts in succeeding years. By the 1980s, Air Products would supply equipment for the liquefaction of 85 percent of the world's supply of LNG.

Despite the strategic shift in other areas from equipment to consumable product sales, in LNG Air Products found itself in the busi-

Giant Air Products heat exchangers being prepared for shipment to the Esso LNG facility in Libya.

ness of making and selling equipment on a worldwide basis. The firm had debated whether to sell or license its LNG technology, and realized that more money would be made by selling the equipment.

Finally, it should be noted how, in the 1960s, both research and process design depended increasingly on the computer, which could save thousands of expensive man-hours. In addition, computers could accurately predict design parameters so that only a few actual tests had to be executed in the laboratory. That meant additional savings. Indeed, in the 1960s, the computer was changing more than the way research was carried out. Carroll Claitor, who had played an important role in the Engineering Department since the 1950s, spearheaded the computerization of Air Products. The production, storage, and demand schedules for merchant bulk liquids were computerized so as to minimize production and distribution costs; the firm also computerized most of its routine accounting and costing functions; and the inventorying and ordering of cutting and welding supplies were put under the control of a computer.[24]

Agricultural Chemicals

While research and development played an important role in creating investment opportunities in the gas business in the 1960s, Air Products also continued a modest buildup of its chemicals operations. Thanks to this buildup, chemicals would eventually become a substantial second leg of the company's business in the 1970s. The logic of this diversification derived from the company's deepening involvement in the field of petrochemicals. Air Products got closer to the petroleum industry with its oxo-alcohol venture and its acquisition of Houdry. The next logical step appeared to be integration into the production of ammonia and into the manufacture and sale of agricultural chemicals. Prominent in the entry into agricultural chemicals was the use of Air Products' engineering talent from the Cryogenic Systems Division, together with the experience derived from selling processing equipment to the synthetic ammonia business in the 1950s.

In the early 1960s, it seemed that markets for chemical fertilizers were golden. Ammonia was the key commodity in chemical fertilizers. And ammonia was made from nitrogen and hydrogen, about which Air Products knew a great deal. Balanced against this technical advantage was the liability that this was another market in which Air Products had no experience. Also, the golden opportunity was recognized by many companies, and soon there was an excess of productive capacity.

The company's entry began with the decision in 1964 to synthesize ammonia, the basic substance used in the production of chemical fertilizers, for which there was a large demand in the South, Midwest, and overseas. To compensate for a lack of experience in ammonia production, a team of engineers was brought in from Kellogg to work with Air Products in the construction of its 600-ton-per-day anhydrous ammonia plant near New Orleans. Joe Cost, Gordon Kiddoo, and Dick Checksfield worked with the Kellogg people, who also assisted in starting up the plant. Natural gas was purchased on long-term contract from Shell and Tenneco. About 60 percent of the output was sold on a twenty-five year, take-or-pay basis to the Southern Nitrogen Company for the manufacture of chemical fertilizers. Dave Mac-Reynolds, an experienced ammonia salesman, was recruited to Air Products to sell the rest of the New Orleans ammonia output. MacReynolds and the ammonia operation were placed in the Houdry management organization.

The New Orleans facility was designed as an integrated gas and chemical complex. Since the production of ammonia required nitrogen and hydrogen for which the company had other markets in the region, Air Products included in the complex a 1,000-ton-per-day oxygen-nitrogen generator as well as a 32-ton-per-day liquid hydrogen plant. The latter facility enabled Air Products to supply NASA in Mississippi, Alabama, and Florida. As a result of the know-how developed during prior work for the military and NASA, Air Products was able to piggyback the plant to provide liquid hydrogen for commercial markets in the Southeast and Midwest.[25]

Building one complex to satisfy the gas needs of NASA and the merchant market, and its ammonia operation, gave Air Products the advantage of economies of scale in manufacturing and distribution. Delivery costs could be held down because of the ammonia facility's location on the inland waterway. The site permitted low-cost barge transport to the entire Gulf Coast, to agricultural markets throughout the Mississippi and Ohio river valleys, and to overseas markets. Operations in New Orleans, in time, would be expanded to make additional quantities of merchant gas and to produce carbon dioxide.

Carbon dioxide is a by-product of the synthesis of ammonia. The liquefaction of carbon dioxide allowed Air Products to create another synergy. In 1967, the company constructed a liquid carbon dioxide plant at its New Orleans chemical and industrial gas complex, selling the product under long-term contract to Liquid Carbonic, the country's largest merchant supplier.

Inauguration of the integrated industrial gas and ammonia works near New Orleans, Louisiana. Left to right: Jim Norwood, Ed Donley, Leonard Pool, and Bill Scharle.

Air Products decided to expand its agricultural chemicals business beyond ammonia, by diversifying into pesticides, for which there was a growing demand. It considered reselling pesticides made by other companies. To gain the marketing experience and organization it lacked, in 1967 Air Products bought the Adkins-Phelps Company, a small manufacturer of herbicides and fungicides, located in Arkansas. Adkins-Phelps was also a retailer of other agricultural chemicals and seeds in the Mississippi delta area. The acquisition provided Air Products with ready-made manufacturing and sales organizations, and with customers. Early in 1968 Frank Ryan transferred from Industrial Gases to run a new Agricultural Chemicals Division.

The division was put together from the New Orleans ammonia plant, Adkins-Phelps, and a related Air Products R&D program on agricultural chemicals. At first, Ryan and the company were uncertain about where the division was going to make its expanded range of agricultural chemicals, but they did know that ammonia prices had been excellent in the late 1960s, and Ed Donley, who initiated the venture, was eager to develop the company's chemical business.

It happened that Ebasco (Electric Bond and Share Co.) had just built a natural gas pipeline from Louisiana to the multi-plant complex of its Escambia Chemical Corporation, at Escambia Bay, Florida. Along the pipeline, the company sold some of the natural gas. Federal regulations, however, dictated that Ebasco either become a gas distributor or make chemicals. It could not do both. So, in 1969, Air Products bought the Escambia Chemical Corporation for a price well below book value.

Escambia's production facilities consisted mainly of a multi-plant complex located on a 1,500-acre site adjacent to Escambia Bay near Pensacola, Florida. Escambia's was an integrated chemical works based on natural gas, which produced a wide range of industrial and agricultural chemicals, including ammonia, methanol, amines, dinitrotoluene (DNT), toluenediamine (TDA), and polyvinyl chloride (PVC). In fact, Escambia had been one of the nation's leading marketers of alkylamines (used mainly in the production of pesticides) and a major producer of DNT, a chemical intermediate used in the manufacturing of polyurethane resins. Escambia also had a large number of small farm service centers located in Florida, Alabama, and Georgia. Larry Carey,[26] who had been Escambia's President, was retained and allowed to run the subsidiary semiautonomously. Escambia, which took over Air Products' ammonia sales shortly after the acquisition, also had a quality management and engineering staff which enhanced the worth of the acquisition.

Each step forward on this path carried Air Products farther from its core markets and customary methods of selling its goods and services. By buying Escambia, the company acquired products, facilities, engineering know-how, sales forces, and customers. However, the company also committed itself more firmly to agriculture and to retailing.

It was not long before Air Products began to experience problems in its newly diversified network of chemical subsidiaries. In 1967, the first full year of operation at the New Orleans facility, the financial results were excellent. Production exceeded design capacity and all the output was sold. But in the following year, with the plant operating near capacity, profits suffered from the price attrition which was prevalent throughout the ammonia market. Air Products had not been the only firm to move into this market. As supply increased, demand dropped off due to poor weather conditions during the planting season. This was normal for a business in price-sensitive commodities.[27] Also, profits from agricultural chemicals declined.

In 1969, the New Orleans ammonia plant continued to run at record efficiency and production levels, but severely depressed prices in agricultural chemical markets hurt profit margins on the fertilizers produced by Escambia and on the herbicides distributed by Adkins-Phelps. The following year sales to the agricultural market fell again. Despite the Adkins-Phelps distribution network and sales experience, Air Products seemed unable to turn a profit in this new industry. Nor did others in the business do much better, except perhaps for the cooperative producers. Furthermore, the regulatory environment was becoming more and more of a problem.

Concerned about the losses and the mounting difficulties, Air Products began to back off. Harry Quigley (who had transferred from industrial gases to the Agricultural Chemicals Division) and Frank Ryan examined the firm's agricultural chemicals operations first hand. What, they wondered, was Air Products doing in the retail business? The company's strength had always been in direct sales to industrial customers. Ryan recommended to Donley that the company liquidate Adkins-Phelps. That cleared Air Products from a line of business in which it had no particular skill and certainly no marginal advantage over the competition.

Adkins-Phelps was sold off. Eli Lilly bought the patents and technology for the herbicide tebuthiron, which had been developed in the R&D program, and which was extremely effective against brush on beef cattle ranches in Texas and Oklahoma. As the company left the retail end of the agricultural chemicals business, another cloud appeared on the sales horizon. The oxo-alcohol venture, buoyed by the growing plastics industry, had been profitable throughout the 1960s. By 1970, however, severe price competition was resulting in slim profit margins. Similarly, excess capacity in certain aspects of the plastics industry was beginning to bring down prices and profit margins. The industrial gas business also was showing low prices and poor profit margins. It was not the best of times.

By 1970, Air Products was a very large and, on balance, very successful company. It had integrated vertically and had begun to move toward the divisional structure favored in those years by most multinational, diversified corporations. The family firm of the fifties was well on its way to becoming a large, professionally managed corporation. In the 1970s, when the firm experienced new troubles and triumphs, Air Products would no longer be the day-to-day concern of its founder, Leonard Pool.

Notes

1. Auerbach Report, pp. 1–4.
2. The Auerbach Report, pp. 22–23; Standard and Poor's Industry Surveys, *Chemicals*, 3 November 1960, Sec. 3, p. C 31; 14 November 1963, Sec. 5, p. C 31; 22 October 1964, Sec. 2, p. C 33; 23 November 1967, Sec. 3, p. C 33; 20 March 1969, Sec. 2, p. C 37.
3. Auerbach Report, p. 25; Marshall Sittig, *Nitrogen in Industry* (Princeton, N. J.: D. Van Nostrand, 1965), pp. 98–101, 164–167.
4. "An Analysis of Air Products and Chemicals, Inc.," Financial Analysis by Butcher & Sherrerd, [1965], pp. 2–3; Sittig, p. 97.
5. This was an expansion of the plant built by Air Products in 1959.
6. Lanny Patten, "Air Products Industrial Gases Since 1960," November 1989, p. 11, APHO.
7. Standard and Poor's Industry Surveys, *Chemicals*, 12 December 1974, Sec. 1, p. C 16, reported that the historical annual growth rate of the on-site oxygen business had been about 5 percent, while the merchant business annual growth rate was about 10 percent.
8. Standard and Poor's Industry Surveys, *Chemicals*, 22 October 1964, Sec. 2, p. C 34; 3 November 1966, Sec. 2, p. C 34.
9. Auerbach Report, pp. 27–28.
10. Standard and Poor's Industry Surveys, *Chemicals*, 23 November 1967,

Sec. 3, p. C 34; *Annual Report 1969*, p. 4; This plant came about because Air Products had won an order for an oxygen-nitrogen plant to supply Armco Steel.

11. John R. MacLean, General Manager, Gas Products, Linde Division of Union Carbide, speech given at I.O.M.A. Annual Meeting, 1972, APHO.

12. Auerbach Report, p. 33.

13. R. J. Gotshall to Appropriation Committee, 4 August 1964, APHO.

14. George Hartnett to Andrew Butrica, 23 October 1989, APHO.

15. *Annual Report 1969*, p. 8.

16. *Annual Report 1970*, pp. 10–11.

17. Union Carbide, *1960 Annual Report*, p. 21.

18. E.F. Kurzinski, "The Revolution in In-Transit Refrigeration," *Cryogenic Engineering News*, (July 1967): 22–27; (August 1967): 86–90.

19. E.F. Kurzinski, "Cryogenic Processing and Transportation of Food Stuffs," *Cryogenic Engineering News*, (August-September 1965): 57–58; (October-November 1965): 32–35; (December 1965–January 1966): 32–33.

20. Air Products and Chemicals, *Basics of Cryopumping*, n.p.; R. C. Longsworth, "Performance of a Cryopump Cooled by a Small Closed-Cycle 10-K Refrigerator," in K. D. Timmerhaus, *Advances in Cryogenic Engineering*, p. 658.

21. Primarily such nitrogen-fluorine compounds as nitrogen trifluoride (NF_3), tetrafluoro hydrazine (N_2F_4), and the isomers of difluoro diazine (N_2F_2) as well as such fluorine-bearing compounds as oxygen difluoride (OF_2). APCI, "The Newest Dimension in Gas Technology," [1965], p. 15.

22. "Lee Gaumer Testimonial," film from Chairman's Award Dinner, 9 June 1989, APHO.

23. Lee Gaumer, Jr., U.S. Patent no. 3,763,658, issued 9 October 1973.

24. Auerbach Report, p. 16.

25. "Liquid Hydrogen," NASA-George C. Marshall Space Flight Center News Release, #67–121, 6 June 1967; *Annual Report 1965*, p. 6.

26. Lawrence Carey received a B.S. in mining engineering from Michigan Technological University. He joined Escambia in 1966 and was named President in April 1968.

27. *Escambia Facilities Book*, October 21, 1971, n.p. Harry Quigley earned a B.S. in chemical engineering at Villanova University. He was an experienced project manager when he joined Air Products in 1966.

8

Triumphs and Troubles

In the 1970s, Air Products crossed the final divide between a family business dominated by an entrepreneur-owner and a professionally managed corporation. The impetus for new investments, programs, and policies as well as the day-to-day running of the firm had, for some years now, come from leaders such as Ed Donley, Dex Baker, and Lee Holt. Increasingly, too, the company culture was breeding entrepreneurs within the firm. In the mid-sixties, Leonard Pool was preoccupied with his wife's serious illness and then, tormented by her death, he turned his attention to the improvement of health care in the Lehigh Valley. Ed Donley became President in 1966, and guided Air Products into a more structured managerial mode. However, Leonard Pool remained Donley's mentor and the final arbiter of major decisions. In 1973, Pool finally yielded the helm to Donley, who became Air Products' Chief Executive Officer. That same year, George Pool died of heart failure. Two years later, on December 27, 1975, the founder died.

Donley had some rough seas to navigate. The seventies were full of troubles for industrial gas companies, for American business in general, and for the entire U.S. society. The highly competitive drive for market share of the sixties had left Air Products, and its rivals in the industrial gas business, with excess productive capacity and low profit margins. The war in Vietnam raised fears about the limits of American power and American prosperity, and the attempt to spend on guns and butter, on both defense and welfare programs, led to a spiraling inflation. If these tribulations were not enough, corporate leaders like Ed Donley also faced other problems.

Companies like Air Products had to adjust to changing standards of acceptable behavior. The Clean Air Act of 1970 and kindred legislation signaled a heightened awareness of environmental issues. At the same time, risks associated with the manufacture of PVC challenged the firm's commitment to employee health and safety. In addition, the 1973 war between Israel and the Arab nations led to an embargo on oil shipments to the United States and other suppliers of military aid to Israel. After the embargo, OPEC pushed for higher revenues, and oil prices nearly quadrupled.

Like other American firms, Air Products was greatly challenged by the energy crisis and by changes in environmental and health regulations. However, the firm found fresh opportunities for diversification and investment as a consequence of its attention to energy and environmental issues. By the end of the seventies, in fact, the company's response would form the basis for an entirely new set of growth opportunities. Air Products also greatly expanded its investment in chemicals, and the industrial gas business began to turn around.

The Problem of Succession

Two years after their mother died in 1952, Leonard's youngest brother Walter had some heart problems. Leonard told him, "you know, the Pools are only diers; they just don't live . . . I'm planning my life accordingly."[1] A part of that planning involved giving thought to the selection of his successor. At first, Leonard's choice was his brother, George, a choice common in family businesses. The choice was implicit rather than explicit, for Leonard really preferred to hold the question open and preserve his options.

From time to time in the early sixties, members of the Board of Directors pressed him to choose a successor. "When are you going to cease being a one-man show?" they asked. But Leonard Pool kept his counsel—until his wife's critical illness forced his hand, in 1966. Dorothy had an incurable cancer. Pool finally made one of his hardest choices, deciding not to anoint his brother. The reason was that George had remained too much the gas salesman and too little interested in the technological, management, and financial issues which had come to the fore as Air Products grew into a large corporation. George Pool would have been a good choice in 1950 or even in 1955, but by the mid-sixties someone quite different was needed.

What Leonard Pool had been looking for in a successor was an intimate knowledge of Air Products' culture as well as of people and management skills. He wanted someone who shared his vision of the company, a vision in which growth would be driven by both engineering and sales. There were several strong candidates on the management team, including Dex Baker, Don Cummings, and Lee Holt. However, in Pool's mind, Ed Donley stood out. He had spent long years as Pool's right-hand man. His reputation had been made in sales. And, as Holt observed, "Ed . . . was an engineer by nature, by intuition, and it was a great strength. He always has been a driving force in the company for process engineering and he carried that forward."[2] Pool was fearful that a financial manager—one of the "bean counters"—or Jim Spencer, the company's first legal counsel and a Director, might assume command.

Leonard Pool and Ed Donley both had childhoods marked by financial need, which had led them to abandon hopes of higher education. While Donley went to college, he did so only through a scholarship. The two shared an insatiable desire to read, devouring books on a wide range of subjects. There was also an emotional bond between them. When Donley went through a difficult period, Pool provided psychological support. The experience brought the two closer together, making Donley in a sense the son that Pool never had. Donley himself later reflected that: "I was probably looked upon by others and in some ways by myself as a protégé of Leonard. He was my mentor."[3]

With his wife's health deteriorating, Pool quickly arranged the succession. First, he oversaw a reorganization of the corporate structure that brought it more in line with prevailing practice by introducing the position of Chief Executive Officer. Pool was elected Chairman of the Board and CEO, and Donley elected President. George Pool became Vice-Chairman of the Board and Lee Holt, already a Vice President, took on expanded responsibilities in corporate administration. The chain of succession was marked.

The action pleased investors and outside members of the Board. However, the new arrangement inevitably left some within the company disappointed. Ted Burtis, head of Houdry and a Board member, realized that his future at Air Products was limited and returned to Sun Oil. Don Cummings, Vice President of Industrial Gases, resigned. While Leonard Pool regretted the loss of two of the company's best people, he was confident that Donley was the right choice. He turned to the task of caring for his wife, and had Dorothy admitted to Memorial Sloan-Kettering Cancer Center in New York. Extremely devoted, he stayed by her side in the hospital, sleeping many nights on a cot. For a time, he lost interest in the company.

A Living Memorial

Dorothy died on March 23, 1967. Leonard's immediate reflex was to create a living monument to her. He "reiterated that Dorothy had died, but she had the most competent health care in the world, at Sloan-Kettering Hospital in New York. There was an unfairness in society if a wealthy person could have that care and a working person could not."[4] Determined to improve conditions in the Lehigh Valley, Pool set out to build a new hospital. He believed he was the man for the job, because "it takes big organization, it takes big money to get progress, much as it does in engineering at Air Products."[5] What he did not understand was that the Valley's hospitals reflected community values and slow, consensual decision making, rather than being businesses oriented to profit and growth.

Leonard Pool set his heart on an entirely new teaching hospital, capable of acute care and part of a unified, regional system. His vision quickly generated substantial opposition. Allentown's three hospitals—Allentown, Allentown Osteopathic, and Sacred Heart—had neither big money, nor big organization, nor big medicine. In 1963, Allentown Hospital's postgraduate teaching program in internal medicine had lost its accreditation, and Sacred Heart's program was equally precarious. Bishop Joseph McShea of the Catholic Diocese of Allentown feared that a unified hospital would threaten the practice of Catholic medicine at Sacred Heart. He filed suit to halt development. The Bishop's action instigated a three-year legal battle, shattered community harmony, and threatened to bury Pool's project.

As always Leonard Pool persisted, but this time he had to compromise. His own health was failing. He had a mild stroke and was briefly unable to talk, in 1972. The following year, his brother George died, and Pool blamed himself for the death. He was also having to adjust to his second, much younger wife, Gloria, the widow of Air Products engineer Jack Graeffe, as well as to his step-children. Still, he saw the crusade to its conclusion. The court settlement (August 4, 1972) established that the Allentown and the Sacred Heart sections of a new hospital would take up separate areas and have distinct medical staffs. This administrative structure ensured that the old hospitals would run the new health center and not the reverse, as Pool had hoped. Sacred Heart remained a general community hospital with an obstetrics and gynecology department in conformity with Catholic principles.

Pool's vision of a coordinated, regional hospital system did not materialize, but he did live to see his new, regional institution, the Allentown and Sacred Heart Hospital Center (later the Lehigh Valley Hospital Center), completed in 1974. He contributed over $5 million to the project, and many Air Products managers, lawyers, and engineers also gave generously of their time and skills. On December 27, 1975, Leonard Pool died in his sleep. His will established a $20 million trust in his wife's name, the Dorothy Rider Pool Health Care Trust, to support the Hospital Center. An era had ended.

Modern Management Comes to Air Products

Upon becoming President in 1966, Ed Donley said his agenda was the same as that of President Lyndon Johnson: "Let us continue." "I don't recall feeling that there was any significant change," he later recounted.[6] And yet change did come, step by step, as Donley deliberately nurtured a different style of management. If Leonard Pool was no longer to be the dominant figure, the company could no longer behave in quite the same way. Change was necessary, even though change was not easy. Employees and even senior executives complained of the disruptions wrought in the way they performed their daily duties. Ed Donley had to walk a fine line as he sought to reorganize the company, and to accelerate the process of building more adequate support in functions such as finance, law, human resources, and R&D.

The first significant change was structural. Donley introduced the matrix concept, with its distinction between functional and administrative responsibilities. The matrix was a management concept in vogue in corporate America at the time, and many companies created matrix organizations. Air Products' matrix structure gave to the officers heading the functional groups (e.g., R&D, computer services, administration) control of the staff resources they needed to accomplish their missions. In turn, executives in charge of business areas such as gases or chemicals were given direct authority over particular segments of the functional staff necessary to the efficient accomplishment of their particular tasks. This centralization and division of certain responsibilities had a subtle but deep effect on the company culture. It was a way of placing greater emphasis on the important role of professionals in such areas as R&D, safety, finance, law, and human resources. Corporate staff in these latter areas reported administratively to Lee Holt, who continued to nurture the human resource activities of the company.

The idea of the matrix was one thing. Practice was another. In the merchant and cylinder gas business, regional and district managers enjoyed a high degree of discretionary power, although budgetary questions remained in the hands of Leonard Pool. Managers (most in their thirties) had the responsibility of coordinating both supply and sales, a combination which was unusual in the gas industry. Managing the two together gave a competitive advantage, since dependability of supply is an important marketing tool in regional gas sales. However, field practices were not under adequate control, with the result that safety was among the issues jeopardized. The matrix concept provided a means through which to impose safety and other standards. This centralization ran contrary to the freewheeling nature of George Pool's field organization, and added more levels of management. As a result, there was friction over Ed Donley's innovations. In contrast, engineers responsible for on-site plants, operating through the Cryogenic Systems Division centralized at headquarters, had little difficulty adapting to the matrix idea.

Matrix management could not go too far so long as Leonard Pool was living. Access to Pool was not limited. He practiced what author Tom Peters has called "managing by wandering around." Pool continued his habit of visiting the plants and offices to see first-hand what was happening in what he still perceived to be *his* company. Pool's presence constrained Donley, as did the difficulty of getting employees to accept the matrix concept after they had worked for so many years with less structured modes of communication and control. Reflecting on that battle, Donley related, "A common expression of mine used to be that if I ever got to see St. Peter and he offered me reincarnation, I would say that I wanted to be reincarnated in a world where functional and administrative responsibilities are understood."[7]

The matrix structure had little effect on Houdry and Catalytic. Both were run in a semiautonomous fashion, the former by Wes Hoge, who had succeeded Burtis, and the latter by Dick Klopp, who had been Alan Knight's right-hand man. Escambia, too, was left in the hands of Larry Carey, its President from before its purchase. Carey had his own management team, as did other parts of the chemical business. As long as they brought in a profit—and Houdry, Catalytic, and Escambia were money-makers in the 1960s and 1970s—Donley left their managers in place. When eventually it became necessary to reorganize the whole area of chemicals, the transaction taxed his skills and patience, as we shall see.

Regardless of which functional group was involved, Ed Donley wanted and needed good managers. More than ever, the emphasis at Air Products would be on the recruitment and development of quality people. Donley sought improved administration that would stress the role of engineering and deliberative decision-making in the company's long-range strategy. Throughout the 1960s and even into the 1970s, the rapid growth of Air Products in the United States and overseas strained its ability to develop sufficient numbers of quality managers internally. The company had necessarily to rely heavily on the managers of acquired companies.

Donley saw the people of Air Products as being key to its success. He and other senior officers personally recruited at their alma maters. Air Products hired individuals with M.B.A.s, especially those with engineering training. Many other engineers took M.B.A.s locally at Lehigh University through the company's tuition-reimbursement plan. Donley also gave fresh emphasis to the practice, begun in the late 1950s, of sending top-level executives to the Harvard Business School's Advanced Management Program. The first employees to go had been George Pool, Frank Pavlis, and Ed Donley himself.

A key part of the effort in management development lay in Donley's renewed stress on the Career Development Program (CDP). This program had initially been introduced by Leonard Pool in 1959.[8] Pool had named a committee, consisting of Carroll Claitor, Clyde McKinley, and Charles Shaw, Employee Relations Director, to formulate the means of recruiting and training college graduates so that, in the words of Pool, they could "take a more important part in the affairs of the company." The result was CDP, which rotated graduates through several jobs before they received a permanent assignment.

CDP was a real selling point in recruiting. College graduates no longer saw Air Products as a unique challenge in the way Pool had presented his cause to Frank Pavlis. They were necessarily interested instead in how the company, which was by now very large, could show itself possessed of human scale and could advance their careers. "We try to recruit the highest quality people, then retain and develop them," Lee Holt explained. "In order to do that you have to show them potential for growth. . . . If they don't see it in the company, they won't stay with you long. The larger the company becomes, the harder it is."[9]

Donley also sensed a need to deepen the research culture within the company. He saw applied research and development as one key to continuing growth and diversification. In this he was influenced by his knowledge of how development contracts had aided the growth of Air Products' capabilities in cryogenic systems, and by the successes of AR&D in the Industrial Gas Division. In order to emphasize the need for basic research as well, Donley hired Nat Robertson as the company's first Vice President of Research and Development in 1966. Robertson, a graduate of the Princeton University Ph.D. program in physical chemistry, had many years of experience as a chemist and as a research director. Robertson worked closely with Clyde Mc-Kinley, who continued in his role as Director of the Corporate Research and Development Department.

The short-term developmental work of the Advanced Products, Specialty Gases, and AR&D departments all operated without benefit of matrix ideas, and dovetailed well with the company culture. But such goal-oriented thinking was not as appropriate to the kind of basic research familiar to many chemical companies—the kind of research that had produced Dabco. That research took long-term commitment of substantial financial and human resources without a contracted-for goal. Air Products understood applied research, but had little experience in basic research. While the company had a wealth of engineering talent, it lacked the cadre of scientists needed to sustain basic research.

Despite the opportunities afforded by the matrix structure, Nat Robertson did not succeed in changing the character of R&D at Air Products. Research remained structurally and functionally dependent on the various engineering sections. The company's R&D effort continued to focus heavily on the furnishing of data to the Industrial Gas and Cryogenic Systems divisions. Within the Cryogenic Systems Division, which had its own R&D director in Lee Gaumer, applied research was central to process design and engineering work. As the company dealt with more complex and larger-scale designs, its engineers needed to understand heat and mass transfer phenomena better. For instance, the understanding of distillation tray performance in various configurations became more and more important. By supplying necessary engineering data, the R&D Department performed an important role. Within the Chemicals Division, the situation was somewhat different. There, Houdry had its own R&D facility separated by geography and style from the rest of Air Products.

Donley's hope for a more centralized approach to basic research proved difficult to realize.

Ed Donley made his way with great skill through the years between his official promotion to President and his assumption of unalloyed command upon Leonard Pool's death. He won the full respect of the inner core of long-serving senior officers. His changes in corporate structure and his emphasis on professionalism in the field of human resources helped Air Products to become more efficient even as it grew larger in scale and more complex in scope. The company's values changed more slowly than its structure, of course; but the new techniques helped pilot the firm through diversification and through some difficult years in the 1970s.

Weathering the Storm

By the late sixties, the extremely competitive scramble for market share had left the domestic industrial gas business with excess productive capacity, low prices, and low profit margins. Shipments of some gases were hurt by a slowdown in military spending.[10] Companies sought with limited success to lower costs and raise prices, while federally mandated price controls came and went and OPEC drove up the price of energy, the main cost in making industrial gases. What the industry really needed was greater consumption, but that took some years to materialize. Air Products would succeed in weathering the storm, thanks in good measure to a series of strategies for the industrial gas business that were articulated by Dex Baker.

By 1968, as domestic gas operations were beginning to experience hard times, Baker had returned from Great Britain. It was not easy for Ed Donley to know exactly how best to utilize Baker's very considerable skills, honed by a decade of experience abroad. The solution was to make him Executive Vice President, one of the highest titles in the recently restructured company, but one which initially did not have fully explicated functions. Baker asserted his authority quickly by reorganizing top management responsibilities in the whole area of industrial gases. In the process, it became obvious to Jack Stewart, who had been Vice President and General Manager of the Industrial Gas Division (IGD), that he had become Baker's subordinate. Stewart resigned, giving Baker the opportunity to complete the final stages of a reorganization that would enable him to play a leadership role in industrial gases, both at home and abroad.

Pat Dyer, who had become one of the company's most effective gas people, was promoted from his position as Northern Area Manager to President of IGD. Andy Mellen, who less than a decade earlier had been selling helium and LNG equipment, was named President of the important Cryogenic Systems Division. Austin Walker was promoted to replace Baker as the head of APL. All reported directly to Baker. These changes resulted in new opportunities for career advancement within IGD. Dyer's promotion, for example, brought the talents of Lanny Patten to the fore as he became the General Sales Manager of Industrial Gases, after having progressed through Chicago, Cleveland, and Pittsburgh assignments in the previous five years.

With this reorganized top management, Baker set out to stimulate overseas activity and also to get the domestic gas business out of its doldrums. Baker demanded an analytical approach that emphasized return on investment and product line profitability.

Some of the company's best people were transferred from the United States to spearhead European activities. Mark Halsted left the Operations Department to become General Manager of European operations. Other prominent transferees to Europe were Hap Wagner, who took over sales management, Walt Rector, who headed engineering, and Joe Kaminski in the controllership. In Britain, under Austin Walker and Don Spencer, APL continued to display the sort of entrepreneurial drive it had acquired under Baker. In 1970, it began construction of a 400-ton-per-day carbon dioxide plant at Stanlow, England, heralded as the largest such plant in the United Kingdom. Through a 50–50 joint venture with the British Steel Corporation, APL operated the largest oxygen generator the company had ever made, a 1,500-ton-per-day oxygen-nitrogen plant at Llanwern, Wales. The British subsidiary also manufactured and exported a substantial number of generators. Its impressive export record was recognized three times with the prestigious Queen's Award to Industry (1968, 1972, and 1978).[11]

Through the efforts of Baker and of Pat Dyer, Air Products was also entering other industrial gas markets around the globe as a hedge against the tightening domestic situation. A significant new operation close to home was opened up when, with their help, Lanny Patten pushed the firm into Canada, focusing on Ontario, where there was a market for both generators and gases. Jim Strecansky led the team that won an on-site steel mill oxygen order from Stelco, Canada's largest steel producer. The Stelco on-site generator provided added

In 1970, Air Products began construction of this 2,000-ton-per-day oxygen and 400-ton-per-day carbon dioxide plant at Carrington, England. When completed, it was among the largest industrial gas facilities in Europe.

capacity to piggyback Air Products into the Ontario merchant market. Bob Waring followed by Robin Scott took over as successive managers of the business, which grew and spread throughout Canada.

Not all foreign operations went smoothly; the company had serious problems in Brazil and Japan. Air Products had been selling the occasional generator in South America for over two decades. Those sales encouraged Frank Pavlis, by now Vice President of World Trade, and Ralph Maynard, his international sales associate, to seek and uncover potential acquisitions, joint venture opportunities, and new and used plant deals in South America. Their sales activities were successful, but Air Products' management was cautious about major investments in the region. Inflation, political uncertainty, and uneven business conditions made the risks too high. But then came Whitey (William) Veale, a steadily promoted CDP who was fascinated by opportunities in Latin America.

Veale got Air Products into Brazil in 1973. The venture, a subsidiary called Air Products Gases Industriais Limitada, centered around a 300-ton-per-day liquid oxygen plant installed at São Paolo to serve the merchant market. As management had feared, acceptable profits were slow in developing. Fiscal 1979 saw the subsidiary's first earnings, and it became profitably managed by Fernando Guidao. However, no additional investments or ventures followed in South America.

The Asian market was more difficult to penetrate. The most attractive country was Japan, which had a growing steel industry. One important order came in 1974, when the company won a contract for cryogenic work on an ethylene plant for the Ukishima Petrochemical Co. Ltd. of Japan. It was the first application of a newly developed proprietary technology. Air Products also participated in the Japanese merchant market through a five-year contract, signed in 1970 and guided by Ben Reinoehl, to ship liquefied helium to Japan. Helium is the only industrial gas that is routinely exported. These first shipments were a remarkable technical achievement and the start of the company's world leadership position in liquid helium supply.

On the domestic front, Baker and Dyer set out to enrich and deepen the sales culture. A major undertaking, which became an Industrial Gas Division tradition, was the orientation program devised to acquaint new salespeople and acquired companies with the Air Products story, the company's capabilities, and the values of the gas sales force. This program helped bring greater cohesion to IGD. Everett Mills from the Personnel Department organized and ran the program. Over the years, his presentations, emphasizing integrity, motivation, and the will to succeed, became legendary.

Sales efforts in the government sector also helped to boost industrial gas revenues. The space shuttle program was just getting under way and needed fuel. In June 1975, thanks to the creative efforts of Pat Dyer and Wes Timmcke, the National Aeronautics and Space Administration awarded Air Products a twelve-year, $287 million contract for liquid hydrogen for the shuttle program. In order to meet the increased demand, the company built an additional thirty-ton-per-day plant at New Orleans in 1977.[12]

While the new government fuel contract, coupled with more efficient plant designs, a commitment to strengthening the sales culture, and the entry into new foreign markets, all helped to improve Air Products' position in the industrial gas business, what Air Products and the industry needed most was increased demand to alleviate the problems of excess capacity, inflation, and rising energy costs. As demand rose, supply would become more limited, and prices would rise. By 1974, in fact, demand finally caught up with supply. Sales personnel now had to tell customers that prices were going up, and to give this bad news with the same thoroughness and devotion previously required to win accounts.

In the late seventies, Air Products launched an ambitious program to build capacity and to expand sales at home and overseas. The use of piggybacking declined, and stand-alone plants became the rule. These plants were designed with an emphasis on cost of production and distribution. Gains in plant productivity came from a task force headed by IGD's Bob Jones and by Nirmal Chatterjee of the Cryogenic Systems Division. At the same time, Air Products salespeople found that, instead of being David taking on Goliath, Air Products was a major player. In the sixties, the firm's sales force was on the offensive. In the seventies, it had to defend its markets while still striving to grow.

In the seventies also, gas sales profited in unexpected ways from the energy crisis that hurt so many U.S. firms. High energy prices meant increased consumption of merchant and on-site industrial gases, which replaced more expensive natural gas in numerous processes. Industrial gases also found new uses in the intensified search for oil. Environmental concerns in their turn opened up a new, if small, business in oxygen for wastewater treatment. In these various ways, Air Products profited from both the energy and environmental crises.

Barges loaded with liquid hydrogen getting ready to leave the New Orleans complex for a NASA delivery.

Energy and the Environment

One way in which the energy crisis helped to boost industrial gas sales was by spurring exploration for oil and gas in the North Sea. The exploitation of North Sea deposits required sustained, deep-sea diving from offshore rigs. That meant a booming demand for diving gases. APL established facilities at Bargeddie in Scotland in 1974, and organized a wholly owned subsidiary (Air Products Helium Services Limited) to service diving operations. Later, the company supplied a barge-mounted nitrogen plant to be used for repressuring offshore oil wells.

Air Products also found that it could sell additional nitrogen and hydrogen to the steel and chemicals industries. Metalworking industries had come to rely on natural gas to create special atmospheres for controlled annealing, sintering, and carburizing. Air Products already had been providing some nitrogen and hydrogen for those purposes as early as the 1950s. Starting in 1974, the company's AR&D Department developed mixtures of nitrogen and hydrogen to substitute for natural gas. Similarly, food processors, heat treaters, and metalworking and electronics customers began to purchase additional hydrogen as an alternative to reformed natural gas. Hydrogen also was in demand for use in refineries to produce higher-value products, such as gasoline and jet fuel, from crude oil. Synthetic gas projects also demanded the provision of industrial gases in tonnage quantities. In 1977, for instance, Air Products signed an on-site contract to supply 2,500 tons-per-day of oxygen and nitrogen from its LaPorte site to the Syngas Company, a joint venture of the Du Pont Company and National Distillers, Inc.

High prices made the natural gas business itself more lucrative than ever. Sales of the company's MCR heat exchangers for liquefying natural gas rose. APL built a ten-million-cubic-feet-per-day natural gas liquefaction works for the British Gas Council at its Canvey Island Terminal (1972). In the United States, Air Products invested in natural gas "peak-shaving" ventures. Peak shaving involved purchasing natural gas in the warmer months, when prices were low, and liquefying and storing it until the winter, when prices normally rose.[13]

Air Products had entered this business in 1965, when it started operating a peak-shaving facility for the Alabama Gas Corporation near Birmingham, Alabama. In the early 1970s, Air Products began two peak-shaving operations in New England under long-term contracts. These ventures were highly successful and trouble free. None-

theless, because the potential liabilities and the cost of insurance far
outweighed their profitability, Air Products divested itself of all responsibility for these domestic liquefied natural gas facilities in the
1980s.[14]

A traditional field of environmental concern, wastewater treatment,
also propelled Air Products into a new market niche in the early
seventies. Like the company's activity in the LNG equipment business, its entry into wastewater treatment was an initial failure that
turned into a later success. And like the LNG example, wastewater
treatment profited by entrepreneurship from within the company.
By the end of the eighties, moreover, the modest wastewater treatment business would prove to have been the first step to creation of
the firm's third leg: energy and environmental systems would join
industrial gases and chemicals as a recognized area of Air Products'
endeavor.

The company had tried to enter the wastewater treatment business
as early as the 1950s, when Leonard Pool sensed a possible market
for oxygen. Carl Anderson later recalled that something went wrong
in the field trials at the Allentown sewage plant and sewage sprayed
all over Pool. Experiments were halted. Eventually, Air Products
backed into this field by way of its British subsidiary.

It was George Hartnett who seized the initiative on behalf of APL
by taking over a license from Smith & Loveless, a major American
manufacturer of self-contained, shop-assembled aerobic treatment
plants. APL sales expanded in Britain, then in the Middle East and
Africa, particularly Nigeria. After 1969, the British-based wastewater
treatment business operated under the name Satec, Limited. The
firm successfully marketed sewage systems for small communities as
well as a secondary waste-treatment system utilizing oxygen. Satec
supplied a number of British municipalities and exported to thirty
countries in Europe, Africa, the Middle East, and South America.
Once again, innovation from within one of the divisions was successful, driving Air Products into a new and profitable industry.

APL also found a separate market for its oxygen generators in the
wastewater-treatment business. In 1976, the subsidiary contracted to
erect a 180-ton-per-day, computer-controlled oxygen generator for
the city of Copenhagen. Other orders in Western Europe and the
Middle East followed. By then, Air Products had licensed the five
basic patents for the technology from Linde and was selling wastewater-treatment systems under the trade name Oases. Commercialized in 1972, Oases was a high-rate, secondary treatment system for

removing conventional pollutants. Each Oases system was accompanied by an oxygen generator. Oases involved large-ticket, capital-goods sales to a few customers, the type of market in which the company's Cryogenic Systems Division knew how to succeed.

Wastewater-treatment systems were viewed in the early 1970s as a key technology in reviving the industrial gas business. Linde went so far as to predict that more oxygen would be used for waste treatment in the eighties than was consumed by the steel industry, which was still the number one buyer of oxygen.[15] The prediction was not fulfilled, but wastewater treatment was a growing business thanks to the availability of federal funds.

The Oases system was introduced at a time when the municipal wastewater-treatment business was taking off. In 1973 alone, over fifty municipalities in the United States, spurred by a grant program of the Environmental Protection Agency, were planning treatment plants using oxygen. The federal program also stimulated demand from industry. Air Products, which tailor-made Oases systems for each industry's or municipality's needs, won a noteworthy share of this business in the face of competition from Linde, which had pioneered the field.[16]

Satec and the Oases system took Air Products into environment-related businesses. The firm's Catalytic subsidiary also had a broad-based environmental expertise. In keeping with the tenor of the times, Catalytic organized an Environmental Systems Division to offer customers services from laboratory analysis through process design to construction and operation of treatment facilities. The ability to correct pollution problems at their source enabled Catalytic to make environmental work a significant portion of its business. The Environmental Protection Agency selected Catalytic to develop technology and cost figures when the agency set effluent guidelines in 1978.

Catalytic also had a branch involved in the energy business, in the field of nuclear power. The subsidiary parlayed the knowledge it had gained through defense-related work into contracts in the commercial sector. Before Air Products acquired it, Catalytic was already providing engineering support for the Atomic Energy Commission and, after being acquired, it undertook projects at the government nuclear facilities at Miamisburg, Ohio, and Shippingport, Pennsylvania. Catalytic had such a large volume of nuclear-related work that, in 1969, it created a subsidiary, Suntac Nuclear, to provide electric utility companies and government agencies with engineering, maintenance, modification, and refuelling services. The growth of commercial, nuclear-fueled power plants stirred up public debate. That debate in turn focused attention on the effects of radiation, which led to demands for better handling and disposal of radioactive materials. These concerns generated further business opportunities for Catalytic.

Difficulties with Diversification

While the Oases venture and Catalytic business in the fields of energy and the environment brought Air Products into entirely new fields, Dexter Baker, as Executive Vice President, also sought to expand certain more traditional aspects of industrial gas operations.

The company already had a modest trade in gases and equipment for the metalworking trade and it was well aware of the medical market for gases. The 1961 merger with Southern Oxygen had resulted in an enlargement of Air Products' welding and equipment operations, and of its small business in medical gases and equipment. George Pool had united Southern Oxygen and certain Air Products operations to form the KGM Equipment Company and the Medical Gas Department in the Industrial Gas Division, both in 1962. The Jet Cut Corporation (1966) and Exomet, Incorporated (1967) were added to the KGM Equipment Company. In its turn, the Medical Gas Department benefited from the mushrooming expenditures by hospitals across America. By 1969, the nation's annual expenditures for health care were in excess of $56 billion and represented about 7 percent of the gross national product.[17]

Welding and medical products appeared to offer promising opportunities. In both, the name of the game was aggressive selling to an expanding array of small customers, with widely differentiated needs.[18] Despite its successes with cylinder gases—a market also made up of many small customers—Air Products would find it extremely difficult to adapt its marketing strategies. The company would take some hard knocks in the welding business, and eventually abandon the medical field.

In 1969, Baker reorganized the firm's activities in these two areas by creating the Welding Products Division and the Medical Products Division. Several million dollars were spent on acquiring companies in both areas, thereby rapidly increasing and broadening Air Products' involvement. This move was consistent with management's desire to find fresh investment opportunities. The Welding Products Division purchased the Arcair Companies (1969), Automation Industries

(1970), Whittaker (1974), and Compuline (1974), and in 1970, added non-destructive testing equipment through a joint venture, TekTran, with North American Rockwell Corporation, which had developed the technology for the aerospace program. The division now manufactured such cutting-edge equipment as exothermic and heat-insulation products for the metals and construction industries, automatic welding equipment, as well as ultrasonics and eddy current non-destructive testing systems. The Welding Products Division, which also sold products to industrial gas distributors, was reorganized as the Material Sciences Division under Vice President Gerald Frieling, who had been hired from Texas Instruments in 1969 to run this business segment.

The Medical Products Division was headed by Vice President James Ruff, who was brought in from American Hospital Supply. The Division sought to enter inhalation therapy and anesthesiology, fields in which the company had no marketing experience. At that time, however, Leonard Pool was keenly interested in hospitals and health care. Consequently, Air Products purchased The Foregger Company, Inc., in 1970, paying a very high price. Foregger was a leading manufacturer of supplies and equipment used in surgical and dental anesthesia. The Medical Products Division set out to offer "everything for the operating room" including gases. It acquired a broad line of intensive care equipment and disposable hospital items as well as a business from the Bristol Myers Company.

The Material Sciences and Medical Products divisions suffered from numerous problems. The corporate overhead that was charged to each division meant that several of the newly acquired companies began to go into the red. Their growth was not rapid enough to bear the added charges. IGD and Material Sciences salesmen found themselves pitted against each other. The coordination and camaraderie that existed in the cylinder and bulk gases operations were missing. Deeply entrenched competitors like Linde proved difficult to dislodge. Moreover, Air Products paid too much for some of the acquisitions. In late 1978 and 1979, the difficult decision was taken to disband and sell off the two divisions. After ten years and substantial investments in both fields, Air Products was, for all practical purposes, out of those businesses. Lateral diversification into areas with many small customers, through purchase of variegated minor companies, required a more compulsive commitment than the company was able to muster, in light of its many other plans and problems.

Table 8
Chemicals Group Sales and Operating Profit, 1961–1989

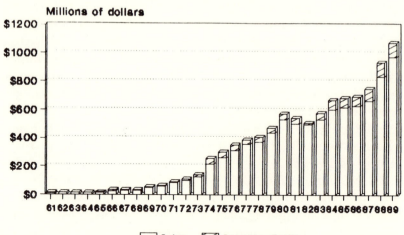

Operating profit is defined as profit
before interest expense and income tax.

A Chemical Formula for Success

In contrast to the, at best, lackluster performance of the Materials Sciences and Medical Products divisions, the company's chemicals activities expanded and proved profitable. Moreover, they were profitable in a period of immense difficulties for the chemical industry. Air Products was clearly no longer just an industrial gas company: the Chemicals Group was becoming the enterprise's second leg (Table 8).

In 1969, in order to expand and run the chemicals business, Ed Donley persuaded his colleagues to agree to the hiring of Dick (Richard) Fleming. Fleming had been a chemical engineer in R&D at Sun Oil, until he became President of Avisun, a subsidiary that manufactured polypropylene. Avisun was sold to Amoco, based in Chicago. Fleming, reluctant to leave the Philadelphia area, joined Air Products as Vice President of the newly formed Chemicals Group and started a major acquisitions search.

Dick Fleming discussed Air Products' strengths with Frank Ryan and Harry Quigley. They noted that Air Products did well at regional gas distribution and at buying major slices of companies, such as Houdry and Escambia. So Fleming, Ryan, and Quigley looked for major divisions of companies that were for sale.

Fleming focused on the Chemicals and Plastics Division of Airco (the name of Air Reduction after 1971), centered in its Calvert City, Kentucky, works. Started in 1953, Calvert City had been planned as a miniature Ruhr Valley, where coal and electricity would be turned into calcium carbide and acetylene, and the acetylene transformed into a wide range of organic chemicals. However, in the 1960s, ethylene, derived from the nation's abundant supplies of natural gas, had become available as an equally satisfactory and cheaper starting point for many organic chemicals. The lower production costs of ethylene made the acetylene-based chemistry of Calvert City obsolete for large-volume products like vinyl chloride and vinyl acetate.[19] As a result of this technological obsolescence, Air Products was able to pick up Airco's chemical operations at a bargain price in 1971.

Integration of the different chemical operations owned by Air Products posed a major challenge. Prior to this purchase, Fleming had a small number of people reporting to him: Wes Hoge of Houdry, Larry Carey of Escambia, and Frank Ryan in the Agricultural Chemicals Division. Airco's chemical business was larger and more complex than any previous acquisition. In accordance with the matrix pattern, Fleming centralized his group. Management personnel from the Airco chemicals office in New York, from the Escambia office in Pensacola, from Houdry in Philadelphia, and from Air Products in Allentown were brought together in a single office complex near Valley Forge, Pennsylvania. The accounting, employee relations, engineering, legal, R&D, and planning functions were consolidated. Quigley was put in charge of planning, and Carey ran manufacturing. R&D was headed by Mayo Smith, an Escambia employee who had come to Air Products before the Escambia purchase (Table 9).

The Chemicals Group would have access to the accumulated expertise of the Cryogenic Systems Division. CSD managers, headed by Lee Gaumer, brought to the Chemicals Group their experience in liquid hydrogen, hydrogen purification, on-site liquid plants, the Esso (Libya) LNG project, specialty designs, liquid carbon dioxide, and the New Orleans ammonia complex, as well as a broad knowledge of air separation plants. Joe Cost of the Cryogenic Systems Division was transferred to be the group's engineering coordinator. This integration of Air Products' process engineering skills with the chemical knowledge of the acquired companies was a key factor in the success of the Chemicals Group.

That success did not come easily. The early policy with the chemicals acquisitions, as with Catalytic, had been to leave original man-

The Calvert City, Kentucky, works, acquired as part of the Chemicals and Plastics Division of Airco in 1971.

Table 9
Chemicals at Air Products, 1961–1976

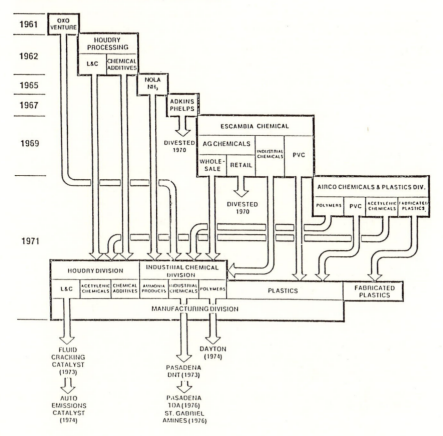

agement in place. This policy had some negative effects. Though the very title of the corporation, Air Products *and* Chemicals, signalled the possibilities for either synergy or divisiveness, the gas side of the business was quite separate from both Catalytic and the Chemicals Group. Equally, Catalytic and Chemicals were out of touch with each other, and Chemicals was divided internally. The result was a high degree of territoriality. "Houdry people" were different from "Air Products people," and from "Escambia people," or "Airco people." In 1971, the cleavages within the Chemicals Group became particularly evident when, for the first time, operations were centralized at Valley Forge.

Employees from the various chemical subsidiaries did not know each other. Their offices had been scattered about the country. Bringing everyone together at Trexlertown would have forced a more direct confrontation with the mainstream culture of Air Products. At Valley Forge, the chemical subsidiaries were integrated, but at the same time they were separated from company headquarters and thus quite naturally developed their own culture. A significant factor was the basic differences between the industrial gas and the chemicals businesses. In chemicals, there was no one central competitor, like Linde. Unlike air, raw materials for the chemicals operation had to be purchased through contracts with feedstock suppliers. Also, there were many different customers to cater to. Suppliers could be competitors: for instance, Union Carbide, a competitor in amines, sold Air Products its amine feedstock. The Chemicals Group was successful under Fleming, but increasingly it seemed like a separate company.

In 1976, Ed Donley grasped the nettle. The Chemicals Group was brought into the corporate headquarters complex. Dick Fleming soon left, realizing that his opportunities for advancement were limited. His leaving opened the way for the promotion of Frank Ryan to Vice President of the Chemicals Group in 1980. By then the group had changed significantly, and its growth areas were no longer Houdry's Dabco or plastics-related chemicals. Industrial chemicals and polymers were the star players. The successes in those areas were a result of the firm's dominant position in specialized market niches, and of reliance on its process engineering expertise. But the decline of Dabco, and of Houdry in general, was one less-happy consequence of the triumph of the Air Products' culture. That culture was inhospitable to the style of research on which Houdry had depended for its innovations.

The Dabco line and Houdry's catalyst and chemical process businesses demanded basic research. Houdry expenditures on basic research in the early sixties were double those of the rest of Air Products. After its acquisition, Houdry lacked a "champion" within its host company. One consequence was that the Houdry research budget shrank. The subsidiary began to concentrate on incremental improvements in its products and processes. That was the kind of research and *development* that Air Products valued. The company's management was dominated by the engineering side of its culture, centered on project completion, problem-solving, and incremental improvements. This kind of R&D was very successful in the firm's AR&D Department and its Cryogenic Systems Division. It was not, however, the kind of basic, long-term research that was needed to keep Houdry's businesses viable. As a result, those businesses declined.

Houdry's process licensing activities were mostly overseas. Dabco's market strength was based on its patent position. The use of polyurethane foams in the manufacture of domestic and foreign automobiles in the seventies boosted sales. But that and other markets shrank as research at rival firms brought new products to the market. In 1982, after Wes Hoge retired, Air Products folded what was left of Houdry's licensing operations into the Cryogenic Systems Division.

By the end of the seventies, similar declines had taken place in the small molded plastics and polyvinyl chloride (PVC) businesses. Molded plastics had been run independently by John Tinnon, who had managed the business under Airco. This profit center produced and sold flexible and rigid vinyl plastics which were molded into everything from handlebar grips to hose for vacuum cleaners and swimming pools.[20] However, after sales began to plummet, Air Products sold off the business. The PVC operation also proved unsatisfactory. PVC had been a high-growth chemical used for plastic piping and siding and a host of other industrial and consumer products. Air Products was a latecomer to this market. The purchase of Escambia had provided a small, well-managed PVC business. After significant engineering alterations, and even after the installation of pollution control devices, the Escambia plant was one of the lowest-cost producers of PVC.

In contrast, the Calvert City plant had many problems and was even shut down temporarily by the Environmental Protection Agency. The management retained after the Airco acquisition failed to bring down production costs and the business was unprofitable throughout the late seventies and into the eighties. In the third quarter of fiscal 1981, there was a $44 million non-recurring charge against earnings resulting from a revaluation of the assets of the Calvert City facility. In fact, much of the Group's profits were being wiped out by the PVC operation. In 1982, Air Products wrote off the assets of its Calvert City PVC facility and trimmed related operating expenses. Thereafter, the facility was operated solely "for cash," by creating a paper subsidiary and by taking advantage of certain tax laws.

By 1978, however, it was clear that the Chemicals Group had a profitable and growing core business in certain specialty chemicals. That business had been acquired from Escambia and Airco, and managed by Frank Ryan. The chief industrial chemicals were alkylamines and methylamines, toluene diamine (TDA) and dinitrotoluene (DNT), emulsion polymers, and polyvinyl alcohol. Air Products enjoyed leadership positions in these specialty chemicals. The company found itself a major U.S. manufacturer of dinitrotoluene (DNT). DNT is a compound used to make TDA (toluene diamine), a key ingredient in the production of toluene diisocyanate (TDI). TDI in turn is used in making polyurethane foams, elastomers, and protective coatings. Air Products rapidly established itself as the world's largest producer of polyurethane intermediates, utilizing Escambia's process technology and Air Products' engineering expertise.

Air Products entered into negotiations with Olin, Dow, and BASF-Wyandotte and emerged with an agreement to make DNT and TDA for those three customers on a long-term basis. A large TDA and DNT facility was constructed at Pasadena, Texas. Hydrogen and carbon monoxide generated at the company's industrial gas facility at LaPorte, Texas, were fed to the Pasadena site by pipeline. Pasadena was a single, environmentally sound, cost-effective source of these compounds. In 1976, Air Products had about one-half of the U.S. DNT market. In 1977, the company began exporting TDA.[21]

Air Products also found itself the number one U.S. producer of alkylamines and methylamines after the Escambia and Airco acquisitions. Alkylamines are intermediates for manufacturing herbicides and fungicides, insect repellents, and pharmaceuticals, while methylamines serve mainly as intermediates to produce poultry feed, insecticides, and solvents for synthetic fibers. The planting of more and more acres in corn and soybeans—spurred on by government food programs—swelled the demand for herbicides. The market for poultry food supplements had also grown. Both meant greater demand for alkylamines and methylamines.

Air Products sold those intermediates directly to other chemical manufacturers, much as it sold industrial gases. In 1976, it opened a larger version of its Pensacola works, "the world's largest alkylamines plant," at St. Gabriel, Louisiana. Output was sold on long-term contracts to two of the nation's largest producers of herbicides, Ciba-Geigy and Stauffer, both of which had plants located adjacent to the St. Gabriel works. In 1977, Air Products also began developing export sales of alkylamines and methylamines.

Air Products' emulsion polymers business, based on vinyl acetate and ethylene, also enjoyed a leadership position. Air Products was number one in the U.S. vinyl acetate polymers market, with Union Carbide running second, and number one in selling to the adhesives

The LaPorte, Texas, facility produced hydrogen and carbon monoxide for pipeline customers in the Houston area as well as for the company's TDA-DNT complex at Pasadena, Texas.

The Air Products TDA plant at Pasadena, Texas.

and textile markets.[22] The business, headed by former Airco executive Harold Jaffe, had been acquired from Airco. The polymers were used in adhesives, paints, paper, and textile coatings. They bound non-woven fibers together and made them soft yet strong. Non-woven fabrics were being used extensively for disposable and semidurable products, such as paper towels and diapers. In order to expand production to keep up with fast-growing demand, the company added a new vinyl acetate/ethylene emulsion plant in South Brunswick, New Jersey, built by Catalytic. The vinyl acetate operations had previously been integrated by Airco with a polyvinyl alcohol works. The polyvinyl alcohol was sold under the trade name Vinol, and Air Products was the second largest U.S. producer of the chemical. Vinol was used in the adhesives and textiles industries, and the company saw increasing sales of Vinol during the seventies.

The story was far less straightforward for the company's ammonia business. Ammonia prices escalated enormously in 1974, and ammonia operations at New Orleans contributed significantly to the Chemical Group's profits. Then ammonia prices fell sharply, from $300 a ton in 1975 to $100 a ton in 1979.[23] Conditions like these were trying, to say the least.

In addition to its large ammonia complex near New Orleans, Air Products acquired a smaller ammonia works at Pace, Florida, when it bought Escambia. In 1971, the natural gas supplier interrupted deliveries at Pace. Production costs rose when it became necessary to purchase natural gas at high spot-market prices. A settlement was not reached with the supplier until 1976. A similar problem arose at the New Orleans complex. The company's two natural gas suppliers, Shell and Tenneco, wanted to renegotiate prices. Tenneco interrupted its supply, but Shell continued to supply gas until Air Products and Tenneco reached an agreement. After several years of inconclusive debate, the judge who was hearing the case threw the Air Products and Tenneco people together in a room until they reached agreement, which took only two days. Tenneco received a price increase and Air Products collected substantial damages. Nonetheless, the ammonia business continued to rollercoaster and plans to increase output had to be shelved.

The Chemicals Group had grown significantly and changed markedly over the course of the seventies. By decade's end the group was profitable, although it still had its troubles. While shifting market conditions were among those troubles, environmental and health hazards were major problems for Air Products and the entire chemical industry. The company's chemical (and industrial gas) plants created air, water, and noise pollution, and higher oil prices sharply increased production costs. Government-mandated pollution-control measures and natural gas shortages threatened profit margins. Ed Donley was committed to keeping Air Products a socially responsible firm, but the company's Chemicals Group made that policy expensive.

In 1973, the group operated at eleven locations and at three separate laboratories in the United States and had a joint interest in two plants abroad. At each site, Air Products tried to emphasize effective pollution-control practices and good community relations. In 1973, at its Escambia Pensacola plant, for instance, Air Products built a series of biological treatment ponds through which all wastewaters were processed. This was a highly complex system, in which naturally occurring bacteria and other microorganisms decomposed the plant's waste with the help of oxygen. Over 100 acres of the plant site, including two ponds stocked with fish, were given to the Florida Game and Fresh Water Fish Commission as a wildlife sanctuary, and were opened to the public for bird-watching, hiking, and fishing.

More difficult for Ed Donley and his colleagues was a serious health risk arising from the production of PVC. In January 1974, another manufacturer of PVC reported that three of its workers had died of angiosarcoma, a rare cancer of the liver. The deaths appeared to be a result of occupational exposure to vinyl chloride monomer. The Occupational Safety and Health Administration (OSHA) responded with standards designed to prevent worker exposure. Air Products joined with other producers to challenge OSHA. In the meantime, however, Air Products took the lead in fully complying with the regulations, investing heavily in emission-control equipment at Pace and at Calvert City. The firm retained a distinguished pathologist who developed a diagnostic program that included medical histories, personal examinations, and laboratory tests on 492 employees at both plants. No case of work-related cancer was found, and in 1978, OSHA selected the company to produce a special video program on the safe handling of vinyl chlorides.

In 1976, Air Products also hired a Corporate Medical Director, Lloyd Tepper, M.D. He became the key figure in occupational medicine at Air Products. Tepper had been an associate commissioner of the Food and Drug Administration. His experience in industrial health and toxicology made him ideal for anticipating the medical issues inherent in the firm's chemical operations. Tepper was responsible for evaluating all health-related aspects of the company's operations and for establishing corrective and preventive programs. He organized a mobile monitoring team consisting of a physician, a nurse, and an interviewer. The team made periodic site visits in order to provide employee health examinations at plants lacking a medical facility.[24]

By 1978, Air Products had overcome many of its troubles. On balance, moreover, there were more triumphs than troubles. The company was doing a growing business at home and abroad, at a time in which the American business system as a whole had seen productivity gains dwindle and almost disappear. The firm's hungry opportunistic style, its engineering expertise, and its hard-driving sales force were key elements of success in the post-Pool world of Air Products. Donley, Baker, Holt, and the rest of the firm's managers had good cause to be optimistic about the future. Indeed, in 1978, Air Products would achieve yet another milestone that reflected its success. The company became a Fortune 500 corporation.

Notes

1. Walter Pool interview, 25 January 1976, APHO.
2. Lee Holt interview, 11 August 1988, APHO.
3. Edward Donley interview, 11 December 1987, APHO.
4. Edward Donley interview, 29 January 1988, APHO.
5. Walter Pool interview, 25 January 1976, APHO.
6. Edward Donley interview, 29 January 1988, APHO.
7. Ibid.
8. Leonard Pool to "All Department Heads," 12 June 1959, APHO.
9. Lee Holt interview, 11 August 1988, APHO.
10. Standard and Poor's Industry Surveys, *Chemicals*, 20 March 1969, Sec. 2, p. C 37; ibid., 26 November 1971, Sec. 1, p. C 30.
11. APL also received the Queen's Award for Export Achievement in 1987 and 1989. The Airopak group at APL received the Queen's Award for Technology in 1988. Joseph Kaminski had a B.S. in mechanical engineering from Stevens Institute of Technology and an M.B.A. from Dartmouth. He joined Air Products in 1965 as a project engineer. James Strecansky joined Air Products in 1962, with a B.S. in chemical engineering from Manhattan College.
12. "Liquid Hydrogen Contract Awarded to Pennsylvania Firm," NASA News Release, no. 75–192, 30 June 1975.
13. Lee Gaumer interview, 27 June 1989, APHO.
14. Air Products still operates the Hopkington, Massachusetts, plant under contract.

15. Standard and Poor's Industry Surveys, *Chemicals*, 25 October 1973, Sec. 1, p. C 27.

16. *Annual Report 1973*, pp. 5–6.

17. Union Carbide and Carbon Corporation, *Annual Reports 1950–1970*.

18. Dennis Domchek, "Industrial Gases: New Application Markets," paper for Chemical Marketing Research Association, Munich, Germany, 15–17 October 1979, pp. 1–3, APHO.

19. Peter H. Spitz, *Petrochemicals: The Rise of an Industry* (New York: John Wiley & Sons, 1988), pp. 400–415.

20. *Annual Report 1974*, p. 13.

21. Air Products and Chemicals, Inc., "Presentation to Security Analysts," 16 June 1976; *Annual Report 1977*, p. 8, APHO.

22. Air Products and Chemicals, Inc., "Presentation to Security Analysts," 16 June 1976, APHO.

23. Presentation by Air Products and Chemicals, Inc. to the New York Society of Financial Analysts, 13 November 1979, APHO.

24. *Annual Report 1974*, p. 2.

PART IV

A FORTUNE 500 CORPORATION

Air Products' sales exceeded $1 billion in 1978 (Table 10). As the company reached that benchmark, the business system in America was entering a wrenching period of intense competition, renewed energy shortages, and high unemployment. The deep recession of 1981–1982 would add to the problems of an economy in need of renewal and reform.

The challenges facing Air Products' management and employees were formidable. The industrial-gas business, hit once again by excess productive capacity, low prices, and intense competition, also saw new challenges in a growing globalization as American firms pushed further into European and fast-growing Pacific Rim markets, while facing fresh competition at home from the foreign-based giants of the industry. The company now was under closer scrutiny from institutional investors. Two Chief Executive Officers, Edward Donley and Dexter Baker, shared the task of continuing the dramatic growth Air Products had experienced during the previous four decades. In tackling that task, Donley and Baker enriched the company culture through their emphasis on the human resource functions of the firm, and on "getting close to the customer." They would continue to give technical innovation, engineering expertise, aggressive salesmanship, and an opportunistic entrepreneurial style a central role in corporate strategy.

The search for new investment opportunities would prove perilous, as the company pursued federal contracts in the short-lived synfuels industry, and expanded its engineering activities at an inauspicious moment. Yet, out of these uncertainties would emerge a recognizable third business area, that of environmental and energy systems. That new area was created largely by the entrepreneurship that the company culture encouraged, and which its officers sought to cultivate. And if the corporation had become one that Leonard Pool would barely recognize, Air Products would continue to build on his legacy.

Table 10
Air Products Sales and Profits, 1978–1989

Millions of Dollars

$3000
$2500
$2000
$1500
$1000
$500
$0

78 79 80 81 82 83 84 85 86 87 88 89

■ Sales   ▨ Profits Before Taxes

9

Maturity

Air Products reached $1 billion in sales and listing in the Fortune 500 in 1978. The strategy of deferring short-term profits for long-term growth had been successful. So, too, had been the continued emphasis upon high-quality engineering, on innovative technology and financing, on a "hungry" style of entrepreneurship, and on skillful marketing to industrial and government customers. Where the corporation moved away from its core business, it had sometimes been successful (chemicals) but more often had encountered serious problems (retail sales, material sciences, medical supplies). In the industrial gases field it had become a major player in the United States and abroad; in a number of specialty gases Air Products was the dominant firm in growing markets. In chemicals the company had experienced outstanding success in certain areas. The challenge to Ed Donley and his management team in the early eighties was to build on these achievements without locking the firm into markets that were experiencing slower growth.

Growth, Finance, and Human Issues

Growth was an integral part of the company culture. In the beginning it had been a sheer necessity for Leonard Pool to postpone dividends in favor of investing for the future. That necessity soon became a virtue. When the company went public, Air Products was marketed as a growth stock, offering capital gains rather than immediate income. Over the years the need to grow became automatic, a reflex. As Lee Holt reflected, "I guess it's been built into our psyche from the very beginning. We're just not content with not doing it. I think there is a psychology here that you either grow or you die. You don't stand still. . . . Markets don't stand still. If you don't keep ahead of your markets, and the areas that you're serving, you don't survive. The world is not stable, it's constantly changing, and you have to change with it."[1]

This was clearly Ed Donley's business philosophy too. He reaffirmed growth as an element in the company culture in the eighties. However, he was willing to reinterpret how it would be achieved. He continued to stress the need for adequate managerial structures. At the same time, he reemphasized the company's orientations to technology, to innovation, and to entrepreneurship. Synfuels, chemicals, and R&D would be among the areas where he would push major developments in the early 1980s. He also had to pay close attention to Wall Street.

From its very first days, Air Products had faced pressing financial issues, and responded with ingenuity. Personal loans, government contracts, stock offerings, and indentures had all played their part in financing the company's growth. Leonard Pool had kept a tight hand on financial affairs, as comptrollers came and went. Then, in the late fifties and sixties, the indenture had provided both a means through which to gain greater financial resources and a vehicle through which a more orderly approach to finance was nourished. Ed Donley's appointment as President, then as CEO, opened the way to a full staffing of the financial functions within the company, under the overall direction of Lee Holt.

Among the issues that Donley and Holt faced was how to respond to the country's changing tax laws. For many years, the capital gains tax rate had been significantly lower than the earned income rate. Accordingly, many investors had looked for capital appreciation rather than dividends. That fitted well with Air Products' strategy of deferring income to achieve growth. The stock did very well in the 1970s; there were two-for-one stock splits in 1973 and in 1976. But as the company continued to grow, it found it harder to sustain the same compound growth rate. Moreover, the federal government began, during those same years, to equalize the tax rates on capital gains and earned income.

With an eye toward these developments and toward the new role in the stock market of institutional investors, Donley raised the div-

Through his introduction of the matrix structure and an emphasis on safety, social responsibility, and the importance of human resources, Ed Donley played a fundamental role in shaping the corporation's organization and culture.

idend in September 1977, from 20 cents to 40 cents per share. He boosted the dividend in the following years, bringing it to 80 cents a share in 1980, and to $1.27 a share in 1985, when the stock again split two-for-one. The new policy made the dividend rate dependent on earnings growth. In the eighties, Air Products would continue to emphasize growth, but it would no longer do so to the exclusion of adequate dividends. In this as in other regards, the company had exchanged the style of a tightly held family firm for the stock market–sensitive approach of a major corporation.

The company also changed the way it financed growth, introducing measures that improved debt ratios and other figures important to institutional investors. The indenture lost its central place in financial strategy. Air Products' cash flow, underpinned by the large number of on-site, take-or-pay contracts, had itself become the company's most significant financial resource. Even so, Holt worked closely with John Mountain[2] and Ron Barclay[3] to see that wherever possible debt was used to advantage. For instance, on-site construction was increasingly financed with privately placed project loans.

Despite its size, Air Products remained a company where employees mattered. The key to the firm's engineering and sales success was its ability to attract, develop, and retain outstanding engineers, salesmen, and other professionals, and to create opportunities for them to develop productive and rewarding careers within the corporate structure. In addition to utilizing the Career Development Program, a career grid was developed, which laid out all the positions in the company. Employees were encouraged to be active in planning their careers. Air Products continued to send senior managers to Harvard's Advanced Management Program. Other employees attended local colleges and universities through the company's tuition-refund program. Looking back on his own administration, Donley summed up: "I would say that the most important thing that I did was to re-emphasize over and over again the importance of human resources."[4]

The company's emphasis on people did not stop with its employees. The notion of giving back to the community introduced by Pool became "social responsibility" under Donley. Air Products contributed money, and employees volunteered time, to help local causes in the communities where the company had plants and offices. The Public Affairs Department played a central role in honoring and encouraging this commitment. In 1968, the Corporate Contributions Committee was founded to oversee this process. In the late seventies, the committee, under the direction of Bill (William) Kendrick, the new Director of Public Affairs, articulated a corporate philanthropy statement and created the Air Products Foundation.

Ed Donley summarized the corporation's attitude:

> The bottom line of the company's concern with social respon-sibility is this: business needs a healthy society if it is to survive and prosper. Although the company recognizes that its first re-sponsibility is to succeed in its business and make a profit, it also recognizes that it can no longer simply respond to the de-mands of the marketplace. It also has an obligation to respond to the broader expectations of society, fostering an environment conducive to growth and opportunity for all.[5]

Air Products also remained concerned about safety. In the 1970s, the company's accident record had deteriorated. Donley was entirely dissatisfied with the firm's performance and launched a company-wide effort to correct matters. Thibaut Brian, Vice President of En-gineering, and Bill Scharle, Vice President of Operations and Engi-neering in the Process Systems Group (as the Cryogenic Systems Division was now known), made a careful study of safety practices in the chemical industry. Several companies offered instructional ma-terials and ran seminars. Air Products decided that Du Pont, with the nation's premier safety record, had the best program. Air Prod-ucts' engineers adapted the Du Pont program to the specific needs of Air Products.[6]

By making it a corporate function, Donley assured that safety mat-ters would be handled in a uniform manner throughout the company. Safety in each division and in each subsidiary was overseen and re-viewed from one corporate office. The result of the renewed emphasis on safety was a downward trend in serious injuries. By 1990, Air Products had the best safety record in the industrial gas business and was second only to Du Pont in the chemical industry.

Renewal in the Industrial Gas Business

During Ed Donley's time as CEO in the seventies and eighties, industrial gas operations remained the firm's chief money-maker. Dex Baker had pursued industrial gas markets with vigor in the seventies. Air Products became the worldwide leader in liquid helium as well as in liquid hydrogen.[7] However, the company experienced a signif-icant setback in industrial gases in the early eighties. With the recession of 1981–1982 profitability dropped, demand (mainly for oxygen) fell off, electricity costs climbed rapidly, and the whole industry suffered once again from overcapacity.[8] Donley and his colleagues began to view the domestic industrial gas business as having matured. The search intensified for new areas for investment and diversification.

In actuality, energy costs moderated and demand increased after the recession was over. Less satisfactory to Air Products was the way small industrial gas firms, eager to find a market, cut prices to the bone in order to underbid the established leaders in the industry. Even so, the company achieved market-share gains and volume growth, while improving profitability. Individuals such as Ed Sherry, who was later to become Director of Energy Supply, deftly negotiated special deals with utilities in order to obtain the lowest price possible on electricity. Older, less energy-efficient plants were replaced with facilities that cost less to operate and required fewer employees.[9] Though it was no longer a "young tiger" but rather a mature player defending its established position as the country's second largest producer, Air Products had not lost its hungry style.

Especially helpful was the way the Process Systems Group brought to bear its engineering expertise, and used the computer to cut energy costs. In 1978, Paul Prutzman led a team which installed computer control systems in several industrial gas plants to help reduce the energy consumed. In the Industrial Gas Division, Pete Sipple worked to reduce energy consumption still further in the early eighties by implementing a computer sourcing and delivery system, which increased the efficiency of the truck fleet. Additional energy savings came when gas plants in the United States were linked to a central energy-monitoring system at corporate headquarters. Plant managers were provided with efficiency evaluations of compressors and other process equipment from analyses run on the company's mainframe computer. The system, unique in the gas industry, helped to optimize production and distribution on a nationwide basis. In 1983, Air Products won the National Energy Resources Organization's annual energy conservation award, for its technological advances in the use of computers to produce industrial gases.

The company also developed computer-aided design (CAD) and computer-aided manufacturing (CAM) technologies. CAM technology, coupled with capital investment in more productive manufacturing systems, saved time and money. CAD dramatically reduced the time it took to move a plant design from the drawing board to the field. Air Products advanced its CAD technology from two-

Air Products became a world leader in liquid helium, with shipments to Japan and Europe.

Table 11
U.S. Production of Oxygen and Nitrogen, 1947–1982

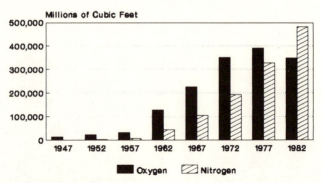

SOURCE: U.S. Census of Manufactures.
Nitrogen figures exclude quantities
produced in the manufacture of ammonia.

dimensional programs to simulate three-dimensional displays, using cathode ray tube screens with color and hidden-line removal, to map out complex process-piping designs. By 1981, computers had become such an integral part of Air Products that it organized Management Information Services (MIS) as a corporate staff function and promoted Peter Mather to be its Vice President.[10]

As Air Products was computerizing its industrial gas operations, demand patterns were undergoing major changes. Merchant supplies now accounted for a third of the industrial gas market in the United States, and the merchant segment was continuing to grow faster than traditional on-site tonnage activity. The heart of the on-site business was no longer oxygen and its use in the steel industry. The 1974–75 recession reduced on-site production by 11 percent. Subsequently, the U.S. steel industry went into a serious decline as a result of intense foreign competition. That decline lowered oxygen demand about 4 percent annually between 1979 and 1984. Falling demand in the on-site oxygen business also squeezed the supply of argon, which was generated as a co-product.[11]

In contrast, nitrogen production continued on its remarkable up-swing. In the decade from 1969 to 1978, consumption had averaged a rise of nearly 13 percent a year. In 1980, nitrogen replaced oxygen as the number one industrial gas in the United States, and by 1990 it was far ahead (Table 11). The major forces powering this expanding use of nitrogen were its replacement of natural gas as a blanketing agent in metalworking and in the electronics industry, its role in chemical processing, and its use as a freezing agent, especially in food processing. Oil fields were also yielding new applications, as nitrogen was used to stimulate gas and oil flow.[12]

As noted in Chapter 8, the OPEC oil embargo had spurred exploration for oil and natural gas at offshore sites on the California and Gulf coasts, and in the North Sea. The growing demand for deep-sea diving gases and equipment helped Air Products make notable sales to diving operations. In 1981, Pat Dyer negotiated the purchase of Gardner Cryogenics, a company founded by former Air Products' employee Bill Gardner. Headquartered in Bethlehem, Pennsylvania, Gardner was a leading manufacturer of diving gases (including helium) and related equipment, in Britain as well as in the United States. The acquisition vaulted Air Products to the leadership of worldwide helium markets.

Repressuring oil wells on land was another energy-related technology much in demand in the early 1980s. Air Products was a leader in this technology. By 1982, the firm had almost 6,000 tons-per-day of nitrogen under contract for oil-field projects. In the Jay field of the Florida panhandle, Air Products supplied the largest tertiary-oil recovery project of its kind. Nitrogen was injected into the field to increase the recoverable crude oil by some fifty million barrels. In February 1983, Air Products brought on-stream the Exxon LaBarge plant, the world's largest single-train nitrogen generator for an enhanced oil recovery project. Upgrading heavier and sour crudes into lighter, higher-value products provided another area for energy-related gas sales.

Air Products also experimented with multi-customer pipelines, a delivery method pioneered by Air Liquide in France, Germany, and the Benelux countries, and by Big Three Industries in the United States. Big Three sold oil-field chemicals, equipment, and related services, as well as industrial gases and welding equipment. In 1980, the firm had a pipeline network stretching nearly 900 miles, mainly in the Gulf Coast region of Louisiana and Texas.[13]

In 1981, two employees in Strategic Planning tried to interest Air Products in the idea of a multicustomer pipeline, but the risks appeared too high.[14] However, the firm eventually installed pipelines where it had a growing number of customers in a small area. The electronics boom in Silicon Valley provided Air Products with one such opportunity. The small automated nitrogen generator installed in 1965 had led to Air Products having about 1,000-tons-per-day of high-purity nitrogen capacity at its plants in Santa Clara, Sunnyvale, and Mountain View, California, by 1988. These plants were eventually

The acquisition of Gardner Cryogenics, a leading manufacturer of diving gases and related equipment, put Air Products in a leading position in that growing field.

The air separation plant at Santa Clara, part of a multiple-customer pipeline serving Silicon Valley.

equipped to serve companies at forty locations through a complex pipeline network. A far smaller, multicustomer pipeline was started in 1982, to serve the petroleum and petrochemical industry in Louisiana, where Big Three dominated the market.[15]

Toward a Global Industry

Domestically, the industrial gas business was hard sledding in the early- and mid-eighties. One partial solution was to look overseas. Even as U.S. firms, led by Air Products, escalated their penetration of the lucrative European and the fast-growing Pacific Rim markets, the foreign-based giants of the industry were returning the compliment by invading the U.S. market.

Air Products maintained a strong position overseas. In 1980, about one-third of its industrial gas sales were in Europe. Air Products' European market was mostly cylinder (40 percent) and on-site (30 percent) sales. The merchant business in liquid oxygen and liquid nitrogen (20 percent) and in argon, hydrogen, helium, and specialty gases (10 percent) was where Air Products succeeded the most, with more than a fifth of those markets. In Britain alone, Air Products attained half of the liquid oxygen market.[16]

The company had reorganized and begun to expand its industrial gas business in Europe as early as 1972, with the arrival of Mark Halsted. Halsted had found that each subsidiary's merchant gas business was run separately. He collected Continental merchant operations under Al Bull,[17] a native German engineer who had been with the company and its overseas branches since 1967. Halsted integrated and computerized Continental merchant gas sales, so that gases could be shipped across national boundaries to take advantage of price differences and to beat the competition. Air Products also consolidated its Continental subsidiaries. In 1977, the firm bought the shares that Société Générale de Belgique owned in their joint venture, thereby making the Belgian, Dutch, and French subsidiaries wholly owned.

After the 1980 retirement of Frank Pavlis as Vice President of World Trade, the firm's European subsidiaries and APL were consolidated into a single corporation, Air Products Europe, Inc. The new corporation soon entered the Spanish and Irish gas markets. In 1984, a subsidiary was set up in Dublin to sell gases to that nation's growing industrial sector. The firm also acquired a minority interest in the Sociedad Española de Carburos Metálicos, S.A., the second largest industrial gas company in Spain. An Air Products subsidiary, Prodair, became the second largest industrial gas producer in France (though still far behind Air Liquide) after acquiring a 65 percent interest in Oxygène Liquide, an important regional gas supplier. More and more in Europe, Air Products was competing with both the "local" national and the big international industrial gas companies.

In the early eighties, Pat Dyer and Joe Kaminski made the Pacific Rim the major strategic thrust of overseas expansion. In 1981, as part of a joint venture in South Korea, Air Products brought on-stream a 130-metric-ton-per-day[18] oxygen, nitrogen, and argon plant. In 1984, a second joint venture was launched with Korea Industrial Gases, Ltd. However, it was Japan that offered the most significant market on the Pacific Rim, indeed, the world's third largest industrial gas demand. Japan was a notoriously difficult market to enter and Air Products' efforts in the 1970s had not led to a continuing presence there. But in 1983, Air Products pushed the door open a bit when it began some joint activities with Daido Oxygen, one of Japan's major industrial gas companies.

From the United States, Dyer and Kaminski had earlier gotten Air Products into the Mexican industrial gas market in a big way through the creation of a joint venture. In 1980, Air Products acquired an interest in two related Mexican companies, CryoInfra, and CO_2 de México, which together formed the largest industrial gas supplier in Mexico. Markets in Mexico were expanding as a result of that country's burgeoning oil and gas industry, and the development of its industrial base.

At the same time that Air Products was pushing into fresh foreign markets, European firms were invading the domestic industrial gas market. That invasion was led by the British Oxygen Company (BOC), one of the largest industrial gas producers in the world. Through one of its subsidiaries, BOC made an offer in 1973 to purchase 35 percent of the stock of Airco, the number three American firm after Linde and Air Products. The Federal Trade Commission (FTC) objected, and ordered BOC to divest. BOC, however, appealed in court, and won. The firm wasted little time buying out the remainder of Airco.[19] The court victory opened the door for other foreign companies to buy up U.S. industrial gas concerns.

In October 1975, Messer Griesheim bought Burdett Gas Products (Norristown, Pennsylvania), and in 1978, AGA of Sweden took over Burdox, Inc. (Cleveland, Ohio). Later, the Liquid Air Corporation, a U.S. subsidiary of Air Liquide, based in San Francisco, made overtures to Allegheny Ludlum for the purchase of its Chemetron sub-

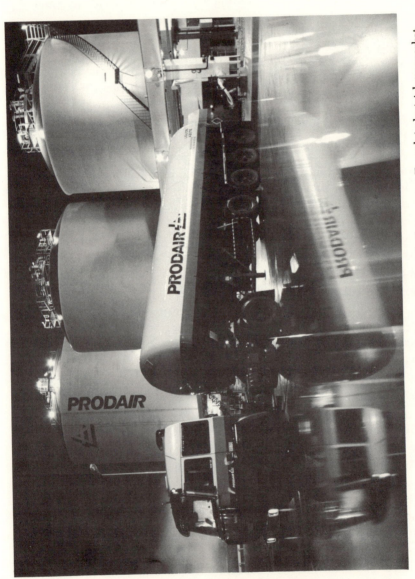

Prodair was the name of the expanded Air Products subsidiary in the growing French industrial gas market. It and the firm's other European operations put Air Products in an excellent position to exploit the expected opening of economic borders in 1992.

sidiary (the former National Cylinder Gas Company). The FTC objected on the grounds that the purchase would eliminate direct competition in a number of regional markets. To complete the takeover, Air Liquide had to agree to sell off several plants. Then, Air Liquide acquired Big Three Industries, making it the third largest industrial gas producer in the United States, ahead of BOC's Airco.[20] Two of the country's four largest industrial gas firms were now controlled by foreign companies. Industrial gases had truly become part of the global marketplace.

Building on Success

The aggressive, global market in industrial gases was, in dollar terms, far smaller than the world market in chemicals. However, for Air Products industrial gases still accounted for more sales and profits than chemicals. Between 1978 and 1986, gas sales were 51 to 59 percent of total sales; chemical sales were 32 to 38 percent. Air Products would continue to expand its investment in chemicals in the eighties, as the Chemicals Group developed its three key areas, amines, polyurethene intermediates, and emulsion polymers.[21]

Despite the fact that chemicals are subject to greater cyclical swings than industrial gases, members of the financial community were impressed with the potential of the Chemicals Group. This reaction, when coupled with the extremely competitive situation in the domestic industrial gas business, strengthened management's resolve to make major new investments in chemicals.[22] It appeared that, during the 1980s, the company could no longer count on unusually rapid growth in the industrial gas sector, which appeared to be a mature market. There were few independents left to acquire. Besides, Air Products itself was a large corporation that had to be concerned about antitrust. As Donley and Ryan recognized, the situation in chemicals was quite different. Air Products was a comparatively small player. It could acquire other companies without arousing the Justice Department. And the variety of specialty chemicals was enormous. In addition, there was the hope that many important products might arise out of company research. Chemicals were targeted for further, major growth in the eighties.

The Chemicals Group strengthened its position in several high-growth market niches through new products. Those products came from internal research and development, as well as from acquisitions and from licensing agreements. The firm's amine and polymers businesses in particular were driven by new products, under the leadership of Hod Harwell and Don Orr.[23]

Air Products remained one of the world's leading producers of alkylamines. In 1981, more than two-thirds of the corn acreage in the United States was treated with herbicides made from Air Products amines. Research carried out by Dale Dixon and Randy Daughenbaugh yielded new amines for treating water, and for processing natural gas and rubber. In 1985, Air Products purchased the Industrial Chemicals Division of Abbott Laboratories. That purchase and the acquisition of a facility in Wichita, Kansas, added to amine production capacity.

Vinyl acetate-based polymers, used in adhesives and emulsions, was the other high-growth area in chemicals. In 1982, Air Products was the number one supplier of polyvinyl acetate emulsions in the United States. From 1979 to 1984, this business grew two-and-a-half times faster than the Gross National Product. The adhesives industry was turning away from solvent-based systems because of rising prices for petroleum feedstocks. The industry's shift to water-based systems favored Air Products' polymers, which enjoyed a sustained, high-growth market throughout the eighties. In 1984, the company increased its emulsions capacity 40 percent. Research led to a growing line of patented "Airflex" emulsions as well as other water-based emulsion and adhesive polymers. In 1986, Air Products licensed the exclusive North American manufacturing and sales rights from BASF, a German chemical concern, for new, pressure-sensitive adhesives.

Polyvinyl alcohol (PVOH), traded as Vinol, was similarly successful. Air Products was the second largest domestic supplier of PVOH,[24] and research yielded a new grade of PVOH which permitted lower energy requirements in certain operations in the textile industry. By applying its process engineering expertise, Air Products reduced unit costs, broadened its product line, and improved product quality. Process engineering also held down production costs and provided important price advantages in other product lines, helping make Air Products the largest U.S. producer of the polyurethane intermediates DNT and TDA.

Through innovation, and through investment in acquisitions and production capacity, the Chemicals Group increased its profitability. Furthermore, under Frank Ryan's direction, steps were taken to cultivate overseas markets. In 1984, he launched a development department and a technical diversification effort, with the aim of establishing an Air Products chemicals presence in Europe. It was an important first step for the Chemicals Group.

Research Reborn

The emphasis of the Chemicals Group on research echoed changes within the Industrial Gas Division and within management in general. In all of the Gas Group divisions, research had remained focused on short-term, incremental improvements. That was the kind of research in which the group excelled. This applied research and development work was carried out by the AR&D, Specialty Gases, and Advanced Products departments. And it continued to furnish the company with growth opportunities throughout the eighties.

The Applied Research and Development Department, now headed by Dennis Domchek, was carrying out research in a number of areas, including reduction, sintering, carburizing, and hydrogen-nitrogen atmospheres, and new uses for hydrogen, helium, and argon. The stars of AR&D were still the Cryo product lines, although Cryo-Guard (transport refrigeration) was phased out in 1982. The company's equipment for deflashing molded products continued to do well. Nonetheless, there was competition in the United States from systems furnished by such foreign-based firms as Liquid Air and Messer-Griesheim, a mark of the changing industrial gas business in the United States.

Cryo-Quick food-freezing equipment was still the biggest seller, accounting for 80 percent of the liquid nitrogen freezers sold domestically in 1981. The addition of new frozen-food items to restaurant menus, such as chicken, offered new growth for the Cryo line and for liquid nitrogen. Cryo-Quick equipment sales were not always accompanied by sales of liquid nitrogen since competitors undercut Air Products in order to get into the market. Moreover, in Southern California, where high power rates made liquid nitrogen expensive, and on the Gulf Coast, where carbon dioxide was plentiful and cheap, many consumers adopted liquid carbon dioxide freezing. Even McDonald's, Air Products' long-time customer for liquid nitrogen for freezing hamburger patties, chose rival liquid carbon dioxide units on occasion, to freeze chicken parts.

The Specialty Gases Department under manager Bill Ent had its own set of successes and difficulties. Basically, the department was in a strong position, as it focused on new areas of research and product development under Andy Woytek, a chemical engineering graduate of Pennsylvania State University. One such area concerned new uses of fluorine-based products. The department combined in-house with company-funded research at Pennsylvania State University to develop

At the new Specialty Gases facility at Hometown, Pennsylvania, researchers created new, award-winning processes and products.

a process for making tetrafluoromethane through the direct fluorination of carbon. Produced at the department's Hometown facility, tetrafluoromethane was consumed in the plasma etching of silicon chips for large-scale integrated circuits.

In addition, Jerry Recktenwald and Dale Dixon of the Specialty Gases Department developed the award-winning Airopak process, which substituted blends of fluorine and nitrogen gases for air when blow-molding plastic containers. Airopak containers could be substituted for metal or glass and used to package agricultural chemicals, cleaning fluids, paints, motor oil, and even gasoline because the treatment process created an impermeable barrier which prevented the product from evaporating through the container's walls. Airopak brought in attractive profits and boosted merchant sales of fluorine and nitrogen. The company found a market for nitrogen trifluoride, made by the direct fluorination of ammonia, as a silicon wafer plasma etchant. Another large market was represented by the Department of Defense, which consumed this specialty gas in laser-weapon research.

The electronics and defense industries also were major buyers of equipment from the Advanced Products Department (APD), headed by Dick Meier. In 1983, APD developed a refrigerator to cool the superconducting magnets used in MRI (Magnetic Resonance Imaging) medical diagnostics. MRI technology generates images of body organs and is able to accomplish multiple-depth "slices," without the potential hazard of ionizing radiation. Through 1985, as APD was entering the market, about 250 MRI systems were installed worldwide, offering a major market for liquid helium.

Nat Robertson had left in place the decentralized structure and the applied orientation of R&D at Air Products. His efforts to deepen the culture of basic research were unsuccessful. He stepped aside in 1976, taking the position of Senior Vice President. Ed Donley took the opportunity to hire another research director from outside the company. The new Vice President for Research was Bob (Robert) Lovett from Exxon. Lovett took a new tack, bringing together various support services into a central research department under Clyde McKinley. The new research department maintained a library, conducted analytical and thermodynamic work, undertook research for departments that lacked their own facilities, and supplemented the research carried out in other departments. Thus, for example, the corporate laboratories carried out chemical and specialty gas research.

The existence of a central research facility meant that different departments could share expensive instruments. Thus management could justify and fully utilize state-of-the-art analytical equipment and techniques. By the 1980s, there was a great emphasis on analytical work. That emphasis reflected the important role of specialty gases, as well as the company's ongoing commitment to safety. Development work on specialty gases implied analyzing concentrations in parts per million. Impurities like methane required especially close attention, because they could freeze out in the process plant and plug up the equipment, or cause explosions.[25]

Bob Lovett faced the same challenges that Robertson had in instilling a tradition of basic research at Air Products. Donley and his colleagues knew that they were in danger of missing the boat as a technological revolution, even more basic than the emergence of tonnage oxygen generation over three decades earlier, ran through the industrial gas business at the close of the seventies. Industry leaders Air Liquide, British Oxygen, and Linde were developing vacuum-swing adsorption (VSA), pressure-swing adsorption (PSA), and membrane technologies, all non-cryogenic means for separating gases.

These technologies used small units, like the generators Air Products had made in the forties, to produce small quantities of nitrogen, oxygen, and hydrogen more cheaply than traditional air separation plants. PSA plants, for instance, generated less than forty tons per day. These new technologies represented a challenge to the merchant market, although they had their drawbacks. The gases produced were only 99 percent pure, in contrast to the 99.999 percent pure cryogenically generated gases. The new systems could not furnish gases at several different purities or in varying volumes. However, they were suitable for up to 30 percent of merchant gas customers, and annual sales, it was believed, might exceed $1 billion by the mid-nineties.[26]

In order to remain competitive, Air Products *had* to get into the non-cryogenic gas processing field rapidly, and that meant revitalizing research. In 1980, Bob Lovett persuaded Ed Donley to create the Corporate Science Center, charged with conducting fundamental exploratory research crucial to the long-range development of the business. Air Products was by now highly active in seeking closer links with university research. Air Products and Lehigh University cosponsored the second annual meeting of the Council for Chemical Research, a new organization itself committed to drawing the universities and the chemical process industries closer together. Links like these helped in the drive to staff the Center with Ph.D.s in the various sciences. Several areas of research were identified as decisive for the company's future growth. These included catalysis, gas and fluid separations, polymer science, cryogenics, biotechnology, and organic synthesis. Like many other corporations at the start of the eighties, especially those in chemicals, Air Products would bet on its ability to institutionalize the innovative process. The hope was that in-house research would generate both radical and incremental innovations, through which to create whole new product areas and to enhance existing product lines.

Air Products' chief scientist, Jim Roth, was named head of the Center.[27] In 1981, the company brought in a new Vice President of Research, Brian Rushton,[28] when Bob Lovett moved to run Air Products Europe. That same year, management created an Innovation Steering Committee to ensure the development of non-cryogenic processes and other areas vital to the firm's long-range growth. The company was committed to creating a research culture within the corporate walls.

As a result of the creation of the Corporate Science Center and the firm's heroic efforts to catch up, Air Products was able to market internally developed, non-cryogenic gas generators in 1983. Two years later, Air Products had five on-site nitrogen VSA plants in operation. Air Products introduced other non-cryogenic plants for generating oxygen; for separating hydrogen, carbon dioxide, and methane; and for purifying methane.

Air Products was establishing a foothold just in time. Other U.S. and foreign industrial gas companies were entering into partnerships with chemical firms which had developed their own non-cryogenic gas processes. Early in 1988, Air Liquide, the largest industrial gas company in the world, and Du Pont, the recognized leader in membrane technology, announced the formation of a joint venture to develop and exploit membrane separation technology in the United States.[29] Air Products responded later that year by forming a joint research program with Akzo, NV, to develop and commercialize membrane technology for air separation. Akzo was the world's largest manufacturer of hollow-fiber membranes and contributed both its substantial knowledge of polymeric membrane technology and its manufacturing capability.[30] Although it had a late start, Air Products was now a contender, thanks to its recommitment to research.

The Venture into Synfuels

In addition to bolstering its industrial gas position through research in non-cryogenic technologies, Air Products management was on the lookout for investment opportunities related to its core businesses in industrial gases and chemicals. The result was a major move into synfuels. Synfuels promised to be a replay of the tonnage liquid hydrogen scenario of the fifties, in which Air Products had parlayed government research contracts into a leadership position in a new market. Things did not work out as hoped. However, because of the expansion of its engineering activities, initially associated with the move into synfuels, Air Products did gain a nucleus around which to build a third leg for future growth in energy and environmental markets.

In response to the OPEC embargo, which had the country waiting in long lines at the gas station, the federal government became deeply involved in efforts to create gaseous and liquid fuels from coal. In 1980 Congress earmarked $88 billion for a program to produce two million barrels a day of petroleum equivalents by 1992.[31] Like the great majority of informed observers at the time, Ed Donley believed that synthetic hydrocarbon fuels would form a new industry with sales of billions of dollars. Indeed, Air Liquide, Lotepro (the U.S. subsidiary of Lindes Eismachinen), and Linde were also seeking orders for air separation plants for synfuels projects.[32]

Donley saw synfuels as a new investment area and an opportunity to repeat the company's success story of applying process engineering expertise. It was a long time since federally funded R&D had furnished Air Products with the expertise and technology needed to enter a market. Donley believed synfuels to offer such an opportunity, and he wanted a partnership between the company and the government to play its familiar role.[33]

Getting into synfuels required air separation plants of unprecedented size, and a knowledge of coal processing technology. Although plants producing 1,000 tons or more per day of oxygen had been built in the seventies, the new synfuels plants were expected to have far greater requirements. Consequently, the effort required a major commitment of Air Products' engineering resources. Research on solvent refining of coal and other energy-related subjects was supported by federal contracts, but it drained the company's attention away from other opportunities.

Catalytic had long ago gained important know-how in the area of coal-based technologies. Donley had tried unsuccessfully to convince Dick Klopp, Catalytic's President, to use his company as a window on investment opportunities for Air Products. Now, however, it appeared that Catalytic would open up opportunities in the nascent synfuels and energy-related industries. With private and public funding, Catalytic was already undertaking research that helped it learn the emerging technologies of synfuels. For instance, Catalytic found private-sector research money with which to investigate a coal gasification process as early as 1972. If commercialized, the technology would use large amounts of oxygen, entailing the need for many large generators. Catalytic and Air Products also licensed innovations from Japan and cooperated with the British Gas Council in developing a process for making methane and other chemicals from high-sulfur gas and oil. A federal contract followed for a demonstration plant to produce high-BTU methane gas, aromatics, and liquefied petroleum gas from high-sulfur gas and oil in the United States.

Further, Air Products had a Department of Energy contract to study the production of synthetic natural gas from coal. Another government R&D contract was for a study of markets and supply systems for chemical feedstocks made from gasified coal. The coal gasification work led to a contract to supply an oxygen generator for one of the country's first advanced-technology coal gasification systems.[34] Increasing the nation's use of coal meant that greater amounts of noxious sulfur compounds would be released to the air, since American coals generally have high sulfur contents. To deal with this problem, Catalytic carried out contract R&D work on flue-gas desulfurization and after testing in a pilot plant, Catalytic sought access to the technology through a licensing agreement.

Catalytic also acquired a position in the central technology of the energy crisis, the solvent refining of coal (SRC). The idea of SRC was to remove the sulfur from coal before it burned.[35] In 1972, Catalytic completed the design and construction of the Wilsonville, Alabama, SRC pilot plant, the first industry-sponsored SRC demonstration unit in the United States. The plant converted high-sulfur coal into a high-BTU solid fuel containing less than 0.8 percent sulfur and less than .15 percent ash. This plant marked Air Products' first introduction to synthetic fuels. After a twelve-month testing period that demonstrated the feasibility of the process, Catalytic undertook optimization studies to reduce pollutant levels even more and began designing a 900-ton-per-day prototype plant.

Air Products took the Catalytic SRC process to the next step, the design and construction of a demonstration plant to convert 6,000 tons of coal per day into 20,000 barrels of a clean-burning, synthetic crude oil, by 1985. That plant, however, would be far larger than anything the company had ever built. In 1978, through the efforts of Andy Mellen and Jack Pryor in the Process Systems Group (PSG), Air Products created a joint venture, called the International Coal Refining Company (ICRC), with Wheelabrator-Frye, Inc. Wheelabrator-Frye brought to the project important experience and technology in a variety of energy-related and environmental areas as well as necessary engineering-construction talent and resources.[36]

Air Products saw the ICRC joint venture as an extension of its on-site operations. The company wanted to make and sell both synthetic fuels and the industrial gases necessary to make these fuels. In contrast, Linde was content with the more modest idea of providing process technology for synfuels to other contractors, while supplying the air separation plants itself. An article in *Chemical Week* stated that Air Products' synthetic fuels program "could be either strategically brilliant or the greatest corporate risk they've ever taken, because the bucks are enormous."[37]

The ICRC venture demanded immense capital investments. Air Products and Wheelabrator-Frye intended to expand their initial SRC unit into a 100,000-barrel-a-day complex by 1990 at a cost of $4 to $5 billion. Air Products committed some of its best people to the venture, including Jack Pryor, Walt Rector, Wes Timmcke, Rudy Kroc, Stan Morris and Bob Fleming. John Paul Jones, who later would play a vital role in developing Air Products' energy and environmental business, transferred from PSG to head ICRC planning.[38] The whole venture was managed by PSG, headed by Andy Mellen. PSG would play an important role in the unfolding adventure in the years ahead. The joint venture proceeded rapidly with work on the Kentucky demonstration plant, with financial backing from the U.S. and Kentucky departments of energy.[39]

At the same time that Air Products was vigorously entering the new federally sponsored synfuels industry, Donley was serving on the Business Higher Education Forum. A Forum task force studied the country's synfuels needs. Its report showed that, based on congressional authorizations, and given the rule of thumb that 8 to 10 percent of plant costs are salary costs of engineers, the country had only half the engineers it needed to undertake the synfuels program alone! The report and the company's plans for synfuels gave

Donley good cause to be concerned about Air Products' ability to find the talented engineers it would need.

To avert this threatening manpower shortage and to secure the corporation's position in synfuels, Donley began to look for a promising candidate for merger or acquisition. He learned that he might be able to buy Stearns-Roger World Corporation. Stearns-Roger was a Denver-based, employee-owned engineering firm active in mining (ore processing), electric utilities, and the petroleum industry. It had one of the best safety records in the construction industry, and in 1981 had sales of about $1.5 billion. On May 21, 1982, Air Products bought Stearns-Roger World Corporation and its subsidiaries for $210 million in cash.

Stearns-Roger and Catalytic had combined billings that ranked them among the top ten engineering contractors in the nation in 1981. Their activities were geographically complementary, with Catalytic essentially east of the Mississippi and Stearns-Roger to the west. The two organizations were merged to form the firm's new Engineering Services Group. Andy Mellen left PSG, where he was replaced by Bill Scharle, to run the new group.

Mellen soon discovered that Stearns-Roger had good engineers but little new work. Its mining business was lackluster. In the construction of power stations, a third of Stearns-Roger's business, it was losing bids. Another third of its trade was in petroleum and natural gas processing. The drop in crude oil prices in 1982 and the associated glut of natural gas quickly soured that market.[40] In short, what Andy Mellen faced was a crisis situation. The only bright note was Stearns-Roger's work for Arco on the Kuparuk crude oil recovery project (the Alaska Pipeline), which lasted through 1985. Kuparuk was the largest single project that Stearns-Roger had ever undertaken, and it put Engineering Services at the forefront of modular engineering and construction.

In addition to the recession of 1982–1983, other serious problems were becoming evident. Political support for synfuels weakened in 1983 as the Reagan administration increasingly turned away from what it perceived as a characteristic liberal program. Congressional appropriations were slashed.[41] Retrenchment became the order of the day, and the engineering construction business entered a long recession.

Andy Mellen undertook a number of urgent reforms. He introduced computerized systems to help the company hold its leadership position in contract maintenance. He tried to improve profits by reducing overheads. He cut employment, and pushed his marketing efforts into such high-growth industries as electronics. Design and engineering contracts were won in the microelectronics industry from manufacturers such as IBM and AT&T. Mellen upgraded the group's skills in order to offer a fuller capability in construction, and he explored ways to create greater synergies between Engineering Services and the other groups in Air Products. These moves were intended to reduce the break-even point and allow the new group to operate profitably in a less than favorable business environment. Even so, crisis loomed.

Before taking his new assignment, Mellen had been asked by Donley to keep an eye out for new investment opportunities. Now, however, events were forcing him to become an entrepreneur and create those opportunities himself. The highest priority was to revitalize the Stearns organization by creating work for it. Catalytic itself remained profitable at this time, at least partially because of its contract maintenance work. As part of the overall strategy, the Engineering Services Group was reorganized as Stearns-Catalytic World Corporation in early 1984.

Mellen pressed the establishment of cogeneration and waste-to-energy projects, which would later, with flue-gas desulfurization, form the core of Air Products' environmental and energy businesses. PSG had already built gas-fired cogeneration systems for some of its industrial gas and chemical plants. Now Air Products would sell coal-fired cogeneration plants to the public. PSG and Stearns-Catalytic did the selling together. The effort succeeded with a contract to build a cogeneration plant in Stockton, California. The plant was to supply steam and electricity to an industrial customer, CPC International, and excess electricity to a utility, Pacific Gas and Electric. The project combined Stearns-Catalytic's design and construction experience with PSG's operating and project management skills.

As head of PSG in the seventies, Mellen had looked at the emerging market for waste-to-energy facilities as an opportunity for on-site projects, but had dropped it from consideration because of the very considerable. engineering tasks involved. The facilities were too large for Air Products' human resources at that time. Now, with the acquisition of Stearns-Roger, that was no longer true.

Wheelabrator-Frye, Air Products' partner in the ICRC joint venture, had a license for a Swiss waste-to-energy process.[42] Mellen and Jones were convinced that this was an excellent new field for PSG, so they began negotiations for a joint venture based on the Swiss license. Gradually, the focus shifted away from the original topic as the two companies became excited about alternative waste-to-energy technologies. Though the negotiations were never concluded, Mellen remained committed to realizing his dream. In 1984, he succeeded, and Air Products formed a joint venture with Browning-Ferris Industries, Inc., called American Ref-Fuel. The joint venture used the proprietary technology of Deutsche Babcock Anlagen. This "roller grate system" technology had already been incorporated in more than fifty waste-to-energy facilities around the world. American Ref-Fuel's aim was to design and build trash-fueled electric power plants.

Despite these innovative undertakings, Mellen was fighting a losing battle. Stearns logged major operating losses as sales fell from $88 million in 1983 to $59 million in 1984. Sales revived modestly the next year, but in 1986, sales fell again, reaching $41 million. The subsidiary lost $4 million.

Accomplishments and Prospects

Ed Donley was due to retire in 1986. He knew that the vitality of the company in such areas as gases, chemicals, and environmental and energy systems was masked by the sharply deteriorating performance of Stearns-Catalytic. The venture into synfuels had been short-lived, but hardly unrewarding. The intention had been, in Donley's words, to create a "replica of what we had done on a much smaller scale, with the gas business twenty years earlier. I thought that those technologies would become commercialized, and we'd have a major position in this new industry."[43]

But the attempt to replay the strategy of learning a new area of technology through federally financed R&D contracts was not working out. "What I didn't realize was the way the situation was going to change. Oil was to become at least temporarily available in large quantities and the whole thing was going to collapse." Rather than being a replay of the military-funded hydrogen work of the late 1950s, synfuels turned out to be more akin to the Helium Conservation Program. Congress launched the enterprise but, when conditions changed, the government phased out the program.

While the termination of the synfuels program by Congress was something the company could survive, its losses from Stearns were more troubling. Reluctantly, Ed Donley decided to bite the bullet. Once launched on necessary house cleaning, he acted with vigor. Stearns-Catalytic was sold to United Engineers and Constructors, a subsidiary of Raytheon. Various other items of housekeeping were attended to. Air Products sold off its South African affiliate in response to political pressure for divestiture, even though the subsidiary was financially profitable. The firm also restructured several small product lines in the chemicals and equipment businesses; and revalued certain assets. The result was a company shorn of some major problem areas, but also a company with its first dramatic slump in profits for almost three decades: the 1985 profit figure of $143 million was replaced by one of $5 million in 1986.

As Donley put it, "The day I retired, we had the balance sheet cleaned up with all the bad news all behind us. The new management had a clean slate with no residue from the past era." Perhaps if the whole episode had come earlier in Donley's career, Lee Holt reflected, "he could probably have sweated it out. He's oriented that way."[44] Even so, the corporate strategy of increasing dividends to please institutional and other investors demanded that losing ventures be wiped from the books as quickly, and as profitably, as possible.

The synfuels and Stearns experiences had their positive side. The company had recruited and trained many engineers who moved to other branches of the firm. It was, Donley observed, an example of "government-funded human resources development." The new ventures started with Stearns-Catalytic, moreover, brought Air Products into entirely new technological and market areas. They were the kind of investment opportunities Donley had been looking for. They would soon form a third leg of company business, in the area of the environment and energy.

When Ed Donley turned over leadership of Air Products to Dex Baker, he could take pride in what had been accomplished. Like many other American chief executives, he had taken an entrepreneurial risk in response to the renewed energy crisis. When the gamble failed, he acted quickly. By stopping the losses, he enabled the company to focus its attention on its profitable and growing lines of business.

In 1986, the company was more coherently organized and more professionally managed than it had ever been under its founder. Sales were pushed from $1 billion to nearly $2 billion between 1978 and 1986. Profits had increased more slowly, giving cause for concern. But Air Products was a thriving enterprise with significant strength and technical ability in a number of important fields. Its core businesses—industrial gases and chemicals—were in good shape. Entrepreneurship, sales, and engineering remained central to the company's success. And the firm was launched into experiments in a number of wholly new areas, characterized by their high risk and their potential for high growth.

Notes

1. Lee Holt interview, 11 August 1988, APHO.

2. John Mountain received a B.S. from Temple in accounting in 1956 and an M.B.A. from Southern Methodist University in 1964. Prior to joining Air Products in 1965 he worked for LTV, Thiokol Chemical, and Arthur Young & Company.

3. Ronald Barclay received a B.S. degree in business administration from the University of Pittsburgh in 1956 and an M.B.A. from Lehigh University in 1965. He joined Air Products in 1956 as a market planning assistant.

4. Donley interview, 29 January 1988.

5. *Annual Report 1982*, p. 14. William Kendrick has a degree in business administration from Boston College and a law degree from the New England School of Law. He joined Air Products in 1977 as Director of Federal Relations.

6. William Scharle interview, 30 March 1988, APHO.

7. Standard and Poor's Industry Surveys, *Chemicals*, 24 October 1985, Sec. 1, pp. C 22–23; "The World's Biggest Oxygen Producers Battle for Synfuels Business," *Chemical Week* 127 (September 3, 1980): 24.

8. Standard and Poor's Industry Surveys, *Chemicals*, 24 October 1985, Sec. 1, p. C 23.

9. Standard and Poor's Industry Surveys, *Chemicals*, 24 October 1985, Sec. 1, p. C 23.

10. Michelle Louzoun, "Air Products Turns to Computers and the Chemistry's Just Right," *Information Week* (December 22–29, 1986): 28–30; Peter Mather earned an M.B.A. from Lehigh University in 1977. He joined Air Products in 1967.

11. "Money from Nothing," *The Economist* 308 (September 10, 1988): 88; Standard and Poor's Industry Surveys, *Chemicals*, 30 August 1979, Sec. 2, pp. C 18–19 and 24 October 1985, Sec. 1, p. C 23.

12. Standard and Poor's Industry Surveys, *Chemicals*, 30 August 1979, Sec. 2, p. C 19, and 5 November 1981, Sec. 2, p. C 17, and 21 June 1984, Sec. 2, p. C 23.

13. Merrill Lynch, "L'Air Liquide," 1988, p. 6, APHO; Standard and Poor's Industry Surveys, *Chemicals*, 3 July 1980, Sec. 3, p. C 6, and 4 September 1975, Sec. 2, p. C 16.

14. Paul Lovett and Richard C. Wardell, Strategic Planning, "The Impact of Pipelines on APCI's Oxygen and Nitrogen Business," 19 May 1981, APHO.

15. "Money from Nothing," p. 88; *Annual Report 1983*, p. 8.

16. "The World's Biggest Oxygen Producers Battle for Synfuels Business," p. 28.

17. Alfred Bull received his Diplom-Chemiker in 1959 from the Berlin Technical University and his doctorate in 1961 from the Technical University of Aachen. He joined Air Products in 1967 as District Manager of Ruhr, Germany.

18. Equivalent to about 144 tons per day.

19. *British Oxygen Company Report and Accounts*, 1971–1980; Edward Russell-Walling, "Strong-Man Clears the Air at BOC," *Financial Weekly* (February 19, 1987): 37. For a history of BOC, see The BOC Group, *Around the Group in 100 Years* (London: BOC, 1986).

20. Merrill Lynch, "L'Air Liquide," 1988, p. 6; *Moody's Industrial Manual*, 1980, vol. 1, p. 1; "The World's Biggest Oxygen Producers Battle for Synfuels Business," p. 26.

21. Frank Ryan, "Chemicals in Air Products' Portfolio," pp. 32–33, in Air Products, *Financial Conference* (Trexlertown, Air Products, 1982).

22. Frank Ryan interview, 25 August 1989, APHO.

23. Howard Harwell received a B.S. in chemical engineering from Yale University. He joined Air Products in 1969. Donald Orr received a B.S. in chemical engineering and an M.S. in industrial administration from Purdue University. He joined Air Products in 1965, and was named Vice President of the Industrial Chemicals Division in 1983.

24. *Annual Report 1982*, pp. 2, 13.

25. Clyde McKinley interview, 10 March 1988, APHO. Robert Lovett had a Ph.D. in chemistry from the University of Delaware.

26. "Money from Nothing," p. 88.

27. "The Science Center: Where the Product is Technology," *Today* (June 1985): 4–5.

28. Brian Rushton received an associateship in the Royal Institute of Chemistry (A.R.I.C.) in 1957 from the University of Salford, England, and an M.S. from the University of Minnesota in 1959. He earned a Ph.D. in physical organic chemistry from the University of Leicester, England, in 1963.

29. Merrill Lynch, pp. 5–6.

30. "Money from Nothing," p. 88.

31. Ernest J. Yanarella and William C. Green, *The Unfulfilled Promise of Synthetic Fuels* (Westport, Conn.: Greenwood Press, 1987), pp. 22–23.

32. "The World's Biggest Oxygen Producers Battle for Synfuels Business," pp. 23, 25; Edward Donley interview, 29 January 1988, APHO.

33. Edward Donley interview, 29 January 1988.

34. *Annual Report 1978*, pp. 11–12.

35. "The World's Biggest Oxygen Producers Battle for Synfuels Business," p. 24.

36. *Moody's Industrial Manual*, 1980, vol. 2, p. 4332.

37. "The World's Biggest Oxygen Producers Battle for Synfuels Business," p. 24.

38. John Paul Jones joined Air Products in 1972 and was a CDP. He has a B.S. in chemical engineering from Villanova.

39. "The World's Biggest Oxygen Producers Battle for Synfuels Business," pp. 23–24.

40. "Plunging Oil Prices Tarnish a 1982 Investment," *Chemical Week* 138 (May 14, 1986): 5.

41. Yanarella and Green, pp. 23–24.

42. *Moody's Industrial Manual*, 1980, vol. 2, p. 4333.

43. Donley interview, 29 January 1988, APHO.

44. Lee Holt interview, 11 August 1988, APHO.

10

Planning for Growth

When Dexter Baker became CEO in December, 1986, he developed an ambitious plan for growth. There were solid grounds to be optimistic. America, and American industry, were in a phase of renewed confidence and prosperity. The problems spawned by the Vietnam War were receding into memory. The energy crisis and double-digit inflation had disappeared. The global marketplace for goods and services, and for companies, was becoming faster paced. Corporations attuned to innovation and entrepreneurship could expect to grow. *Forbes* and *Business Week* extolled Air Products' stock as a good investment, and there were indications that the German chemical firms Bayer and Höchst were interested in buying the company.[1]

After wide consultations with his colleagues, Dex Baker published a ten-year plan for Corporate Growth. The plan announced that Air Products aimed to triple in size, from $2 billion to $6 billion in sales by 1996. The keystones of growth would be low-cost production, technological innovation, vigorous marketing and salesmanship, a program of acquisitions, and a continuing push toward globalization of the firm's business. Crucial to all would be the strengths residing in the corporation's people and in its well-grounded culture of entrepreneurship, engineering, and sales. In Baker's view, one of his most important functions was to nourish that culture. He had always been oriented to human as well as to technical resources. While he had an engineering background, he had long emphasized the sales side of the company's values. According to Ed Donley, who had originally

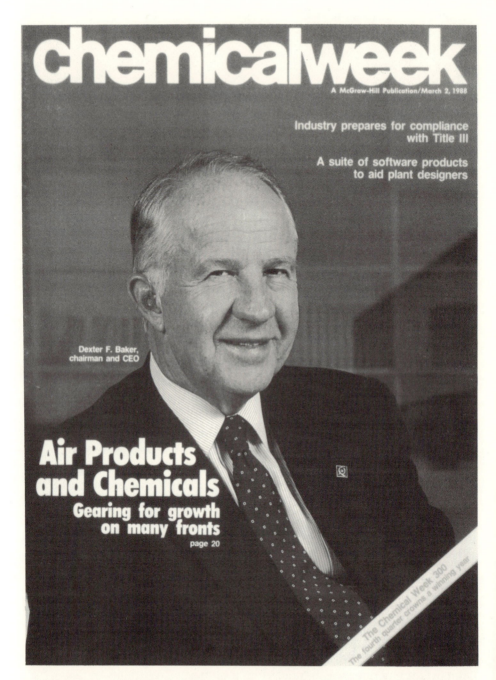

On December 1, 1986, Dexter Baker became Air Products' third CEO. Baker has made corporate values the essential underpinning of a bold ten-year growth plan through a strategy of getting closer to the customer. (Reproduced by kind permission of Chemical Week Associates.)

hired him, "Dexter probably turned his mind a little more to sales than I did."[2]

When Baker assessed the company's position, he was pleasantly surprised by the strengths of its traditional markets. The industrial gas and chemicals businesses were growing faster than expected. Together with his management team, he decided to refocus investment on these two core businesses and on a third, newly defined area of opportunity in the environmental and energy markets. In due course, Air Products sold off its joint venture in industrial biotechnology, Apcel, Limited, and later its small venture in advanced ceramics.[3]

Sales objectives were central to the plan for growth. One essential aim was to get closer to the firm's customers. Although technology and finance would remain important, Baker intended to push Air Products ahead by building on the already considerable skills base of the company's employees. That meant devoting still greater attention to human resources and to nurturing the people who would deliver the innovations, the low-cost production, the customer service, and the entrepreneurial drive needed to propel Air Products along the path he was charting.

Gases Around the Globe

The gas business (centered in the Industrial Gas Division and the Process Systems Group) was doing better than ever. Industry-wide shipments in the United States had grown at a rate about twice that of GNP in the seventies and early eighties; now they were increasing at three times GNP, and GNP itself was growing steadily.[4] Air Products was determined to reap its full share of the opportunities. In addition to its leadership position in liquid hydrogen and liquid helium, the firm had become the leading U.S. supplier of nitrogen. It had for some time now been the second largest producer of industrial gases in the United States after Linde, a position achieved through the development of fresh applications for industrial gases and through many years of aggressive salesmanship and forceful exploitation of its low-cost production.

In the late eighties, the Industrial Gas Division (IGD) was headed in turn by Vice Presidents Pat Dyer, Lanny Patten, and Stan Roman, and the Process Systems Group by Bill Scharle, followed by Bob Gadomski. Nitrogen and hydrogen were the mainstays of the business, with oxygen, argon, helium, and specialty gases contributing

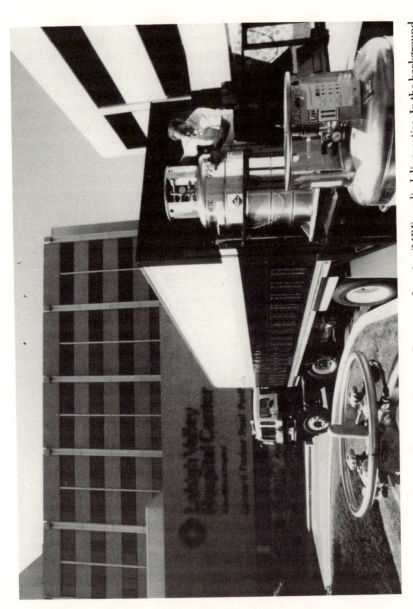

A shipment of liquid helium for use in Magnetic Resonance Imaging (MRI) medical diagnostics. In the background is the Leonard Parker Pool Pavilion of the Lehigh Valley Hospital Center.

important but smaller percentages of sales. Nitrogen sales were sustained by growing demand in the electronics and food industries. In addition to California's Silicon Valley, where Air Products was the leading supplier of industrial gases, the company was providing substantial amounts of gas to the new semiconductor manufacturing center emerging in Arizona's "Silicon Desert" near Phoenix, where the company tripled the capacity of its Chandler plant.[5]

Although sales of liquid hydrogen to NASA dropped sharply after the *Challenger* explosion in 1986, the subsequent decision to continue the shuttle program brought with it an extension of Air Products' supply contract. In recognition of the superior performance of the firm's liquid hydrogen sales, operations, and distribution teams, NASA gave commendations to employees in Chuck Anderson's Government Systems Department and to the managers of the firm's liquid hydrogen facility located outside of New Orleans. Other federal programs, including the Strategic Defense Initiative, the Superconducting Super Collider, and the National Aerospace Plane, promised to increase demand for extremely low temperature "slush" hydrogen, and for liquid helium.[6]

The fastest-growing demand for liquid helium was in the private sector, in magnetic resonance imaging (MRI). IGD helium business, managed by George Diehl, developed a novel service out of its close relationship with the leader in MRI equipment, General Electric, and quickly extended it to Siemens, the second largest supplier. General Electric and Siemens customers were serviced by Air Products technicians, who delivered helium and nitrogen for MRI systems at the point of consumption. In 1988, to support its growing position in the MRI market, Air Products completed helium transfill facilities in New Jersey and on the West Coast, and in 1989, Lee Gaumer and Nirmal Chatterjee in PSG led the retrofit of the National Helium plant in Liberal, Kansas, which substantially reduced operating costs of the facility from which Air Products intended to derive most of its crude helium in the future.[7] A helium liquefier was also brought onstream at Bracknell, England, and the largest liquefier in Europe started operation at the Vilvoorde, Belgium, plant of Air Products' Gardner Cryogenics subsidiary, making the company the Continent's most reliable supplier of gaseous and liquid helium.[8]

Air Products' Airopak business was also flourishing, both at home and overseas. The Airopak process used fluorine and nitrogen blends to treat blow-molded plastic containers. European expansion of Airopak was especially remarkable. The business grew with the opening of plants in Monzon, Spain, and in St. Etienne, France, with the addition of blow-molding machines at the Crewe facility in England, and with the purchase of a one-third interest in the SEP Group, a blow-molder in Belgium and the Netherlands.[9] As early as 1987 APL, the British subsidiary of Air Products Europe, produced its five-millionth treated container, and in 1988 it received the Queen's Award for Technical Achievement.

Sales of equipment by the Process Systems Group (PSG) also provided fresh opportunities. The group demonstrated the roles that research and acquisition would play in Air Products' strategy for growth. PSG shipped its patented liquefied natural gas heat exchangers to Indonesia and Australia.[10] Its Gardner subsidiary had a record year in 1989, introducing patented improvements in storing cryogenic liquids. Advanced Separations (a PSG department established in 1987)[11] acquired a number of non-cryogenic technologies, including the Separex membrane gas separation system, and organized a team of field specialists to facilitate their sale. In 1989, Air Products introduced a new generation of pressure-swing adsorption units under the trade name Spectrum.[12]

A key aspect of Baker's plan for growth was the further globalization of the firm's business. Overseas gas markets, in fact, held even greater promise than the United States. By 1990, worldwide demand for industrial gases approached $16 billion. In almost every corner of this huge market, Air Products faced tough competitors. Leading the field were Air Liquide and the British Oxygen Company. Air Products was number four in the world, just behind its main American rival, the Linde Division of Union Carbide.[13] The struggle for market share was particularly sharp in Europe, where the industry giants had once respected each other's domains. Companies tried to position themselves to take advantage of the growth anticipated following European economic consolidation. AGA and Air Liquide dissolved their fifteen-year partnership; Air Liquide invaded West Germany; AGA bought a French and a Norwegian firm; and the British Oxygen Company won its first contract on the Continent. That contract was for the supply of nitrogen and oxygen to Dow Chemical's complex in Terneuzen, Holland, right in Air Products' backyard.[14]

To handle these fresh challenges, Dex Baker made extensive personnel changes in Europe. In 1987, Chris Ryan became the Managing Director of APL. In 1988, when Bob Lovett returned to the States to become Vice President of the Chemicals Group, Hap Wagner, a twenty-five-year Air Products veteran, became the President of Air

Products Europe. With the Single European Market set for 1992, Baker put Al Bull in charge of a special committee to prepare for altered economic conditions. To speed up the flow of information between Trexlertown and Europe, in 1987, Corporate Telecommunications (itself a new function) installed a satellite link for voice and data transmission.

APL, which observed its thirtieth anniversary in 1987, was setting records in gas and equipment sales. In 1988, Digital Equipment Corporation awarded APL contracts for the supply of equipment and gases to its silicon chip manufacturing facility near Edinburgh, and in 1989, APL was awarded a contract for high-purity methane for five nuclear power stations. The on-site business placed on-stream an air separation plant near Hull, England, which required the largest single investment ever made by Air Products in the United Kingdom.

APL's sales performance overseas was equally exemplary, winning the Queen's Award for Export Achievement in 1989 for the fifth time.[15] Among the most notable projects was the shipment in 1987 of the longest distillation tower APL had ever made to the Nippon Steel Corporation of Japan.[16] In 1989, the subsidiary was chosen to supply the world's largest nitrogen generation and compression facilities for the North Sea operations of Phillips Petroleum. APL was also manufacturing large-scale non-cryogenic equipment, developed in the United States, for the European market. Its first vacuum-swing adsorption oxygen unit was brought on-stream at an Austrian paper mill in 1987, and the next year APL began building the world's largest-capacity membrane unit for hydrogen purification, at Esso Petroleum's Fawley refinery.

Air Products Europe's own operations were equally buoyant, with the winning of important contracts and geographic expansion. In 1987, a sixty-ton-per-day plant was sold to supply oxygen and nitrogen for the Ariane rocket operations of the European Space Agency,[17] and in 1989, after several years of negotiations, the European Transonic Windtunnel consortium awarded a contract for design and engineering services. In France, the 65 percent interest acquired in Oxygène Liquide greatly strengthened the competitive position of Air Products, and complemented the operations of Prodair, the company's French subsidiary, managed by Alain Régent. The German Air Products subsidiary, under Stefan Schaefer, built a new merchant plant at Hattingen, entered into a joint venture with the Tyczka industrial gas company, and purchased a number of small industrial gas companies.[18] The Belgian subsidiary supplied equipment for the Giotto satellite which studied Halley's Comet, and in the Netherlands, Air Products Europe expanded its hydrogen and carbon monoxide facility and built Europe's first large-scale liquid hydrogen unit near Rotterdam.

The transnational approach of Air Products Europe was typified by its construction of a large-scale air separation plant in Strasbourg in 1988, near the headquarters of Oxygène Liquide. The plant, which was built in partnership with a German industrial gas producer, supplied liquid products for merchant customers in France and Germany, as well as piping gaseous oxygen across the Rhine River to a German steel mill.

Air Products Europe was also busy expanding into Austria, Portugal, and Italy. Operations in Austria began with the establishment of a hydrogen purification and distribution facility. The move into Portugal was part of a wider expansion by Air Products' Spanish affiliate, the Sociedad Española de Carburos Metálicos, which acquired a Portuguese producer as well as two Spanish companies, and started up liquid plants near Valencia and Seville. Air Products also opened an industrial gas sales office in Milan, as it sought opportunities to establish a position in Italy.

These various developments, aggressively pursued, made Air Products into Europe's third largest supplier of industrial gases by 1990. Substantial growth took place outside Europe. In Canada, the acquisition of Inter-City Gas of Calgary and other independents expanded Air Products' base, while Evan Mongelard led the effort that resulted in Air Products' winning a multi-million-dollar contract to supply Alcan with all its industrial gas requirements. The company also continued to sell gases in Mexico, Puerto Rico, and Brazil, while mounting a special effort to increase its role in the most rapidly growing industrial gas market in the world: the Pacific Rim.

Pat Dyer and Joe Kaminski had earlier overcome considerable initial skepticism in Trexlertown, as they began to develop joint ventures on the Pacific Rim.[19] Joint ventures had not traditionally been a strong suit for Air Products. But they were a necessary way of doing business if the company was to challenge the entrenched positions of British Oxygen and Air Liquide in many Far Eastern markets. Korea had provided one early success, as the joint venture with the Lee family became South Korea's largest supplier of industrial gases. Also successful was the Thai joint venture, Bangkok Industrial Gas Company, incorporated in 1986, which involved the Bangkok Steel Industry Company and four other investors.

Thailand was followed by Malaysia in 1988, when Joe Kaminski moved Air Products into acquiring a 30 percent interest in Super Oxygen, the country's second largest industrial gas supplier. The most striking undertakings in the Pacific Rim, however, were those in China and Japan. With the opening of China to Western capital, Air Products entered into a joint venture with Chun Wang Industrial Gases in 1986. The agreement marked the first investment in the People's Republic by a major Western industrial gas company. In 1988, Air Products commissioned a facility at Shekou to generate high-purity nitrogen and hydrogen, as well as oxygen plants for steel works in Shanghai and in Liaoning Province.[20] The company accelerated its efforts to penetrate Japan, also buying a stake in a second large Japanese company, Daido Sanso, of Osaka.

By 1990, Air Products was thus firmly established as a supplier of industrial gases and equipment on a global basis. This first leg of Air Products' business—the area in which Leonard Pool had launched his enterprise in 1940—provided over $1.6 billion in sales and $300 million in profits in fiscal 1989. Making those profits "out of thin air" was a far larger and more varied enterprise than it had been half a century earlier. Upstart Air Products was no longer the late entrant, but a central player in what was now a global marketplace. Remarkably, the company had succeeded in developing those economies of scope and scale, and that depth of management and marketing talent, which together distinguish an industry's leading firms from their less fortunate competitors.

Chemicals

Growth opportunities in the Chemicals Group also looked promising throughout the late eighties. In fiscal 1989, sales rose to a record high of almost $1 billion.

When Baker promoted Frank Ryan to President of Air Products in 1988, Bob Lovett replaced him as Vice President of the Chemicals Group, assisted within the Group by Don Orr as Vice President, Business Divisions. One central task of Ryan, Lovett, and Orr was to strengthen international activities. Reflecting the fact that Air Products did not become Air Products *and* Chemicals until 1961, the Chemicals Group had much work still to do if it was to emulate the success of the industrial gas operations on a global scale. Not only was chemicals a smaller, newer, second leg of the company's business, but the whole field of chemicals was very much bigger, more complex, and more variegated than that of industrial gases. Furthermore, that field was full of large, long-established multinational companies.

In the sixties and seventies, with the exception of ventures undertaken by Houdry, the chemicals activities of Air Products were almost entirely confined to the domestic market. For many years the firm relied on agents and distributors, as it slowly began to develop its business in Europe. Victor Bonanni was put in charge of the European effort, and by 1989, export chemical sales from the United States reached a record $110 million. At the start of 1988, Air Products finally established its first overseas manufacturing facility, when an acquisition team headed by Leo Daley acquired the Anchor Chemical Group, a British company and a world leader in epoxy curatives. This acquisition gave Air Products a manufacturing foothold in Europe.[21] In 1989, the Chemicals Group signaled its growing global ambitions by opening sales offices in São Paulo, Brazil, and Tokyo, Japan.

To fulfill its goals as set forth in the ten-year plan, the Chemicals Group also mounted domestic programs of acquisitions and research. By 1988, over 20 percent of chemical sales were from products Air Products had not offered five years earlier. One example was PACM, a product of in-house research used in non-yellowing polyurethane for no-wax flooring, low-maintenance coatings, and automotive finishes. A technological breakthrough in catalytic hydrogenation was behind the firm's decision to become a major producer of PACM. A manufacturing facility at Wichita, Kansas, completed in 1988, made Air Products the world's largest supplier of this chemical.[22]

The company remained a leading producer of alkylamines. New products (such as morpholine, diethylene glycolamine, and triethylamine) had been added in 1985, and amines manufacturing capacity was increased in 1986.[23] A year later, the group added further capacity at the St. Gabriel complex, using technology developed internally by lead process engineer Brian Heft. In 1989, a twenty-million-pound-per-year polyamines plant was brought on-stream at St. Gabriel, and construction of a $5 million product development lab was completed at Pace, Florida.[24]

The amines business remained a highly opportunistic one, in which Air Products sought to expand in part by moving downstream in the product cycle. That strategy applied equally to the second strong area of the company's chemical activity, in certain polymers. Air Products' leading position in the adhesive and emulsion field was handled through the Polymer Chemicals Division of the Chemicals Group, headed by Andrew Cummins. The line of polymers was expanded through a 1986 licensing agreement with BASF, the giant German chemical concern. The agreement gave Air Products exclusive U.S. rights to manufacture and sell certain polymers for pressure-sensitive adhesives.[25] The group's position was further enhanced by a line of water-based systems in the summer of 1988, when the firm bought the Valchem division of United Merchants and Manufacturers, Inc.[26] Earlier that year Air Products purchased a facility in South Carolina in order to manufacture acrylic emulsions. Research also made a significant contribution by expanding the line of patented Airflex emulsions.[27] In 1988, equipment and process improvements at the South Brunswick, New Jersey, plant led to a major improvement in emulsion polymer quality.

Meanwhile, Air Products continued its strong and growing position in the polyurethane intermediates, DNT and TDA. The Polyurethane Chemicals Division was managed by Hugh Gallagher. In 1986, the Pasadena, Texas, facility produced its five-billionth pound of DNT and one billionth pound of TDA.[28] Overseas sales rose as the company found customers in South America and the Far East. Although by this time the original Dabco patents had long expired, the Chemicals Group worked hard to retain a position in the field of polyurethane additives, and introduced fresh products from research and acquisitions under the Dabco name. Adding to the 1985 purchase of M&T's polyurethane catalyst business, in 1987 Air Products bought the specialty additives businesses of Rhone-Poulenc and Akzo, two European chemical firms. Research expanded the company's line of polyurethane chemicals, including non-volatile, highly uniform TDI prepolymers and a line of water-based mold-release agents.

In the production of polyvinyl alcohol (PVOH), the Chemicals Group cut operating costs and increased export sales. To meet a growing demand, PVOH production facilities were expanded, and the result was an important contribution to Air Products' earnings in the late 1980s. In 1989, Air Products announced plans to build a seventy-million-pound-per-year plant on the Gulf Coast, in a bid to become the country's largest producer.

True to the experience of the sixties and seventies, the chemicals business remained an important, opportunistic area for Air Products throughout the 1980s. If chemicals were by then a recognized core business, it was one that contained within itself three central sectors in amines, polyurethane chemicals, and polymers, as well as what sometimes threatened to become a bewildering array of other activities. Indeed, bringing a sense of strategy and tactics to the various options which chemicals presented for both risk and growth was a central task of the corporate planning function, headed successively by Hap Wagner (1982–1986), Andy Mellen (1987), and Joe Kaminski (1987–1990).

By 1990, three things seemed clear. First, Air Products was firmly established as a *chemical* company, with many opportunities before it to move more fully onto the global stage. Second, the heart of its chemical skills lay in its knowledge of process equipment, and in its strong positions in the manufacture of certain categories of chemicals. Third, the firm would have to be very disciplined in deciding on which possible products and processes were worthwhile targets for research or for acquisition. Air Products was by now large enough, diverse enough, and international enough in its chemical activities for promising opportunities to be far easier to find than commensurate financial or human resources. This reality was signaled both by the divestitures of the firm's biotechnology and advanced ceramics ventures, and by changes in Air Products' overall strategy in R&D.

Refining R&D

One avenue of innovation in the late eighties was through the work of the Applied Research and Development Department (AR&D), itself a part of the Industrial Gas Division. The Cryo-Quick system of freezing food with liquid nitrogen was improved and adapted to the needs of an increasing variety of food applications. In 1987, AR&D introduced Freshpak food-preserving atmospheres and, in 1989, brought out the Freshpak Test Kit, an innovative way for food packagers to test modified atmospheres to improve shelf-life and appearance. The department also worked with other company units to produce novel products and processes. One example was the Mega-class gases, developed in 1988 in conjunction with Specialty Gases, IGD Engineering, and Engineered Products. These gases, delivered usually to electronics customers, were of very high purity and supplied as liquids.

To speed the creation of new products and processes for the European market, a small Technology Centre was opened in 1987, at the Brunel Science Park in West London. In 1989, the Centre launched the Cryostream freezer, which used liquid nitrogen to produce small, individual, free-flowing pellets from a liquid food product.[29]

The Corporate Research Center also continued to refine its function of contributing to corporate growth through the creation of market-oriented products. A major tenet of the philosophy of Brian Rushton, Vice President of Research and Development, was that no matter how basic, research must be coupled to the strategies of the firm. In 1988, the Corporate Science Center and the Technical Diversification Department were merged to form the Corporate Science and Technology Center (CSTC). The aim was to bring basic research more clearly into line with the firm's sharpened focus on its core businesses, and thus to improve the integration of commercial development considerations with the science and technology resources of the Science Center.[30]

CSTC made important advances in the company's technology base, including development of technology for controlled release of polyurethane-foam catalysts that overcame stability problems, and the commercialization, with Specialty Gases, of a means of producing high-purity zirconium tetrafluoride. CSTC also identified several novel polymeric materials for the company's second-generation nitrogen-membrane processes; achieved a breakthrough in understanding how the adsorbents used in pressure-swing processes separate gases; and made progress in developing a new family of polyamines.

CSTC also looked outside the company for ways to fund research and to acquire technologies, thus drawing on one of Air Products' oldest traditions. In 1987, for instance, CSTC received government contracts for work on a hypersonic aerospace vehicle proposed by the Air Force, contracts to develop liquid-phase methanol technology for the U.S. Department of Energy,[31] and a Gas Research Institute contract to develop steelmaking processes.[32] In 1988, CSTC's Contract Research section secured a $1.2 million agreement with the U.S. Department of Energy to identify, fabricate, and test novel membrane technology. In order to better identify technologies being developed outside the firm, in 1989 Merrill Brenner of CSTC created a service called Aptech, a clearing house that searched out externally developed technology available for licensing.

The Environmental/Energy Systems Division

In addition to expanding the company's core businesses in industrial gases and in chemicals, Baker and his colleagues set about creating a third business leg for Air Products. A new operating group, the Environmental/Energy Systems Division (EED), was set up in 1988, run briefly by Jim Strecansky, followed by Andy Mellen, and then taken on by John Paul Jones, who had joined Air Products in 1972 as a CDP and made his way up through positions in ICRC and Stearns-Catalytic.

EED focused the attention of the firm and the investing public on Air Products' innovative capabilities in the two closely related areas of the environment and energy. EED projects carried the company's engineers into high-temperature, rather than low-temperature, processes. Much that was new had to be learned and applied. Through that learning Air Products was transformed from being a buyer of energy into a buyer and seller of energy and energy services, such sales becoming an important aspect of the Environmental/Energy Systems Division.

The ventures grouped in EED were all associated with environmental concerns and thus with the federal legislation of the eighties. The heart of the division was in its waste-to-energy activities, in cogeneration, and in flue-gas desulfurization. These technologies all required large amounts of capital, most of which was raised in the public sector. They all involved on-site projects, which allowed Air Products to exploit the operational and managerial knowledge of its Process Systems Group. At the same time, they built on some of the insights the company had won in its synfuels ventures. The engineering expertise in large undertakings gained through the Stearns-Catalytic experience was especially relevant.

Other steps toward the field of energy services had been made much earlier, when Mark Halsted and Ed Sherry in PSG began negotiating electricity-supply contracts for on-site generators and when, in 1978, Don Shire established a consolidated function for Energy and Materials. The purchasing of energy was combined with a range of other activities (supply, sales, forecasting, planning, and regulatory matters).[33] The strength of this function was to prove important as plans developed to turn Air Products into a seller of energy and energy services.

In the late 1980s, the accumulated experience of Air Products in energy-related areas began to bear fruit. Under Chris Sutton, who ran the cogeneration activities of EED, the $100 million Stockton, California, facility was completed in 1988, and construction was started on a similar plant in Cambria County, Pennsylvania, in 1989.

The American Ref-Fuel joint venture with Browning Ferris Industries (BFI) was also promising. Through it, Air Products acquired access to BFI's waste-to-energy technology as well as to its experience with a wide range of waste-management operations, including collection, transfer, recycling, and development of sanitary landfills. Because of its expertise in the recycling industry, BFI could assist in marketing materials not burned in the waste-to-energy plants. In 1990, American Ref-Fuel had eight waste-to-energy projects in various stages of planning, construction, or operation. Collectively, they could generate enough electricity to supply over a quarter of a million homes. The venture's first facility, at Hempstead, Long Island, came on-stream in the summer of 1989. American Ref-Fuel was also building New Jersey's largest waste-to-energy plant, in Newark, to serve the refuse disposal needs of twenty-two municipalities in Essex County. Construction was also scheduled for an even larger project in Bergen County, New Jersey, capable of burning 3,000 tons of refuse a day and generating 80,000 kilowatts per hour of electricity.[34]

The sponsors of these American Ref-Fuel projects were local governments (like the town of Hempstead, Long Island) or public authorities (such as the Port Authority of New York and New Jersey), which floated bond issues to supply significant portions of the capital. American Ref-Fuel provided the remainder through equity financing. Each waste-to-energy project was built, owned, and operated by a separately organized company. The long-term (twenty to twenty-five year) service contracts often had integrated waste services (ash disposal, ferrous materials recovery) piggybacked onto them. In all cases, the Air Products on-site concept was taken one step further. The electricity generated as a by-product in these facilities was sold to local utilities at an established rate on long-term supply contracts, lowering costs for refuse disposal.

The on-site, own-and-operate concept was also being applied in the flue-gas desulfurization business, which was created as part of the sequence through which Air Products sold Stearns-Catalytic. In the 1970s, Stearns had built an electric power plant for Hoosier Energy of Indiana, employing as a subcontractor Mitsubishi Heavy Industries America, Inc. Mitsubishi had built about half the flue-gas desulfurization scrubbers sold in Japan, and many for the German market.

Andy Mellen told Mitsubishi that Air Products would like to form a joint venture in flue-gas desulfurization, because he anticipated that acid rain legislation would create a demand for scrubbers. Although Mellen had initially advised Mitsubishi Heavy Industries America to stay with Stearns after its acquisition by United Engineers, it soon became clear that United Engineers was not interested in promoting flue-gas desulfurization. So Mellen invited Mitsubishi to enter into a

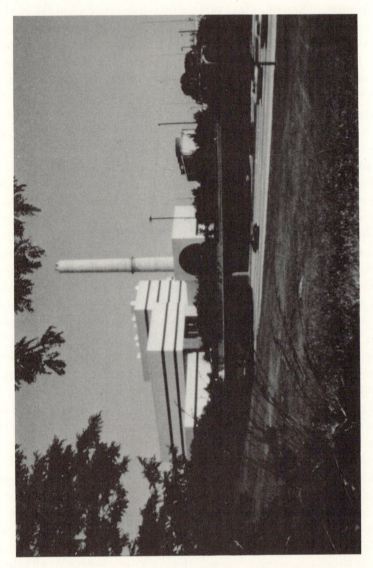

The first American Ref-Fuel facility, Hempstead, Long Island, New York.

joint venture with Air Products to develop this line of business. The result was Pure Air, an Air Products–Mitsubishi 50–50 venture headed by Bob Conley, who had worked for ICRC and Stearns-Catalytic.

Pure Air's technology was entirely Japanese. R&D was carried out at Mitsubishi's Technical Institute in Hiroshima. The Mitsubishi process had already been successfully operated in a wide range of plants with sulfur dioxide emissions in the United States, Japan, and Germany. Pure Air's own first project was for Northern Indiana Public Service Company's Bailly Generating Station, near Gary, Indiana, and was scheduled for completion in June 1992.[35] Pure Air on the Lake, a subsidiary of Air Products, would design, construct, own, and operate the system under a twenty-year service contract. For the first time in the industry, a company furnishing flue-gas desulfurization equipment would also own and operate it for the customer. The partnership was funded by the utility and by the Department of Energy (DOE) through its Innovative Clean Coal Technology Program. DOE's aim was to provide a solution to the problems of acid rain. Pure Air technology would allow Bailly to burn the high-sulfur coal indigenous to Indiana while minimizing atmospheric pollution.

In addition to the Pure Air, American Ref-Fuel, and cogeneration businesses, EED took over responsibility for the wastewater-treatment and landfill-gas processing activities developed and acquired by PSG. Rounding off EED's activities was GSF Energy, Inc., acquired as Getty Synthetic Fuels, in September 1985. GSF owned and operated plants for extracting and processing the gases generated when bacteria break down refuse in landfills. Business was carried on as with other on-site projects. Air Products owned and operated the facilities on long-term service contracts and sold the output on long-term supply contracts. Typical of these operations was the facility in the Hackensack Meadowlands of New Jersey. When completed in April 1990, the plant had a capacity of six million cubic feet of gas per day. The town of Kearny and the Hackensack Meadowlands Development Commission helped to fund this project for turning waste material into a valuable product, while protecting the environment.

Federal as well as state legislation supported these varied efforts. The Resource Conservation and Recovery Act of 1976 established regulatory guidelines for landfills, restricting methane concentrations and landfill-gas migration. In addition, the State of New York passed a law requiring utilities to purchase electricity from small producers at a minimum price. These laws encouraged investment in alternate energy schemes such as waste-to-energy and landfill-gas-recovery facilities.

The Power Generation and Marketing Department was organized in 1987 to support the company's initiatives in waste-to-energy, cogeneration, flue-gas desulfurization, and related areas. The department sold the electricity produced by these varied enterprises, its price being a critical factor in a project's viability. In addition to negotiating and administering sales and transmission agreements, the department prepared supply, demand, and price forecasts.

These new businesses in the related areas of energy and the environment had an important impact on Air Products. A company that had been a large-scale consumer of electricity was evolving into a seller of energy and energy services. Its on-site concept and its knowledge of process engineering were finding fresh applications. More than that, Air Products was developing a new core area of operations, which interacted creatively with its skills in chemicals and in industrial gases.

People, People, People

Other shifts in strategy were taking place as Dex Baker took the helm, in December 1986. Looking ahead, he and his colleagues saw that Air Products would have to give even more attention to its people, to managing and to achieving the fullest development of its human resources. The Air Products tradition of valuing its employees had started long before with Leonard Pool and "Pool's Philosophy." In the early days, Pool regularly thanked employees as he walked around the firm's shops and offices. Ed Donley had carried on this tradition, and in 1978, when sales exceeded $1 billion for the first time, he had stressed the role that "the extraordinary dedication and competence of our employees played in the firm's success."[36]

The recurring emphasis on the people of Air Products was evident in the evolution of the employee-relations function. Originally, this operation had been concerned primarily with union-linked issues. Then, under Jim Boyce, the focus had shifted to "employee services." A change in name to Human Resources was introduced by Don Shire in 1986, reflecting the newer concern with employee development and employee benefits. The company's professional managers saw ever more clearly that Air Products' greatest resource was its people, and that there was a corresponding need to pay attention to that resource.

The Human Resources Division has constantly asked "how can we change the status quo to make things better for our employees?" In seeking to improve life at Air Products, Shire and his colleagues sought to break down the barriers between professional or "exempt" and non-exempt workers. Certainly, the barrier between union and non-union employees has been coming down. Since Air Products started offering its employees the opportunity to change to staff status with Air Products employee benefits, there have been twenty-nine union decertifications involving over five hundred employees in the United States and Canada.

The changed approach to human resources emphasized two-way communication. As the corporation grew steadily larger and more complex, there was an inevitable danger that employees would feel that what was going on was somehow secret. Management needed to improve communications. Seemingly small changes marked the fresh philosophy. An electronic bulletin board called "Corpnews" was introduced to disseminate company news instantly and worldwide, in 1985. Employee-oriented publications were brought out to keep everyone in the Air Products family abreast of the latest company news. In 1988, Public Affairs and Human Resources set up a network of television monitors to provide rapid communication, and "Coffee Talks" management presentations were organized. In November 1989, in an expansion of two-way communications between executives and employees, Dex Baker gave his first face-to-face talk to employees on the future direction of the company, with videotapes being sent to all field locations.

One keystone of the human resources philosophy was employee development. As Baker had declared in 1986, "we are committed to providing an environment that stimulates professional growth, through varied developmental assignments and formal training and education. In turn, each of us has primary responsibility to realize our own potential."[37] The company already had in place a number of programs, including a Deferred Stock Plan and an Innovative Rewards and Recognition System. Baker added the Chairman's Award for Excellence. This award included $50,000 in cash and stock bestowed in recognition of a significant technical, scientific, commercial, or professional achievement or for a pattern of notable achievements over an individual's career. The first winner of the prize was Lee Gaumer, whose engineering achievements included

Lee Gaumer accepting the Chairman's Award for Excellence from Dexter Baker. The award is given for major technical, scientific, commercial, or professional achievement and includes the glass sculpture shown here.

innovative work on helium, liquefied natural gas, and other cryogenic process designs.

Baker made it clear to all employees that Air Products was determined to create opportunities for entrepreneurs within the corporation, to give individual initiative free reign. Just as Pool had bet on Baker, whom he sent to England to head up APL, Baker was "betting on other bright young people who want to grow and have good ideas and have the desire to execute those ideas."[38] This kind of entrepreneurship had enabled Air Products to create the cogeneration, waste-to-energy, and flue-gas-desulfurization enterprises. In order to further entrepreneurship, Air Products created a Venture Compensation program. Management designated Venture Managers who were leading a business initiative into a fresh market or a novel technology. A Venture Board was established, consisting of Air Products officers, to afford the Venture Manager access to resources. The program was designed to simulate, within a Fortune 500 corporation, the type of risk-reward relationship found in a small, start-up business.

The company's management understood that encouraging entrepreneurship meant taking risks and living with failures. Corporate growth could not depend on the success of every initiative. After all, throughout its history, Air Products had failed in a number of ventures. Nevertheless, its successful undertakings sustained the business, enabling it to continue experimenting. The missile fuel business was a success. Agricultural chemicals flopped. This is the nature of innovation and it was innovation that had kept Air Products a profitable, growing company. With the firm's broad-based portfolio of businesses serving a number of different markets, senior managers believed that Air Products could well afford to take risks. Being able to fail, Baker said, "is one of our most significant strengths and a principal source for optimism as I look at our company's future."[39]

Another key area of concern lay in the area of career development. The career development program (CDP) of 1959 had set a precedent, signaling the corporation's awareness that its destiny no longer depended on chance or the lone individual, however gifted. Over the years, the number of management training programs and workshops had greatly increased. By 1990, a younger generation of corporate leaders was emerging at Air Products, products of the Career Development Program, of training activities, and of the firm's strong culture of growth and risk taking.

Ironically, but not surprisingly, it was at the very apex of the corporation that career development was least well planned. In the beginning, Leonard Pool had preferred to keep the issue of succession in abeyance for as long as possible. Donley and Baker had been chosen from among his top lieutenants, and the replacement of the former by the latter in 1986 had been widely anticipated. By the late eighties, the company was far beyond the Pool era. It did not, however, have clear mechanisms in place to arrive at an orderly transition. The selection of Frank Ryan as President in 1988 had been a difficult choice from among a narrow field of candidates. Ryan's resignation in 1990, and the earlier loss of a number of executives, including Bill Scharle, Andy Mellen, Pat Dyer, and Lanny Patten, highlighted the difficulties in planning for orderly succession at the top. Management realized that a turning point was at hand, and that future Presidents and CEOs would have to be chosen by thoughtful, deliberative methods from among the extensive group of talented vice presidents and senior managers nurtured through CDP and other management development programs.

The Customer Is the Boss

The company would only be successful to the extent that its products and services continued to fulfill customers' expectations. Here the firm's long-standing commitment to quality had a key role to play. As Air Products became larger and more complex, preserving quality as a corporate value across the board also became more difficult. Gone were the days when a single individual, like Carl Anderson, could inspire and direct quality work in all areas. Motivated in part by the book *In Search of Excellence*, Air Products introduced its own "Quality Process." The Chemicals Group was the first to have a quality program, utilizing the system developed by Philip Crosby Associates. Starting in 1986, the other operating groups and corporate staff joined in a similar effort, based largely on the 3M Managing Total Quality approach.[40]

Air Products employees all around the world received training in the Quality Process, and in September 1988, thousands took part in Quality Day, marking the successful completion of the first phase of the Quality Process.[41] Al Greene, a former manager of manufacturing in the Chemicals Group, was named Corporate Director of Quality.[42] Quality Managers and a Quality Steering Committee were appointed for the Gas, Process Systems, and Chemicals groups. In a videotape shown to all employees, Baker emphasized his position: "Let it never be said that Air Products is second to any company in the quality of its products and services."

The goal of quality was one important aspect of getting closer to the firm's customers. In stressing the importance of customers, Baker built on certain traditional aspects of the Air Products culture. From the company's beginning, the engineering dimension of the culture had been firmly in place. It emphasized efficiency, planning, safety, and orderly development. This part of the culture had helped Air Products achieve low production costs in the industrial gas business. It also helped the firm remain innovative in technology. While it contributed significantly to the firm's growth, the engineering side of the company culture tended on occasion to be formalistic, bureaucratic, and control-minded. As a result, some observers inside and outside Air Products thought that the company's management style had over the years become too conservative, too rigid, and too centralized.

Baker sought increased flexibility. He praised the sales orientation, the focus on customers. One of the challenges was "making sure that we don't become so bureaucratic and so control-oriented that we stifle people."[43] The sales side of the company's culture was traditionally more flexible, open, and informal. It was centered not on technology, but on the idea that the customer was the boss. That meant listening to the customer, getting to know the customer's needs, and meeting the customer's expectations.

The activities of the electronics business area illustrated how an emphasis on the sales side of the culture could enable Air Products to grow. The aim in electronics was to become a fully integrated supplier of gases, chemicals, and related systems through acquisitions, agreements, and research. Thus the firm acquired a minority interest in UTI Instruments, which marketed quality-assurance instrumentation such as printed-circuit-board fault-detectors and mass spectrometers. The company also purchased the California-based division of the J. C. Schumacher Company which dealt with solid and liquid dopants, and in 1988 entered into an agreement with the Athens Corporation to market that company's chemical purification systems for semiconductor-wafer cleaning.[44] Air Products also stepped up the production of specialty gases, announcing in late 1989 the doubling of production of tetrafluoromethane at Hometown. Also key to serving

Quality Day was an all-day, first-of-its-kind program held in a tent erected on the Trexlertown campus. Through skits, songs, and speeches, the program aimed to educate the employees about the essentials of quality performance and motivate them to do quality work.

the electronics industry were the firm's exceptionally pure Mega-class gases and its novel, point-of-consumption Megasys gas-delivery system.

These developments positioned Air Products to serve its electronics customers well. The results soon became evident. In 1989, the company signed a first-of-its-kind, Megasys contract to manage every aspect of the supply and use of gases at Motorola's semiconductor manufacturing facility in Arizona.[45] Previously, the responsibility of Air Products and other industrial gas firms had ended at the point of delivery. The Motorola contract extended this responsibility to the point of consumption. Now employees were to be permanently stationed inside the factory to assure a continuous supply of gases of the highest quality. In this case, Baker had literally succeeded in getting Air Products close to the customer.

The importance of the electronics industry to Air Products' future was underscored in late 1989, when the firm created a separate electronics business area with its own R&D and sales organizations. By 1990, the company was negotiating additional Motorola-type contracts in the United States, France, and Italy.

Air Products sought to apply the same formula to cylinder gas sales. Those sales had remained relatively steady for a number of years. Overhead (distribution and selling) costs were high for cylinder gas compared to bulk sales. Air Products had traditionally kept its production costs down, giving it a healthy margin even in lean times, while making sales on the basis of its excellent service. Innovations, such as palletized cylinder delivery, continued to keep down costs and improved safety. However, the operation was organized on the basis of products (individual gases) and geography (regions and districts) rather than with a focus on the particular needs of the individual customer, whatever those needs might be. In late 1989, the firm announced the creation of a cylinder gas sales unit, distinct from bulk merchant sales. Here as elsewhere, growth and change went hand in hand. By creating a special organization to handle this one segment of gas sales, Baker planned to put Air Products closer to the customer in the years ahead.

Conclusion

As Air Products grew larger, so did corporate headquarters.[46] The architecture of the original Trexlertown buildings, fastidiously overseen by Leonard Pool, reflected neither opulence nor a feeling of

Corporate headquarters at Trexlertown, 1990.

self-importance, but the simple, stark values of the engineering side of the corporate culture. By 1990, Trexlertown had also come to symbolize something rather different, namely the move by much of American business from the city to the suburbs. The suburban feel of the corporate headquarters was strengthened by its setting, resembling a university campus, a center for the application of advanced skills in management, science, and engineering.

By 1990, Air Products had developed a secure identity, and a clear position in its three chosen fields of operation. Its hungry and opportunistic style; its financial and engineering capabilities; its very considerable human resources—all combined to put the company in an excellent position to realize its ambition to build aggressively on its established positions in industrial gases and chemicals. Increases in energy costs also seemed likely to boost the firm's energy business, as well as the sale of industrial gases. Environmental concerns, particularly the problems of waste disposal, clean air and water, and acid rain, were increasing, and those concerns could easily translate into a high-growth market in the 1990s for the Environmental/Energy Systems Division.

The fifty years since 1940 had seen Air Products develop those economies of scale and scope which would allow it to compete as a member of the first division, in the new global marketplace. With sales approaching $3 billion, the firm could afford to undertake the research and development needed in a rapidly changing world, in such challenging areas as non-cryogenic gas processing technology. Its extensive, world-wide sales force and its cadres of skilled managers meant that the company could respond creatively to shifts in the marketplace. Its aim was to meet the many challenges that lay ahead by entrepreneurship from within, by carefully crafted acquisitions, and by the type of management that would keep the company in touch with its customers, its mission, its setting, its people, and its culture.

With his emphasis on getting closer to the customer, Dex Baker gave the employees of Air Products the central role in the firm's strategy. In his words, "we must make bets on people as well as programs and technology. If we are wise in the kind of bets we make, some will succeed (hopefully, more will succeed than fail), and out of that process the company will generate opportunities for its continued growth and development."[47] Air Products had been making these kinds of bets for half a century. By 1990, its track record was enviable and its resources considerable. As a result, the firm's managers, employees, stockholders, and customers had every reason to be optimistic about the future of this successful enterprise.

Notes

1. "Why Air Products May Float Even Higher," *Business Week* (June 17, 1988): 80; "Keeping the Cow, Selling the Milk," *Forbes* 143 (March 20, 1989): 40–41.

2. Ed Donley interview, 29 January 1988, APHO.

3. "Air Products Licenses CVD Technology," *Today* (November 1986) 123: 5; "Industrial Microbiology Complex Opens," *Today* (February 1986) 116: 11.

4. Standard and Poor's Industry Surveys, *Chemicals*, 24 October 1985, Sec. 1, pp. C 22–23 and 13 October 1988, Sec. 3, pp. C 21–22; "Money from Nothing," *Economist* 308 (10 September 1988): 88; Alice Agoos, "Industrial Gases Travel an Upward Road," *Chemical Week* 138 (January 1986): 45–47.

5. "Atmospheric Gases Make it Big in Electronics," *Chemical Week* 135 (14 November 1984): 40–41. Stanley Roman joined Air Products in 1967 as a CDP, with a B.S. from the U.S. Naval Academy. Robert Gadomski came to Air Products in 1970 as a CDP. He had a B.S. in chemical engineering and an M.S. in industrial administration from Purdue University.

6. "NASA Commendations for Air Products' Hydrogen Team," *Today* (November 1988) 131: 3; Universities Research Association, *Supercollider R&D, March 1988* (Washington, D.C.: Universities Research Association, 1988); Universities Research Association, *Matter—The Superconducting Super Collider* (Washington, D.C.: Universities Research Association, 1989).

7. While Air Products does not own the National Helium Plant, the firm will operate it under a fifteen-year lease for the owners.

8. "Innovation Creates a New Market for Helium," *Today* (May 1988) 129: 4–5.

9. "How a Technical Idea Became a Commercial Reality," *Today* (June 1986) 120: 7–10; "More Successes for Airopak Containers," *Today* (August 1988) 130: 11.

10. "Cryogenic Heat Exchanger Ordered for Indonesia," *Today* (April 1987) 125: 16; "Still Setting a Torrid Pace in Heat Exchangers," *Today* (May 1988) 129: 10.

11. "Advanced Separations Department Formed," *Today* (July 1987) 126: 17.

12. "Gearing Up for PSA Demand," *Today* (December 1989) 135: 12.

13. "Why Air Products May Float Even Higher," p. 80; "Money from Nothing," p. 88.

14. "Money from Nothing," p. 88.

15. Previous years were 1968, 1972, 1978, and 1987.

16. "Acrefair Ships Longest Column," *Today* (April 1987) 125: 6.

17. "Project from European Space Program," *Today* (July 1987) 126: 13.

18. "Air Products Germany," *Today* (May 1985) 108: 3–5.

19. "Korea Industrial Gases: Performance and Promise," *Today* (July 1987) 126: 10–11.

20. "Air Separation Plants for China," *Today* (May 1985) 108: 3–5.

21. "The Anchor Acquisition," *Today* (May 1988) 129: 8.

22. "Specialty Amines Business Expands," *Today* (July 1987) 126: 17.

23. "Air Products Begins Production of Morpholine and Diethylene Glycolamine," *Today* (February 1985) 106: 10.

24. "Air Products and Louisiana have Built a Relationship Beneficial to Both," *Today* (December 1989) 135: 8–10.

25. "Air Products Acquires Polymer Technology from BASF," *Today* (June 1986) 120: 5.

26. "The Valchem Acquisition," *Today* (November 1988) 131: 15.

27. "New Airflex Emulsion Introduced," *Today* (April 1987) 125: 14; "Technology Pact Leads to Innovation Success," *Today* (October 1987) 127: 8–10.

28. "Pasadena Plant Marks DNT, TDA Milestone," *Today* (November 1986) 123: 12.

29. "The Megasys System Takes Air Products into the Customer's Semiconductor Fab," *Today* (December 1989) 135: 4–5; "Turning Out Mega-Class Gases at Glenmont," *Today* (March 1989) 133: 7; "European Technology Centre Opens," *Today* (April 1987) 127: 7.

30. "The R&D Merger," *Today* (May 1988) 129: 8–9.

31. The liquid-phase methanol program is part of a larger DOE-sponsored research effort in indirect coal liquefaction to demonstrate the feasibility of catalytically converting coal-based synthesis gas rich in carbon monoxide into methanol. "Liquid-phase Methanol Unit Successful," *Today* (February 1986) 116: 14.

32. The Gas Research Institute is a not-for-profit organization whose membership comprises natural gas pipeline and distribution companies. It plans, manages, and develops financing for R&D programs designed to advance gas technology. "Research Meeting Hosted at T-town," *Today* (July 1987) 126: 17–18.

33. Tom Feare, "Air Products: How they Buy," *CPI Purchasing* (January 1984), reprint, APHO.

34. "Ref-Fuel Proceeding on Several Contracts," *Today* (June 1986) 120: 13.

35. "Indiana Utility Chooses Unique FGD System for Control of Acid Rain Emissions," *Today* (December 1989) 135: 13.

36. *Annual Report 1978*, p. 3

37. Ibid.

38. Dex Baker interview, 30 March 1988, APHO.

39. Baker, "Plan for Corporate Growth," 1986, APHO.

40. "Crossing the Bridge from Awareness to Action," *Quality Works* (Fall 1989): 4–6; Bill Scharle interview, 30 March 1988, APHO.

41. "Quality Day Gets Rave Reviews," *Today* (November 1988) 131: 6–7.

42. "Greene Named Director of Quality and Productivity Systems," *Today* (March 1986) 117: 10.

43. Dex Baker interview, 30 March 1988, APHO.

44. "Air Products Buys Schumacher Chemical Systems Unit," *Today* (November 1986) 123: 9; "Schumacher's Double Approach to Semiconductor Safety, *Today* (May 1988) 129: 11–12.

45. "The Megasys System Takes Air Products into the Customer's Semiconductor Fab," *Today* (December 1989) 135: 4–5.

46. "Expanding Company Headquarters," *Today* (November 1988) 131: 14.

47. Dex Baker interview, 30 March 1988, APHO.

Technical Appendix

Air Separation Technology

Oxygen and nitrogen are common chemicals. Together they make up most of the air we breathe, yet only in the last century has there been a commercial market for those gases. In 1990, the sale of oxygen, nitrogen, and other industrial gases constituted a $16 billion business. The technology that made possible that immense market was first introduced on a commercial scale by Carl von Linde in Germany and by Georges Claude in France, around 1900. A major revolution took place in the 1930s and 1940s, when a means for generating large amounts of cheap oxygen was introduced. By 1980, another technological revolution had taken place. The low-temperature, or cryogenic, technologies pioneered by Linde and Claude were being challenged by non-cryogenic technologies utilizing the adsorbent and permeability properties of certain chemical substances.

As commercialized by Linde and Claude, air separation took place in four stages: 1) compression of the air; 2) the removal of carbon dioxide, water vapor, and other impurities; 3) liquefaction of the air; and 4) separation of the air into oxygen and nitrogen. Removal of the impurities was critical, since water vapor and carbon dioxide frozen in the liquefaction process would obstruct the equipment. The various air separation processes were called *cycles* and were based on the application of thermodynamic principles, that is, the manipulation of conditions of pressure and temperature. Both Linde and Claude began by liquefying air, then devised distillation columns to produce oxygen-enriched air, and finally, oxygen.

Figure A.1
Simplified Linde Cycle

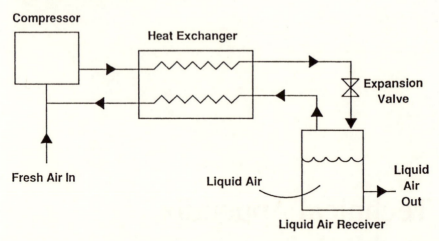

In its simplest form, the key components of the Linde cycle (Figure A.1) were the heat exchangers and the expansion valve. Air, compressed to 200 atmospheres or nearly 3,000 pounds per square inch, was cooled in a heat exchanger. In Linde's original heat exchanger, cold water cooled the incoming air to the temperature of the water. In later versions, after cooling with water, cold air or nitrogen from a later step in the process did the cooling. In the next step, the high-pressure, cooled air passed through an expansion valve, which caused it to become colder and to liquefy. The expansion valve operated on a scientific principle known as the Joule-Thomson effect, discovered early in the nineteenth century. Gases cool when their pressure is reduced while passing through a very small nozzle. Scientists call this way of cooling a gas adiabatic expansion.

The Claude cycle (Figure A.2) achieved greater energy efficiency through a number of measures, notably the inclusion of a device called an expansion engine. In the Claude cycle, air was compressed to only 40 atmospheres or about 600 pounds per square inch, one-fifth the pressure used in the Linde cycle. Using less pressure meant saving energy and money, and gave the Claude and related cycles the generic name "low-pressure cycles," in contrast to the "high-pressure" Linde and similar cycles.

Another vital, energy-saving feature of the Claude cycle was the use of an expansion engine. It was, in essence, a piston which reciprocated inside a cylinder. In fact, on his first liquid air machines, Claude actually used modified steam engines as expansion engines. In the expansion engine, the air was cooled through expansion, as in the expansion valve, and the air set the piston in motion. Creating that motion removed the energy initially added to the air through compression, and the air leaving the expansion

Figure A.2
Simplified Claude Cycle

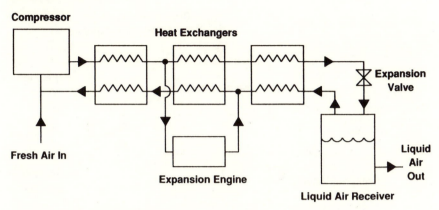

engine was dramatically colder. Scientists refer to this cooling as isentropic expansion.

Once Linde and Claude liquefied air, they sought a means for separating it into its constituent parts, primarily oxygen and nitrogen. They both devised distillation columns for this purpose. While their columns varied in design, in their most basic form, they consisted of evenly spaced trays, designed to bring liquid and vapor into intimate contact. As liquid air entered the column, the difference in boiling points of nitrogen and oxygen caused them to separate. Nitrogen boils at minus 320.4°F and oxygen at minus 297.35°F. The column trays were designed to allow the oxygen to flow to the bottom of the column and the nitrogen to evaporate toward the top of the column. The higher the nitrogen rose in the column, the lower would be its oxygen content. Similarly, the farther the oxygen dropped, the less nitrogen it contained. Oxygen was drawn from the bottom of the distillation column as a liquid and vaporized for use as a gas. Nitrogen gas was often vented as waste, but in variations developed later, it was used to cool the heat exchangers. Other variations in column design allowed for the separation of the rare gases argon, helium, xenon, krypton, and neon, which were removed by distillation in separate columns.

The development of generators capable of cheaply making unprecedented tonnage quantities of oxygen set off a wave of excitement that led *The Saturday Evening Post* to announce in 1947 that "The Oxygen Age is Just Ahead."[1] The development of tonnage oxygen plants grew out of incremental improvements made by a large number of individuals. Key figures were Matthias Fränkl and Peter Kapitza, who introduced, respectively, the regenerator and the expansion turbine.

In the regenerators, compressed air was cooled and the carbon dioxide and water vapor removed (Figure A.3). The regenerators were arranged in

Figure A.3
Tonnage Oxygen Plant Regenerator System

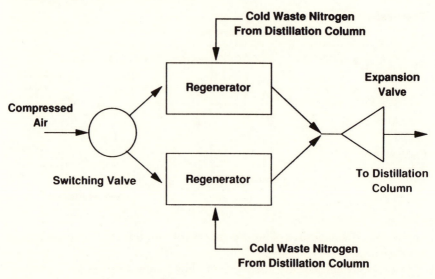

pairs (only one pair is shown in the figure) and were constructed so that they could alternately absorb and give up heat. Air from the compression stage entered one set of regenerators, which were cooled in advance by cold waste nitrogen from the distillation column. The regenerators chilled the air, freezing out the carbon dioxide (as dry ice) and water vapor (as frost). Free of carbon dioxide and water vapor, the air passed through an expansion valve, partially liquefied, then entered a distillation column. As one pair of regenerators discharged cold air, an automatic valve switched incoming hot air to another pair of regenerators, allowing the first pair time to be cleansed of dry ice and frost, before receiving another batch of hot air.

To cool air in the heat exchangers, tonnage plants used the cool air created by an expansion turbine, as well as waste nitrogen and oxygen product from the distillation column. An expansion turbine is much like the turbines used in electrical power plants. Kapitza used a high-speed turbine turning at 40,000 revolutions per minute, but faster, larger, and more-efficient turbines came into use later. The expansion turbine lowered the temperature of the air in the same way as the expansion engine.

Tonnage plants were cheaper and more energy-efficient for a number of reasons. One advantage of the regenerators was that, for the most part, they replaced the expensive equipment and chemicals normally used to remove moisture and carbon dioxide from incoming air. In general, tonnage plants consumed less power than conventional plants since the pressure of the compressed air in tonnage plants was about 85 pounds per square inch, as compared to 400 and even as high as 3000 pounds per square inch in high-

Figure A.4
Oxygen VSA System

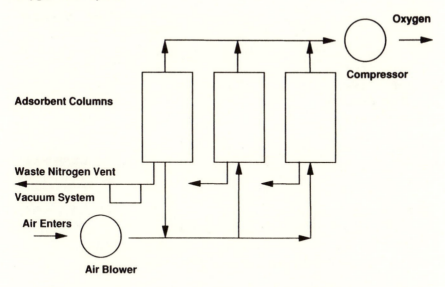

purity, high-pressure plants. The use of turbo-compressors in the compression stage produced further savings in initial investment cost and space for the compressors.

By 1980, a new generation of air separation technologies had emerged. Pressure swing adsorption, vacuum swing adsorption, and membrane separation technologies used the adsorbent and permeability properties of certain chemical substances. They produced gases in smaller quantities and were less energy-efficient than the cryogenic methods pioneered by Linde and Claude, but their capital investment costs were lower. These new systems represented a substantial technological revolution, and very well may effect more far-reaching changes than those brought about by the advent of tonnage oxygen nearly a half-century ago.

Vacuum Swing Adsorption (VSA) systems produced 20 to 100 tons of oxygen per day, with a purity of 93 to 95 percent (Figure A.4). VSA oxygen systems started with air that was filtered to remove dust. Unlike cryogenic methods, the air was not compressed. An air blower fed air into the adsorbent columns, where nitrogen, moisture, and carbon dioxide gas were removed from the air by adsorption. Adsorption is when gases or liquids adhere to the surface of a substance. The adsorbent substance used in the VSA oxygen system was a crystal material known as a zeolite molecular sieve. The sieve selectively adsorbed nitrogen and other molecules on its surface, but allowed oxygen molecules to pass through the column. When the zeolite was unable to adsorb any more nitrogen, the adsorber column was evacuated by a

Figure A.5
Nitrogen PSA System

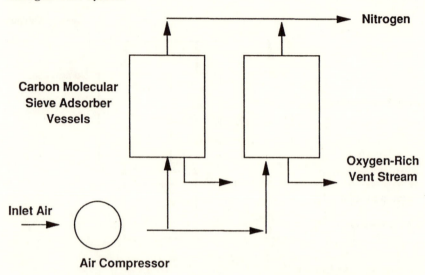

vacuum system, and the waste gases were vented to the atmosphere. Several columns were used, so that while one was producing oxygen, the others were being evacuated. A compressor was used to raise the oxygen to the pressure required by the customer.

Pressure Swing Adsorption (PSA) technology could generate one-half to 40 tons per day of 95 percent pure nitrogen (Figure A.5). In a PSA nitrogen system, the compressed air was sent to the carbon molecular sieve (CMS) adsorber vessels. The carbon molecular sieve had adsorbent properties similar to those of the zeolite molecular sieve used in the VSA systems. The carbon molecular sieve, when fed air under pressure, adsorbed oxygen, and let nitrogen flow through the column. The nitrogen gas was then delivered to the customer by pipeline or stored for later use. Two CMS adsorber vessels were used, so that while one vessel was producing nitrogen, the second was decompressing. During decompression, the adsorbed oxygen and other impurities were vented to the atmosphere. The automatic cycling between the two CMS beds (controlled, along with other operations, by a microprocessor) enabled continuous production of nitrogen.

Membrane technology had applications in air separation and in recovering hydrogen, helium, and carbon dioxide from other gases. Membrane separation operated on the principle of selective permeation, which takes place when a gas penetrates a substance (Figure A.6). Each gas has a characteristic permeation rate, that is, gases flow through substances at different rates. By taking advantage of these different permeation rates, the membrane system was able to separate one gas from two or more. The membrane separation systems utilized layers of polymeric membranes of known prop-

Figure A.6
Membrane System

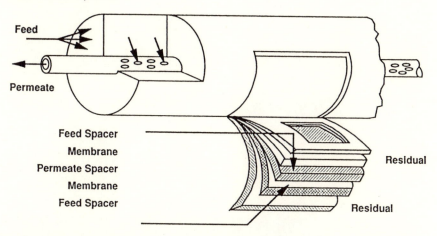

Feed

Permeate

Feed Spacer
Membrane
Permeate Spacer
Membrane
Feed Spacer

Residual

Residual

erties. When a pressurized stream of mixed gases flowed through the separator, the "fast" or more permeable gas, say hydrogen, would penetrate the membranes at a higher rate than the "slow," less permeable gases, like methane or carbon monoxide. The "fast" gas diffused into the permeate spacer in the membrane, then flowed out in the permeate stream. Meanwhile, the remaining gases were channelled through a different gas outlet and either vented to the atmosphere or used in another process.

Note

1. Taken from the title of the article, J. D. Ratcliff, "The Oxygen Age is Just Ahead," *The Saturday Evening Post*, 20 September 1947, pp. 28, 68, 70–72.

Bibliography

Air Products History Office

Most of the material used in preparing this history came from the Air Products History Office. The core collection consists of the approximately one thousand files drawn from the papers of the founder, Leonard Pool, as well as those of his immediate successor, Edward Donley. The History Office also holds transcripts of thirty-five oral history interviews. Additional documents came from a range of corporate offices, including the technical libraries and the office of the Corporate Secretary.

Supplementary materials were obtained from the National Archives and other federal agencies, including the National Aeronautics and Space Administration, the National Air and Space Museum, the U.S. Air Force, the U.S. Census Bureau, and the U.S. Patent Office; from the Charles F. Brush papers, Special Collections, Freihergen Library, Case Western Reserve University, Cleveland, Ohio; from the Hagley Museum and Library; from the Probate Court of Wayne County, Detroit, Michigan; as well as from the libraries of the University of Pennsylvania, Princeton University, Lehigh University, Rutgers University, and of the cities of Philadelphia, Emmaus, and Allentown.

Serial Publications

Air Products and Chemicals, Inc., *Annual Report*, 1945–1989.
Air Reduction, *Annual Report*, 1920–1988.

Aviation Week and Space Technology.
British Oxygen Company Report and Accounts, 1971–1980.
Business Week.
Chemical and Engineering News.
Chemical Engineering.
Chemical Week.
Cryogenic Engineering News.
Iron and Steel Engineer.
Moody's Manual of Investments: American and Foreign.
Poor's Financial Records.
Standard and Poor's Industry Surveys.
Union Carbide and Carbon Corporation, *Annual Report* 1920–1988.

Books

Barba, Preston A. *They Came to Emmaus.* 2d ed. Bethlehem: Lehigh Litho, 1985.
Baruch, Bernard M. *American Industry in the War: A Report of the War Industries Board.* New York: Prentice-Hall, 1941.
Bell, J.H., Jr. *Cryogenic Engineering.* Englewood Cliffs, N.J.: Prentice-Hall, 1963.
BOC Group, The. *Around the Group in 100 Years.* N.p.: 1986.
Carboloy Corporation. *Carboloy Cemented Carbide for Reducing Wear on Tools and Machine Parts.* N.p.: 1936.
Civilian Production Administration. *Alphabetical Listing of Major War Supply Contracts.* Washington, D.C.: Government Printing Office, 1946.
Clark, John D. *Ignition! An Informal History of Liquid Rocket Propellants.* New Brunswick, N.J.: Rutgers University Press, 1972.
Compressed Gas Association. *75th Anniversary of the Compressed Gas Association, 1913 to 1988.* Arlington, Va.: Compressed Gas Association, 1988.
Cox, James A. *A Century of Light.* N.p.: Benjamin Company/Rutledge Book, 1979.
DeLamarter, Richard Thomas. *Big Blue: IBM's Use and Abuse of Power.* New York: Dodd, Mead & Co., 1986.
Durr, Clifford Judkins. *The Early History of the Defense Plant Corporation.* Washington, D.C.: Committee on Public Administration Cases, 1950.
Hall, Karyl Lee Kibler, and Hall, Peter Dobkin. *The Lehigh Valley.* Woodland Hills, Calif.: Windsor Publications, 1982.
Haynes, William, ed. *American Chemical Industry.* 6 vols. New York: D. Van Nostrand Co., 1944–49.
Hellerich, Mahlon H., ed. *Allentown 1762–1987: A 225-Year History.* 2 vols. Allentown, Penn.: Lehigh County Historical Society, 1987.

Holley, I.B., Jr. *Buying Aircraft: Material Procurement for the Army Air Forces*. Washington, D.C.: Department of the Army, 1964.

Kaysen, Carl. *United States v. United Shoe Machinery Corporation: An Economic Analysis of an Anti-Trust Case*. Harvard Economic Studies, vol. xcix. Cambridge, Mass: Harvard University Press, 1956.

Kropschot, R. H., Birmingham, B. W., and Mann, D. B., eds. *Technology of Liquid Helium*. National Bureau of Standards, Monograph 111. Washington, D.C.: Government Printing Office, 1968.

Leslie, Stuart W. *Boss Kettering*. New York: Columbia University Press, 1983.

Licht, Walter. *Working for the Railroad*. Princeton, N.J.: Princeton University Press, 1983.

McClellan, Hassell H. "Air Products and Chemicals, Inc." Harvard Business School Case Study 4–375–370, 1975.

Martin, Geoffrey, et al. *Industrial Gases including the Liquefaction of Gases*. New York: D. Appleton, 1916.

Mottram, R. H., and Coote, Colin. *Through Five Generations: The History of the Butterley Company*. London: Faber and Faber, n.d.

Myers, Richmond E. *Lehigh Valley: The Unsuspected*. Easton: Northampton County Historical and Genealogical Society, 1972.

Noyes, W.A., Jr., ed. *Chemistry: A History of the Chemistry Components of the National Defense Research Committee, 1940–1946*. Boston: Little, Brown, 1948.

Osborn, Richards C. *The Renegotiation of War Profits*. Bureau of Economic and Business Research Bulletin Series, No. 167. Urbana: University of Illinois Press, 1948.

Oxenfeldt, Alfred R. *New Firms and Free Enterprise: Pre-War and Post-War Aspects*. Washington, D.C.: American Council on Public Affairs, 1943.

Reich, Leonard S. *The Making of American Industrial Research: Science and Business at GE and Bell, 1876–1926*. Cambridge: Cambridge University Press, 1985.

Rudge, A.J. *The Manufacture and Use of Fluorine and Its Compounds*. London: Oxford University Press, 1962.

Ruhemann, M. *The Separation of Gases*. 2d ed. Oxford: Clarendon Press, 1949.

Scott, R.B. *Technology and Uses of Liquid Hydrogen*. New York: Macmillan, 1964.

Sittig, Marshall. *Nitrogen in Industry*. Princeton: Van Nostrand, 1965.

Sloop, John L. *Liquid Hydrogen as a Propulsion Fuel, 1945–1959*. Washington, D.C.: NASA, 1978.

Smith, W. Novis, and Santangelo, Joseph G., eds. *Hydrogen: Production and Marketing*. ACS Symposium Series, 116. Washington, D.C.: American Chemical Society, 1980.

Spitz, Peter H. *Petrochemicals: The Rise of an Industry*. New York: Wiley, 1988.

The Story of Fisher Body: A Tradition of Craftsmanship. Detroit: General Motors, 1949.

Thevenot, Roger. *A History of Refrigeration Throughout the World*. Translated by J.C. Fidler. Paris: International Institute of Refrigeration, 1979.

Trayser, Malcolm L. *A Basic Review of Air Products and Chemicals, Inc.* New York: Auerbach, Pollak & Richardson, 1965.

Tussing, Arlon R., and Barlow, Connie C. *The Natural Gas Industry: Evolution, Structure, and Economics*. Cambridge, Mass.: Ballinger, 1984.

Upchurch, Karen, and Crull, Anna. *Commercial Fluorine Compounds: Opportunities and Markets*. Business Opportunity Report C-087. Norwalk, Conn.: Business Communications, 1987.

Van Nimmen, Jane, and Bruno, Leonard C. *NASA Historical Data Book*. Vol. I. *NASA Resources 1958–1968*. NASA Historical Series. Washington, D.C.: NASA, 1988.

War Production Board. *War Manufacturing Facilities Authorized through August 1944*. Washington, D.C.: Government Printing Office, 1945.

White, Gerald Taylor. *Billions for Defense: Government Financing by the Defense Plant Corporation during World War II*. University, Ala.: University of Alabama Press, 1980.

Wilson, David. *The Colder the Better*. New York: Atheneum, 1980.

Yanarella, Ernest J., and Green, William C. *The Unfulfilled Promise of Synthetic Fuels*. Westport, Conn.: Greenwood Press, 1987.

Index

Abbott Laboratories, 248
acetylene, 7, 219
Acetylene Gas and Supply Company, 11, 12
acid rain, 281
Acme Steel Company, 101
Acme Welding Supply Company, 153
acquisitions by Air Products: of Acme Welding Supply Company, 153; of Adkins-Phelps Company, 194; of Airco's chemical operations, 219; of Anchor Chemical Group, 274; of Arcair Companies, 216; of Automation Industries, 216–17; of Catalytic Construction Company, 168; of Chattanooga Welding Supply Company, Inc., 152; of Compressed Gases of Ohio, Inc., 152; of Compuline, 217; of Delta Oxygen Company, Inc., 152; of Escambia Chemical Corporation, 194; of Exomet, Incorporated, 216; of Gardner Cryogenics, 241; of Harris Calorific Sales Company, 72; of Hill Industrial Gas Company, 152; of Inter-City Gas of Calgary, 272; of Jet Cut Corporation, 216; of K-G Welding and Cutting Company, 71; of Keenan Welding

Supplies Company, 152; of Miami Oxygen Service, Inc., 152; of Parco Compressed Gas Company, 72; of Saturn Industrial Gases, 165; of Southern Oxygen Company, 152; in Spain and Portugal, 272; of Stearns-Roger World Corporation, 257; of Steele Gases, 152–53; of Sun Coast Oxygen Service, Inc., 152; of Whittaker, 217
Adkins-Phelps Company, 194, 195–96
Africa, 214
agricultural chemicals, 191–96
Air Force Air Materiel Command, 91
Air Liquide, 98, 179, 189, 241, 245–47, 253, 270
Air Products: accomplishments of, 45; acquisitions by (*see* acquisitions by Air Products); adaptation by, 105; Advanced Products Department of, 184, 251; agricultural chemicals business and, 172, 191–96; Agricultural Chemicals Division of, 194; Air Force cuts costs via, 94; Air Reduction supplied by, 89; air separation business entered by, 101–2; ammonia production by, 105, 191–92, 227; argon business and, 72, 104–5, 176–77,

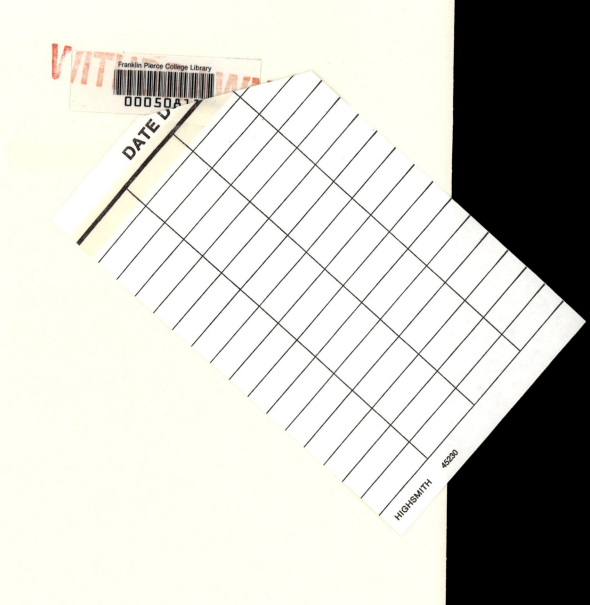